The

Establishment

Clause

BOOKS BY LEONARD W. LEVY

The Law of the Commonwealth and Chief Justice Shaw *(1957)*

Legacy of Suppression:

Freedom of Speech and Press in Early American History *(1960)*

The American Political Process *(1963), ed.*

Jefferson and Civil Liberties: The Darker Side *(1963)*

Major Crises in American History: Documentary Problems *(1963), ed.*

Congress *(1964), ed.*

The Judiciary *(1964), ed.*

Political Parties and Pressure Groups *(1964), ed.*

The Presidency *(1964), ed.*

American Constitutional Law: Historical Essays *(1966)*

Freedom of the Press from Zenger to Jefferson:

Early American Libertarian Theories *(1966), ed.*

Freedom and Reform *(1967), ed.*

Origins of the Fifth Amendment:

The Right Against Self-Incrimination *(1968)*

Essays on the Making of the Constitution *(1969)*

The Fourteenth Amendment and the Bill of Rights *(1971), ed.*

Judgments: Essays on Constitutional History *(1972)*

The Supreme Court under Warren *(1972), ed.*

Blasphemy in Massachusetts *(1973)*, *ed.*

Against the Law: The Nixon Court and Criminal Justice *(1974)*

Jim Crow Education *(1974)*, *ed.*

Treason against God—a History of the

Offense of Blasphemy *(1981)*

Emergence of a Free Press *(1985)*

Constitutional Opinions: Aspects of the Bill of Rights *(1986)*

Encyclopedia of the American Constitution *(1986)*, *ed.*

The Framing and Ratification of the Constitution *(1987)*, *ed.*

The American Founding *(1988)*, *ed.*

Original Intent and the Framers' Constitution *(1988)*

Supplement One:

Encyclopedia of the American Constitution *(1992)*, *ed.*

Blasphemy: Verbal Offense Against the Sacred,

from Moses to Salman Rushdie *(1993)*

Encyclopedia of the American Presidency *(1993)*, *ed.*

Seasoned Judgments:

Constitutional Rights and American History *(1994)*

The
University
of North
Carolina
Press
Chapel Hill
&
London

Second Edition, Revised

Religion

and the

First

The *Amendment*

Establishment
Clause

Leonard W. Levy

© 1994 The University
of North Carolina Press
All rights reserved
Manufactured in the
United States of America
First edition published in 1986
by Macmillan Publishing Company.

The paper in this book meets the
guidelines for permanence and
durability of the Committee on
Production Guidelines for Book
Longevity of the Council on Library
Resources.

Library of Congress Cataloging-in-
Publication Data

Levy, Leonard Williams, 1923–
    The establishment clause : religion and
the First Amendment / Leonard W.
Levy.—2d ed., rev.
        p. cm.
    Includes bibliographical references and
index.
    ISBN 0-8078-2156-x (cloth).—
    ISBN 0-8078-4466-7 (pbk.)
    1. Freedom of religion—United States. 2.
Church and state—United States. I. Title.
    KF4783.L48   1994
    342.73'0852—dc20
    [347.302852]   94-1046
            CIP

98 97 96 95 94
5   4   3   2   1

FOR ELYSE

AMENDMENT I

Congress shall make no law respecting an

establishment of religion, or prohibiting the free

exercise thereof; or abridging the freedom of speech,

or of the press; or the right of the people peaceably

to assemble, and to petition the Government for

a redress of grievances.

Contents

Preface

The establishment clause of the First Amendment ("Congress shall make no law respecting an establishment of religion . . .") does more than buttress freedom of religion, which the same amendment separately protects. Given the extraordinary religious diversity of our nation, the establishment clause functions to depoliticize religion; it thereby helps to defuse a potentially explosive situation. The clause substantially removes religious issues from the ballot box and from politics. Mr. Dooley, Finley Peter Dunne's irrepressible Irish wit, whom Justice Felix Frankfurter called a "great philosopher," said of church and state: "Rellijon is a quare thing. Be itself it's all right. But sprinkle a little pollyticks into it an' dinnymit is bran flour compared with it. Alone it prepares a man f'r a better life. Combined with polyticks it hurries him to it." The establishment clause separates government and religion so that we can maintain civility between believers and unbelievers as well as among the several hundred denominations, sects, and cults that thrive in our nation, all sharing the commitment to liberty and equality that cements us together.

Notwithstanding the establishment clause, religion saturates American public life. Every president swears the oath of office with one hand on the Bible and often says "So help me God." Almost every president has proclaimed days of prayer and thanksgiving to God, and, since 1952, when Congress decreed that a specific date be set aside each year for Americans to pray, the president has annually declared a National Day of Prayer on the first Thursday in May. The Supreme Court opens its session after the bailiff has asked God to save the Court and the United States. Every state legislature as well as Congress starts its daily session with a prayer from a chaplain whose salary is paid with public tax monies. All of us, including schoolchildren, when pledging allegiance to the flag, invoke God on behalf of our nation. Witnesses in court swear to tell the truth, "So help me God." Our money announces that we trust in God. Our churches and synagogues are exempt from taxation. One of our great libertarian enactments, the Virginia Statute of Religious Freedom, calls upon God, as does the Preamble to the Declaration of Independence, both written by Thomas Jefferson, the advocate of a wall of separation between church and state.

Whether the duty we owe our Creator and the manner of discharging it require government aid or whether the establishment clause requires each individual to retain the sovereign power to decide for himself or herself is the subject of this book. A former president of the United States declared a National Bible Year and then lamented that God has been expelled from our public life, enough reason to examine the meaning of the establishment clause as well as the president's mind. The same president, Ronald Reagan, believed that if evolution is taught in the public schools, "the Biblical story of creation should also be taught."

When public officials, including the nation's attorney general, urge a return to the original intent of the clause, an examination of history is especially warranted. Still, the observation of Clinton Rossiter, the conservative constitutional scholar, should be kept in mind. "Most talk about the intent of the Framers," he wrote, "—whether in the orations of politicians, the opinions of judges, or the monographs of professors—is as irrelevant as it is unpersuasive, as stale as it is strained, as rhetorically absurd as it is historically unsound." Rossiter added that men of power who know least about the intent of the framers are most likely to appeal to that intent for support of their views.

Meanwhile, real questions of public policy arise, take on a constitutional dimension, and require resolution by our courts in conformity with the establishment clause. Can any part of our public taxes be spent to cover the costs of parochial schools? Can such taxes underwrite the costs of at least the secular portions of the curriculum, assuming that there are any in schools whose mission is to teach religion when teaching literature, history, biology, and physical education? Can government aid to private sectarian schools or to their pupils be provided without excessively entangling the government with religion as a result of the need to monitor the severing of the secular and the sectarian? Is the textbook, the laboratory, the field trip, the diagnostic test, or the remedial service of a religious character, as judged by government employees? Can children read the Bible in public schools, study comparative religion, see the Ten Commandments posted on the bulletin board, or use school time for devotional exercises of a sectarian or of a nonsectarian religious character (if there are such)? Aside from the unintended profanity of associating the Lord with commercialism, does the motto "In God We Trust" have a legitimate secular purpose and effect that conform to the establishment clause? Can the United States, which is barred from promoting religion, supply chaplains to our armed forces, our federal prisoners, or our representatives in Congress? Does the display of a nativity scene in a public square at Christmastime or of a menorah on the city hall steps at Chanukah violate the clause? Does requiring a kosher butcher to close his shop on Sunday endorse the Christian sabbath, thereby accommodating state policy with the needs of religion, contrary to the principle of separation of church and state? Does aid to religion given impartially and without preference comport with the policy embodied in the establishment clause? Does the exemption of churches from pubic taxation violate the clause? Do interfaith prayers at public school commencements? May a state enforce a statute against consumer frauds by prosecuting sellers of kosher food that an Orthodox Jewish sect claims is not kosher?

What indeed did the clause mean to those who framed and ratified it? Why did they insist on its inclusion in the First Amendment? What does history show about the meaning of the clause? Does its historical meaning shed light on the questions that nag us today? Should we be bound by the original intent? Were those responsible for the establishment clause committed to a high and impregnable wall of separation between government and religion? Was the clause the product of the "secular humanists" of their time—rationalists, Unitarians, and Deists, like Benjamin Franklin and Thomas Jefferson—or were its supporters evangelical Christians, like John Leland and Caleb Wallace, seeking to protect religion from government just as rationalists sought to protect government from religion and both seeking to secure religious liberty?

To such queries nonpreferentialists provide a set of answers that accommodate the needs of religion. Nonpreferentialists are those who believe that if public policy does not prefer one sect or religion above others but treats all without preference, nothing in the Constitution bans government aid and sponsorship of religion. They narrowly interpret the establishment clause, trying to keep it as confined as possible, a constitutional clause of slight importance, subordinate in every conceivable way to the free-exercise clause that guarantees religious liberty.

One nonpreferentialist of distinction, William Bennett, when secretary of education, made a speech on restoring morality to the public schools, as if they were immoral. He advocated that students be allowed to pray voluntarily, as if they could not now do so and as if morality resulted from prayer. Students can, of course, pray whenever they wish, silently, but Bennett wanted to orchestrate prayers under state auspices; he wanted the state to promote religious exercises, which would introduce coercion into religious obligations and, according to the Supreme Court, would violate the establishment clause. It would also violate Matthew 6:5–6 (pray privately). Bennett claimed that so long as no church or denomination receives preference over others, government aid to religion does not violate the amendment's prohibition against laws respecting an establishment of religion.

Bennett holds the narrow view of the establishment clause. History supports the Supreme Court's broad view that government aid to religion, even without preference to any church, violates the establishment clause. Bennett thinks that recent decisions by the Court on public assistance to parochial schools and on religion in public schools are "false to the intentions of the framers" of the First Amendment. The thesis of this book is that nonpreferentialists are wrong about the framers' intentions, not just because the framers had no position on schools, parochial or public, but because the narrow view is based on a misunderstanding of what they meant.

Another nonpreferentialist, Edwin Meese, when attorney general, told the American Bar Association that the establishment clause was designed to prevent Congress from establishing "a national church." He said too that the clause prevents government from "designating a particular faith or sect . . . above the rest," implying that government aid to all without preference to any would be constitutional. He compounded his errors when he said that government neutrality between religion and irreligion undermines religion. It does not; religion flourishes best when left to private voluntary support in a free society.

Chief Justice William H. Rehnquist of the Supreme Court, another nonpreferentialist, flunked history when he wrote an opinion in 1985 in which he sought to prove that the establishment clause merely "forbade the establishment of a national religion and forbade preference among religious sects or denominations." The clause, he claimed, "did not . . . prohibit the federal government from providing nondiscriminatory aid to religion." Thus Rehnquist miraculously converted the ban on establishments of religion into an expansion of government power. He did not consider that the establishment clause prohibits even laws respecting (concerning) an establishment of religion, so that any law on the subject, even if falling short of an establishment of religion, is unconstitutional. He did not know that the clause meant to its framers and ratifiers that there should be no government aid for religion, whether for all religions or one church; it meant no government sponsorship or promotion or endorsement of religious beliefs or practices and no expenditure of public funds for the support of religious exercises or institutions. Rehnquist, Meese, and the nonpreferentialists wish to be bound by the original intent of the framers of the establishment clause because they mistakenly think that the original intent supports their view. In fact, it contradicts their view.

President George Bush, who catered to the Christian right, favored a voucher plan that would enable parents to choose schools where their children would be in a "religious setting and with religious instruction." He also wanted "to put the faith of our fathers back into our schools," and so backed what he called voluntary school prayers. He even said that one could not be president of the United States without faith in God, although the Constitution bans religious tests for federal officeholders. Kenneth Star, Bush's solicitor general, wanted the law to permit government "a non-coercive, ceremonial acknowledgement of the heritage of a deeply religious people." Governments tend to sponsor ceremonial religion that encourages civic virtues like obedience.

The Justice Department under Bush advocated construction of the establishment clause in terms of a coercion test. In the absence of coercion, a government policy would not violate the clause. Such a view, which has not prevailed, would render the clause superfluous, because the presence of coercion would violate the free-exercise clause. Such a view would not only constitutionalize prayer in the schools, especially in ceremonial matters; according to the American Civil Liberties Union, the Bush administration argued "that the government has a right to endorse Christianity as an official national religion so long as it does not force anyone to practice it." Bush scorched the Democratic party in 1992 for failing to mention God in its party platform. The Republican platform ostentatiously supported voluntary prayers in schools and the right to pray publicly at commencements and other community ceremonies. At the Republican convention, spokespersons for the Christian right attributed cultural degeneration—ghetto riots, secular humanism, abortion, pornography, and homosexuality—to what they called the absolute separation of church and state. The establishment clause is a perennially disputatious topic, fraught with emotion.

What did the clause mean in the minds of those who framed and ratified it? The historical evidence on this matter does not speak in a single voice with clarity and insistence. That evidence lends itself to conflicting interpretations. Indeed, my good friend, the Right Reverend Thomas J. Curry, who has reviewed the same evidence as I for the period up to ratification of the First Amendment, holds that the framers retained an image of an establishment of religion quite different from that which I find in evidence. Monsignor Curry and I completely agree, however, that the nonpreferentialist position is historically groundless and without constitutional merit.

Nevertheless, no scholar or judge of intellectual rectitude should answer establishment-clause questions as if the historical evidence permits complete certainty. It does not. Anyone employing evidence responsibly should refrain from asserting with conviction that he or she knows for certain the original meaning and purpose of the establishment clause. The framers and the people of the United States, whose state legislatures ratified the clause, probably did not share a single understanding. Scholars or judges who present an interpretation as the one and only historical truth, the whole historical truth, and nothing but the historical truth delude themselves and their readers. Being sure is more a function of presuppositions than of certainty. The subject of this book is fraught with emotion and partisanship.

Accordingly, I try to recognize and quash my policy preferences when evaluating evidence. My sympathies are clearly with the separationists but are irrelevant to my selection and interpretation of evidence. I go wherever it points and seek to avoid subjectivity. Moreover, my presuppositions are not one-sided. When opinion is at issue, as distinguished from conclusions that must follow from the evidence, I think of myself as a middle-of-the-roader. Others do not. Indeed, many reviewers of the first edition of this book, like Richard John Neuhaus, to my astonishment characterized me as a "strict separationist." Michael McConnell, a law professor who favored the Bush administration's coercion test for use in establishment clause cases, quoted me approvingly on the Supreme Court's difficulty in recognizing an establishment of religion but hastened to add that he stood at a pole opposite mine on most establishment clause issues. One author, Father Richard P. McBrien, an otherwise reasonable man, names me first in his book among the "absolute separationists" whom he placed "on the left."

If people like Neuhaus, McConnell, and McBrien were right, I would not support several of the accommodations to religion that I favor. Strict or absolute separationists, for example, do not criticize the Court's decision against the posting of the Ten Commandments in public schools or approve of Rehnquist's dissent from that decision. Strict separationists do not believe, as I do, that the American Civil Liberties Union too often acts inadvisedly in church-state cases. Strict separationists do not disagree with the Court's opinions as to auxiliary services that aid parochial school students and in particular do not lambaste Justice William Brennan for his opinion in *Aguilar v. Felton* (1985), which prevented New York City from using federal funds to provide highly specialized services to certain disadvantaged parochial school students.

Strict separationists deplored this book. One of them, Albert J. Menendez, an editor of the *Humanist*, finding anomalous my support of public aid to the purely secular functions of parochial schools, exclaimed, "This from a man who praises Jefferson and Madison to the hilt, supports the move to disestablish religious enterprises, and calls for a totally nonsectarian public school system." Menendez is sure that I fail to see that aid to church schools does "exactly" what I condemn in other areas of public life. *Church and State*, a strict separationist publication, found me less persuasive in my analysis of modern church-state issues than in my historical analysis, because I "inexplicably" abandoned strict separation. I thought I had explicated in considerable detail.

Being misunderstood by both accommodationists and strict separationists is tolerable, but not by one whose views are essentially similar to mine. I used to think I was misunderstood by readers because I was not sufficiently clear. I have come to believe that those who differ will distort and refuse to understand; many readers demand clarity and simplicity where the historical record, providing none, shows inconsistencies, lacunae, and complexity. Too many readers want complete adherence to their views, allowing for no exceptions or deviations. Some people seem to read with such blindness that there seems to be no way to shatter the stupefied integument of their biases.

Oliver Wendell Holmes once said that the "chief end of man is to form general propositions, adding that no general proposition is worth a damn." He was wrong on both counts: generalizing is not the chief end of man, and some generalizations are valuable and right. But no general proposition about the establishment clause seems worth a damn unless it is noncontroversial—for example, that there shall be no state church. Anyway, general propositions do not decide real cases.

The establishment clause, like any other controversial clause of the Constitution, is sufficiently ambiguous in language and history to allow few sure generalizations. "Law, like other branches of social science," Justice Benjamin Cardozo observed, "must be satisfied to test the validity of its conclusions by the logic of probabilities rather than the logic of certainty." The evidence demonstrates that by an establishment of religion the framers meant any government policy that aided religion or its agencies, the religious establishments. Even that statement must be qualified; scarcely any clear rule is without exceptions. The exemption of church properties from taxation is certainly a major exception to the rule that aid to religion is unconstitutional.

We live in an imperfect constitutional universe cluttered with ambiguities, mysteries, and inconsistencies. History confounds us. It is delphic and scorns those who seek clarity, certainty, and consistency. Language has a similar effect because words, as Socrates said, "are more plastic than wax is" and therefore are as likely to engender disputes as to settle them. That might not be so if absolutes inhabited the constitutional universe. But no provision of the Bill of Rights guarantees a perfect or unqualified liberty. Chief Justice John Marshall once happily noted that the Constitution has none of the prolixity of legal code. It has rather the virtue of muddy brevity. Even the seemingly specific injunctions of the Bill of Rights do not exclude exceptions, nor are they self-defining.

What indeed in an "establishment of religion" and what is law "respecting" an establishment of religion? History suggests answers but the constitutional text does not. "No law respecting" means no law concerning or touching the subject of, but that still leaves unresolved the meaning of "establishment of religion." The prohibition, one must remember (and what judges forget), is not laid down against establishments of religion but against laws respecting them or on the subject thereof.

Those who wrote our glorious Bill of Rights were vague if not careless draftsmen. Their text offers us no clue as to what constitutes an "unreasonable" search or seizure, or the "probable" cause on which to base the issuance of a warrant. It does not tell us what is an "infamous" crime or what is the nature of the compulsion whose imposition exempts a person from being a witness against himself in a criminal case.

Nor does the text indicate what process of law is "due" before life, liberty, or property may be taken or what is a "public use" and "just" compensation. It is silent on the meaning of a "speedy" trial, "excessive" bail, and a punishment that is "cruel and unusual." The text does not always mean what it says. It does not, for example, really guarantee that the many rights of the Sixth Amendment extend to "all" criminal prosecutions.

If we look to our "first freedoms," we find that the First Amendment (which was originally intended to be the third) tells us nothing about the freedom of speech and press that Congress may not abridge. The very verbs in the First Amendment add to our perplexity. We can understand "no law abridging" but not the use of "prohibit" with respect to the free exercise of religion. Nowhere in the making of the Bill of Rights was the original intent and meaning clearer than in the case of religious freedom. The phrasing was "Congress shall make no law respecting an establishment of religion nor prohibiting the free exercise thereof. . . ." The meaning, I submit, was this: Congress shall make no law concerning religion or abridging the free exercise thereof. The actual phrasing suggests the avoidance of the obvious and the deliberate use of a different verb: prohibiting. But Congress can pass laws regulating and even abridging the free exercise of religion without prohibiting it altogether. The difference here is more than one of degree; it is the difference between diminishing and abolishing. If, then, the text meant what is says, it does not at all protect religious liberty with the amplitude we all assume.

With little guidance from the constitutional text, we may better understand the establishment clause if we understand the American experience with establishments of religion at the time of the ratification of the Bill of Rights in 1791. After the American Revolution seven of the fourteen states that comprised the Union in 1791 authorized establishments of religion by law. Not one state maintained a single or preferential establishment of religion. An establishment of religion meant to those who framed and ratified the First Amendment what it meant in those seven states, and in all seven it meant public support of religion on a nonpreferential basis. It was specifically this public support on a nonpreferential basis that the establishment clause of the First Amendment sought to forbid.

In this revised and updated edition, which is considerably longer than the first, I have added an analysis of Jefferson ideas on church and state; I have fleshed out many of the arguments in chapters 6 through 9; I have added a presentation of the establishment-clause cases of the past seven terms of the Court. And I have taken into consideration a variety of criticisms of the original edition.

Leonard W. Levy
Ashland, Oregon
1993

The

Establishment

Clause

I Colonial Establishments of Religion

On the eve of the American Revolution most of the colonies maintained establishments of religion. Those colonies, although resentful of British violations of American rights, discriminated against Roman Catholics, Jews, and even dissenting Protestants who refused to comply with local laws benefiting establishments of religion. In the five southern colonies, including Virginia, the oldest, largest, and most influential of the thirteen colonies, the Church of England (Anglican) enjoyed the privileges of an exclusive legal union with the state; in the three New England colonies which the Congregationalists domi-

2 | The Establishment Clause

nated, the laws operated to prefer their churches at the expense of others.

The Reverend Isaac Backus, leader of the Baptists in Massachusetts, in the course of a protest against that colony's establishment of religion, informed the governor and council in 1774 that eighteen Baptists from the town of Warwick had been jailed forty miles from home, in Northampton, during the extremity of winter, for the crime of refusing to pay taxes in support of the town's Congregational minister.[1] They were jailed for conscience' sake, Backus declared, at a time when all America expressed alarm at British violations of American liberties. He believed that Massachusetts violated the right to be free from taxation without representation, because its legislature had authorized all the towns to impose "religious taxes." They were as illegal as Parliament's taxation of America, Backus alleged, because the province's charter guaranteed liberty of conscience to all Christians except "Papists." Moreover, Massachusetts law required that Baptists obtain a certificate proving that they regularly attended a church of their own denomination to be exempt from ministerial and church taxes. The towns enacted such taxes for the support of public worship held by "learned and orthodox" ministers (Congregationalists); but these individuals had to pay a tax of four pence (the tea tax was only three pence per pound) for a copy of the certification or legal document that they needed to prove their tax-exempt status. "All America are alarmed at the tea tax; though, if they please, they can avoid it by not buying the tea, but we have no such liberty," Backus complained, and, he added, conscience prevented payment of the certificate tax: government had no lawful authority over religion.[2] Backus had acted on behalf of a Baptist grievance committee formed to fight "oppressions occasioned by nonconformity to the religious establishment in New England."[3] Backus spoke for the Baptist minority that felt persecuted by the Congregational majority.

1. Alvah Hovey, *A Memoir of the Life and Times of Reverend Isaac Backus* (Boston, 1858), pp. 197, 198; dated Feb. 15, 1774.

2. Petition to the General Court, Dec. 2, 1774, in ibid., pp. 215–21.

3. William G. McLoughlin, *New England Dissent, 1630–1833: The Baptists and the Separation of Church and State*, 2 vols. (Cambridge, Mass., 1971), 1:529, quoting Warren Association Minutes, 1769.

John Adams spoke for the Congregationalists when he stated that the establishment to which he gave his support was "but a slender one" that did not infringe religious liberty.[4]

The Reverend Ezra Stiles, president of Yale College, who agreed with Adams, also ignored the fact that Massachusetts imprisoned Baptists and any others who refused obedience to the government in matters of support for religion. In Virginia and other southern colonies, Stiles observed, Baptists "not only pay ministerial Taxes for building churches but are imprisoned for preaching in unlicensed Houses."[5] The decade before the Revolution constituted the "time of persecution" in the history of Virginia's Baptists. Some were beaten by mobs, others fined and imprisoned for their religious beliefs, which prevented them from obeying the laws that established the Anglican (Episcopalian) Church.[6]

To protect the established religion, the Virginia courts regarded certain Baptist conduct as criminal. Preaching in unlicensed houses and preaching without Episcopal ordination were common crimes. For such crimes some Baptist ministers spent up to five months in jail. In a 1771 case, four preachers were convicted of unlawful assembly for having held a religious meeting "under the pretense of the exercise of Religion in other manner than according to the Liturgy and Practice of the Church of England." In another case the crime was defined as "Preaching the Gospel" contrary to the Anglican Book of Common Prayer, for which the criminal spent forty-six days in jail. About fifty Baptists suffered imprisonment for such crimes. Other Baptists were indicted for not attending the services of the established church. The law also made it a crime for any clergyman not licensed by that church to conduct marriages.[7] Young James Madison informed a Philadelphia

4. Hovey, *Backus*, p. 210.

5. Ezra Stiles, *The Literary Diary of Ezra Stiles*, edited by Franklin B. Dexter, 3 vols. (New York, 1901), 1:475.

6. For instances of mob violence, see Lewis Peyton Little, *Imprisoned Preachers and Religious Liberty in Virginia* (Lynchburg, Va., 1938), pp. 41, 43, 47, 49–52, 209, 298, 300.

7. Ibid., pp. 236, 271, 288, 299, 418, 457. Sandra Rennie, "Virginia's Baptist Persecution, 1765–1778," *Journal of Religious History* 12 (June 1982): 48–61,

friend in 1774, "That diabolical Hell conceived principle of persecution rages among some and to their eternal Infamy the Clergy can furnish their Quota of Imps for such business. This vexes me the most of any thing whatever. There are at this [time] in the adjacent county not less than 5 or 6 well meaning men in close Gaol [jail] for publishing their religious Sentiments which in the main are very orthodox."[8]

The established church for whose benefit Baptist preachers faced jail for illegally preaching the gospel was an extension of the Church of England. The Virginia establishment originated with the colony's first charter in 1606, which provided that all ministers should preach Christianity according to the "doctrine, rites, and religion now professed and established within the realm of England." Dale's Laws in 1611 required everyone to be a churchgoer and observe the Sabbath, enjoined the clergy to offer regular religious instruction, and severely punished various offenses against religion including blasphemy, sacrilege, and criticism of the doctrine of the Trinity. Subsequent legislation commanded the public maintenance of every Anglican minister and tithed everyone for that purpose, required "uniformity to the canons and constitutions of the Church of England," allowed only ordained clergymen of the mother church to perform the marriage ceremony, demanded that every clergyman accept the Thirty-nine Articles of faith, and exacted taxes to underwrite the costs of building and repairing churches. The legal code governing this establishment of religion also required vestries in each parish to levy assessments for the benefit of those churches and ordered that the liturgy of the Church of England be followed according to the Anglican Book of Common Prayer. Thus, Virginia's Anglican church was established by law. It was the official church, the only one that enjoyed the benefits of a formal alliance with the government.[9] As the Presbyterian clergy of Virginia declared in a

---

puts the number of persecuted Baptists at seventy-eight for the period she covered. She finds too that the local gentry, including Anglican clergymen, justices of the peace, captains of the militia, and lesser planters, led the persecution.

8. William T. Hutchinson et al., eds., *The Papers of James Madison*, ser. in progress (Chicago, 1962–), 1:106. Hereafter cited as *Madison Papers*.

9. George M. Brydon, *Virginia's Mother Church*, 2 vols. (Richmond, Va.,

remonstrance to the legislature in 1784, the Anglican or "Episcopal Church was virtually regarded as the constitutional Church, the Church of the State" before the Revolution, laden with special privileges that destroyed the equality of all others.[10]

An establishment of religion in the conventional sense denoted a legal union of government and religion, if by "religion" is meant the religion of a single church or denomination, such as Roman Catholicism in Spain, Presbyterianism in Scotland, or Lutheranism in Sweden. Attendance at a state church was compulsory, unless the state indulged the existence of open religious services by dissenters. An establishment of religion had an official creed or articles of faith, and its creed alone could be publicly taught in the schools or elsewhere. Its clergy alone had civil sanction to perform sacraments or allow them to be performed. Subscribers to the established faith enjoyed their civil rights, but the law handicapped dissenters, even if it tolerated their worship, by the imposition of civil disabilities. Dissenters were excluded from universities and disqualified for office, whether civil, religious, or military. Their religious institutions (churches, schools, orphanages) had no legal capacity to bring suits, hold or transmit property, receive or bequeath trust funds. Test oaths usually discriminated against dissenters. Every establishment employed such oaths, although some governments, such as those of the Middle Atlantic colonies that had no establishments, also imposed religious tests on officeholders to make certain that only believers in the gospel would be entrusted with an official capacity.

Conventional establishments of religion existed in the southern colonies of Virginia, Maryland, North Carolina, South Carolina, and Georgia. In each the Church of England was the state church. In South Carolina the Reverend William Tennent, a Presbyterian acting as a spokesman for various non-Anglican denominations, drew up a "Peti-

---

1958), 1:426–81, reprints extracts from diocesan canons and statutes. The laws of Virginia on the establishment are scattered throughout William W. Hening, ed., *The Statutes at Large Being a Collection of All the Laws of Virginia (1619–1792)*, 13 vols. (Richmond, Va., 1809–23).

10. Charles F. James, *Documentary History of the Struggle for Religious Liberty in Virginia* (Lynchburg, Va., 1900), p. 228.

tion of the Dissenters" in 1777, requesting the legislature to disestablish the Church of England, by then calling itself the Protestant Episcopal Church. The existence of an established church, Tennent declared, abridged the "free and equal liberty in religious matters" to which all good Christian subjects were entitled, and by Christian he meant Protestant. He announced his objection to "all religious establishments" because they infringed religious liberty, but he did not favor the complete separation of government and religion. Very few Christians did. Like Tennent, they believed that the state should "give countenance to religion" by protecting all denominations and "do anything for the support of religion, without partiality to particular societies" and without abridging "the rights of private judgment" by exacting taxes to promote religion.[11]

Tennent depicted the establishment in South Carolina from the standpoint of a dissenter. He emphasized that it made invidious distinctions among people of different religious beliefs, merely tolerating dissenters as if they stood "on the same footing with the Jews," unmolested but unequal.[12] It also taxed all for the support of one religion. Invidious distinctions and tax support constituted its chief characteristics. "The law," he declared,

> knows and acknowledges the society of the one as a Christian church; the law knows not the other churches. The law knows the clergy of the one as ministers of the gospel; the law knows not the clergy the other churches, nor will it give them a license to marry their own people. . . . The law makes provision for the support of one church; it makes no provision for the others. The law builds superb churches for the one; it leaves the others to build their own churches. The law, by incorporating the one church, enables it to hold estates and to sue for rights; the law does not enable the others to hold any religious property not even the pittances which are bestowed by the hand of charity for their support. No dissenting

11. Newton B. Jones, ed., "Writings of the Reverend William Tennent, 1740–1777," *South Carolina Historical Magazine* 61 (July–Oct. 1960): 197, reprinting "Mr. Tennent's Speech on the Dissenting Petition, Delivered in the House of Assembly, Charles-Town, January 11, 1777."

12. Ibid., pp. 197, 202.

church can hold or sue for their property at common law. They are obliged therefore to deposit it in the hands of trustees, to be held by them as their own private property and to lie at their mercy. The consequence of this is that too often their funds for the support of religious worship get into bad hands and become either alienated from their proper use or must be recovered at the expense of a suit in chancery.

These are important distinctions indeed, but these are not all. The law vests the officers of the Church of England with power to tax not only her own people but all other denominations within the bounds of each respective parish for the support of the poor—an enormous power which ought to be vested in no denomination more than another. Greater distinction still—where there are parishes the law throws the whole management of elections, the most estimable of all the rights of freemen, into the hands of church officers exclusively. [Church wardens in each parish issued writs for the election of members of the legislature and managed the elections.][13]

A scholar familiar with classic establishments of religion, like the one described by Tennent in South Carolina, concluded in capital letters that an establishment had always and everywhere meant what he found it meant in Europe: "A SINGLE CHURCH OR RELIGION ENJOYING FORMAL, LEGAL, OFFICIAL, MONOPOLISTIC PRIVILEGE THROUGH A UNION WITH THE GOVERNMENT OF THE STATE. That is the meaning given in the *Encyclopedia Britannica*. The phrase has been used this way for centuries in speaking of the established Protestant churches of England, Scotland, Germany, and other countries, and of the established Catholic church in Italy, Spain, and elsewhere."[14] The foremost American constitutional scholar of this century, Edward S. Corwin, advanced the same thesis. Criticizing the Supreme Court's doctrine of the unconstitutionality of government aid to all religions as "untrue historically," Corwin added, "In a word, what the establishment of

13. Ibid., pp. 198–99.
14. James O'Neill, *Religion and Education under the Constitution* (New York, 1949), p. 204.

religion clause of the First Amendment does, and all that it does, is to forbid Congress to give any religious faith, sect, or denomination preferred status." He concluded, "The historical record showed beyond peradventure that the core idea of 'an establishment of religion' comprises the idea of preference, and that any act of public authority favorable to religion in general cannot, without manifest falsification of history, be brought under the ban of that phrase."[15] Thus, we are told, "There is not an item of dependable evidence . . . which shows that the term means, or ever has meant, anything else."[16]

Corwin was wrong. The item of dependable evidence consists of much more than the curious but startling fact that sixteenth-century Transylvania, then part of Hungary, nurtured not only legends of vampires and werewolves but the simultaneous establishment of otherwise warring religions. They were Roman Catholicism, Calvinism, Lutheranism, and Unitarianism.[17] The inappropriateness of using the conventional European model of an establishment of religion as the only definition of an establishment is evident from the provisions of the Quebec Act of 1774. By that controversial statute Parliament established both Anglicanism and Roman Catholicism in Canada. Protestant America, however, received the act in vehemently bigoted terms as an establishment of only Catholicism. The act reconfirmed a previous guarantee of the "free exercise of the religion of the Church of Rome" and stipulated that its clergy might "hold, receive and enjoy their accustomed Dues and Rights" from persons professing that religion. On behalf of the English in Quebec, the next paragraph of the act provided "for the Maintenance and Support of Protestant Clergy within the Province."[18] A minority in Parliament, led by Lord Camden in the House of Lords and by Colonel Isaac Barré in the House of Commons,

15. Edward S. Corwin, "The Supreme Court as National School Board," *Law and Contemporary Problems* 14 (Winter 1949): 10, 20, criticizing *Everson v. Board of Education*, 330 U.S. 1 (1947).

16. O'Neill, *Religion and Education*, p. 204.

17. Earl Morse Wilbur, *A History of Unitarians: In Transylvania, England, and America* (Cambridge, Mass., 1952), pp. 3–98.

18. Charles H. Metzger, *The Quebec Act* (New York, 1936), p. 211.

condemned the act as pernicious to the religion and constitution of England, because it established Roman Catholicism.[19] That view of the matter virtually engrossed the thinking of the act's antagonists. Alexander Hamilton, dismayed because the Quebec Act established Roman Catholicism as well as Protestantism, that is, the Church of England, accepted the validity of the proposition that "an establish-ment of religion is a religion, which the civil authority engages, not only to protect but to support." Hamilton approved of toleration for Roman Catholicism but argued that the act did not remain "passive and improvident" toward it, as toward a merely tolerated religion; the act, rather, was "active and provident" as toward an establishment of religion, because it fixed on ways to support and protect that religion especially by tithes.[20] Hamilton's explanation of an establishment met no known opposition in America, though neither he nor anyone else accepted the Quebec Act for what it was: a statutory provision for a dual establishment of religion.[21]

The classic concept of an establishment of religion as a single state church inappropriately described the American situation; this seems clear from the change in opinion of William Tennent of South Carolina and especially from the change in the character of that state's establishment. Shortly after Tennent had censured the existing establishment in 1777 and had declared himself opposed to "all" establishments as violations of religious liberty, he discovered an establishment that met his approval. He called it a "general establishment" because it recognized and nurtured the legal equality of all Protestants without preferring one denomination over others. The general establishment proposed Protestant Christianity as the established religion of the state.[22] In 1778 the

---

19. William Cobbett, ed., *The Parliamentary History of England [Debates] from the Earliest Period to the Year 1803*, 36 vols. (London, 1806–20), 17:1361–62, 18:657–58.

20. "Remarks on the Quebec Bill," in *The Papers of Alexander Hamilton*, ed. Harold C. Syrett, ser. in progress (New York, 1961–), 1:169–72. Hereafter cited as *Hamilton Papers*.

21. The American reaction to the act is the subject of Metzger, *Quebec Act*.

22. Jones, ed., "Writings of Tennent," p. 203.

constitution of South Carolina created the establishment of religion endorsed by Tennent.[23]

The *Encyclopedia Britannica* and the European precedents notwithstanding, abundant evidence proves that the European form of an establishment was not the only form in America and that the European meaning of an establishment of religion was not the only meaning in America. America in the eighteenth century had broken with the precedents of Europe by providing legal recognition and tax support to more than one church or denomination within a colony and, later, within a state.

Indeed, at the time of the framing of the First Amendment all state establishments that still existed in America were general or multiple establishments of all the churches of each state, something unknown in the Europe familiar to Americans.

The American establishments of religion as of about 1790 authorized the taxation of everyone for the support of religion but allowed each person's tax to be remitted to the church of the person's choice. Without doubt, an establishment of religion still conveyed the basic idea of exclusivity or preference, but that was not the only idea that it conveyed. To the generation that adopted the First Amendment an establishment had also come to mean, in the main, the financial support of religion generally, by public taxation. Granted, religion was then virtually synonymous with Christianity—indeed, in most of America, with Protestantism.

In Europe a state church meant exactly what the term denotes: the church of one denomination, not of Christianity or Protestantism. Christianity or Protestantism may signify one religion in contrast with Judaism, Islam, or Hinduism; Protestantism may, more dubiously, be one religion in contrast with Roman Catholicism. But nowhere after the sixteenth century had Christianity or Protestantism been the solely established religion except in America. An establishment of Christianity or of Protestantism in the American states that permitted an establishment in about 1790 would have been, for practical purposes, a

23. Francis Newton Thorpe, ed., *The Federal and State Constitutions, Colonial Charters, and Other Organic Laws*, 7 vols. (Washington, 1909), 6:3252–57.

comprehensive or nonpreferential establishment, permitting government aid to all churches or to religion generally. No American state at the time maintained an establishment in the European sense of having an exclusive or state church designated by law.

Even before the liberating effect of the American Revolution, America had its Transylvanian equivalents, in which a single political jurisdiction established more than one church. The American experience, always remarkably diverse, comprehended exclusive establishments, dual establishments, and general or multiple establishments of religion. In contrast to the five southern colonies, where Anglicanism alone enjoyed an establishment, four colonies never had an establishment of any kind: Rhode Island, Pennsylvania, Delaware, and New Jersey. In the colonies of New York, Massachusetts, Connecticut, and New Hampshire, however, the pattern of establishment was diversified and uniquely American.

New York's colonial history of church-state relationships provided America's first example of an establishment of religion radically different from the classic European type. New York developed an establishment of religion in general—or at least of Protestantism in general—without preference to one church over others. When the English conquered New Netherlands in 1664, renaming it New York in honor of its new proprietor, the duke of York (James II), they found that the Dutch Reformed Church (Calvinist) was exclusively established as the state church; but after the colony passed to English control, this church lost its governmental support. The "Duke's Laws" of 1664, in the form of instructions to his governor, disestablished the Dutch Reformed Church and established in its place a multiplicity of churches. Any church of the Protestant religion could become an established church. In a sense, of course, this was an exclusive establishment of one religion, Protestantism, but the system involved a general establishment of several different Protestant churches, in sharp contrast to the European precedents that provided for the establishment of one church or denomination only.

Under the "Duke's Laws" every township was obliged publicly to support some Protestant church and a minister. The denomination of the church did not matter. Costs were to be met by a public tax: "Every inhabitant shall contribute to all charges both in Church and State."[24] A local option system prevailed. Each town, by a majority vote of its householders, was to select the denomination to be established locally by electing a minister of that denomination. The head of the state was the head of all the churches. Upon proof that a minister was Protestant, he was inducted into his pastorate by the governor representing the state. In other words, this was an establishment of religion in which there was a formal, legal, official union between government and religion on a nonpreferential basis and without the establishment of any individual church. "Here," remarked a perceptive historian, "is an establishment without a name."[25]

In effect, the "Duke's Laws" allowed the Dutch Reformed Church to remain the established church in most localities, because the Dutch for a while were the most numerous among the settlers. Yet others dominated in a few towns, and as the religious composition of the population changed through constant immigration, the established church of different localities changed. New York's was the only establishment of religion at the time that permitted a very considerable religious liberty.

In 1683 the New York Assembly explicitly confirmed the system of multiple establishments by enacting a "Charter of Liberties." This "charter" stated that "the Churches already in New York do appear to be privileged Churches. . . . Provided also that all other Christian Churches, that shall hereafter come and settle in the province, shall have the same privileges."[26]

However, in 1686 the Catholic James II instructed Thomas Dongan,

24. Quoted in Sanford H. Cobb, *Rise of Religious Liberty* (New York, 1902), p. 326; Cobb's excellent account of church-state relations in colonial New York is on pp. 301–61. John Webb Pratt, *Religion, Politics, and Diversity: The Church-State Theme in New York History* (Ithaca, N.Y., 1967), is still fuller. Thomas Curry, *The First Freedoms: Church and State in America to the Passage of the First Amendment* (New York, 1986), pp. 62–72, 121–24, rejects the multiple-establishment interpretation. Curry's book is the best on the subject for the period between the colonial background and the ratification of the First Amendment, but it is marred by his rigidity.

25. Cobb, *Rise of Religious Liberty*, p. 327.

26. E. B. O'Callaghan and B. Fernow, eds., *Documents Relating to the Colonial History of the State of New York*, 15 vols. (Albany, 1853–87), 1:115; Hugh Has-

royal governor of New York and also a Catholic, to establish the Episcopalian Church of England as the state church of the colony, thereby singling out that church for preferential treatment. Services of the state church were to be based on the Anglican Book of Common Prayer; sacraments were to be administered according to Anglican rites. The ecclesiastical jurisdiction for the entire province was vested in the archbishop of Canterbury; the governor was empowered to remove ministers. Despite these instructions, Governor Dongan took no steps to establish the Church of England. Following the Glorious Revolution in England, London again demanded the establishment of Anglicanism. Governor Benjamin Fletcher tried to implement the royal instructions, but the colonial assembly refused to enact the needed statute. In 1693, however, the assembly, composed almost entirely of non-Anglicans, grudgingly enacted what one historian called "a bill for a religious establishment of an entirely nondescript character, the like of which is not to be found elsewhere."[27] The act stated that in the places thereafter named, "there shall be called, inducted, and established a good, sufficient, Protestant Minister." One such minister was for New York City, one for Richmond County, and two for Westchester and Queens counties. The ministers were to be supported by public taxes. The act did not apply to the remainder of the province of New York.[28]

In effect, the act of 1693 seemed to have established the Anglican Church in the four localities named, but not a word in the act referred to that church. The statute called only for "a good and sufficient Protestant Minister" and specified no denomination. Royal governors and most Anglicans asserted that the statute had established the Church of England; many non-Anglicans in New York disagreed. The legislature that had passed the measure resolved in 1695, to the governor's wrath, that the act permitted a "dissenting protestant minister" to be called to a church within the geographic limits of the act, and "he is to be paid and maintained as the act directs."[29] In other words, non-Anglican

tings and Edward S. Corwin, eds., *Ecclesiastical Records of the State of New York*, 7 vols. (Albany, 1901–6), 2:1073–78.

27. Cobb, *Rise of Religious Liberty*, p. 338.

28. O'Callaghan and Fernow, eds., *Documents*, 1:328–31.

29. Cobb, *Rise of Religious Liberty*, p. 340; Hastings and Corwin, eds., *Ecclesiastical Records*, 2:1114.

Protestants in the four localities could pay their taxes for the support of their own local church, and churches not of the Church of England were in fact built; they and their ministers were maintained by local taxation within the four localities after the act of 1693. In 1695 the legislature declared that the New York City vestry had rightly decided that under the law it could contract for a "Dissenting Protestant minister," that is, a non-Anglican. As a historian of church-state relationships in New York declared, "The concept of multiple establishments remained the dissenters' solution . . . as the seventeenth century drew to a close in New York."[30]

Lewis Morris, himself a strong Church of England man, declared in 1699, "The People were generally dissenters [and] fancied they had made an effectual provision for ministers of their own persuasion by this Act [of 1693]."[31] In 1711, shortly before becoming chief justice of the province, Morris admitted that the act of 1693 was "very loosely worded. The Dissenters claim the benefit of it as well as we."[32] As a result, there was constant argument—the royal governors and the Church of England on one side, the assembly and non-Anglican Protestants on the other—concerning the disposition of tax funds for the support of religion.

Finally, in 1731, the provincial court of New York decided the controversy in a case involving the Jamaica Church of Queens. The church had been built by a town tax as a Presbyterian edifice in 1699. Anglicans, backed by the governor, seized and took possession of the church on the grounds that any property for religious purposes built by public funds must belong to the Church of England as the only established church under the act of 1693. The Anglicans' action set off a long and bitter controversy. The Presbyterians refused to pay the salary of the Anglican minister because, as the Church of England townspeople reported, "they [the Presbyterians] stick not to call themselves the Established Church."[33] After several years of Episcopalian control, the Pres-

30. Pratt, *Religion, Politics, and Diversity*, p. 47.

31. O'Callaghan and Fernow, eds., *Documents*, 5:232.

32. Quoted in Cobb, *Rise of Religious Liberty*, p. 339.

33. E. B. O'Callaghan, ed., *The Documentary History of the State of New York*, 4 vols. (Albany, 1848–49), 3:278.

byterians again took the church. The Episcopalians then sued for possession, once more arguing that a publicly supported church could belong to none but the Church of England, and the Presbyterians lodged a countersuit. The court ruled in favor of the Presbyterians, allowing them to hold the church and collect taxes for its maintenance and for the salary of the minister.[34]

Thus a formal judicial decision by the highest court of the province shows that a multiple establishment of religion existed in New York and that an establishment of religion in New York did not simply mean government preference to one religion or sect over others; it meant public support of religion, especially by financial aid, on an impartial or nonpreferential basis. For much of the remainder of the colonial period, Anglicans managed to pry a minister's salary out of the reluctant inhabitants, but not without constant complaints and a further attempt, defeated by the courts in 1768, to withhold the minister's salary.[35]

Elsewhere on Long Island, the inhabitants supported the non-Anglican town ministers chosen by the majority. Brookhaven certainly supported such a dissenting minister, and, given the scarcity of Anglicans and Anglican ministers in the colony, most towns probably reached their own accommodations with the minister of their choice.[36]

Worthy of note also is the way in which the system of a multiple establishment in New York had changed since its initiation by the "Duke's Laws" of 1664. In the beginning, townspeople by majority vote selected a church as the established church of the town, to be supported by the taxes of everyone regardless of church affiliation. By 1731, however, the multiple establishment had come to mean not only that the several Protestant churches were established, but that in towns with a heterogeneous religious population there were likely to be sev-

34. Ibid., 3:309–11. The Jamaica controversy can be followed in ibid., pp. 205–302. See also Pratt, *Religion, Politics, and Diversity*, pp. 54, 61–62; Cobb, *Rise of Religious Liberty*, pp. 345–48.

35. O'Callaghan, ed., *Documentary History*, 3:311, 330; Pratt, *Religion, Politics, and Diversity*, p. 62.

36. Hastings and Corwin, eds., *Ecclesiastical Records*, 2:1392, 3:1589, 1695, 2141.

eral different established churches, each supported by the taxes of its own communicants.

In the 1750s the organization of King's (later Colombia) College provoked a fierce controversy over the nature of New York's establishment. Anglicans demanded that they control the new school because they enjoyed "a preference by the Constitution of the province."[37] Non-Anglicans rejected Anglican claims of control and preference. A young lawyer, William Livingston, who became a framer of the U.S. Constitution, and two associates, William Smith Jr. and John Morin Scott, organized the opposition. The Triumvirate, as the three came to be known, specifically denied that the Anglican church was exclusively established in the colony. They publicized this refutation in their paper *The Independent Reflector*, and Smith devoted a section to it in his *History*.[38] The Triumvirate insisted that the establishment "restricted no particular Protestant Denomination whatsoever" and that the people were to choose which ministers to establish.[39] Here again is evidence that the concept of a multiple establishment was understood by and also engaged the attention of the inhabitants of colonial New York.

Although New York Anglicans claimed an exclusive establishment of their church, a large number of the colony's population understood the establishment set up by the act of 1693 not as a state preference for one religion or sect over others but as allowing public support for many different churches to be determined by popular vote. Thus, in 1775, Alexander Hamilton, a young New York lawyer, defined "an established religion" as "a religion which the civil authority engaged, not only to protect, but to support."[40]

A widespread belief exists that the New England colonies, excepting

37. William Smith, *A General Idea of the College of Mirania* (New York, 1753; Charles Evans, *Early American Imprints*, no. 7121, microcard), p. 84. Pratt, *Religion, Politics, and Diversity*, pp. 67–71.

38. Milton Klein, ed., *The Independent Reflector* (Cambridge, Mass., 1963), pp. 171–78. William Smith Jr., *The History of the Province of New York*, edited by Michael Kammen, 2 vols. (Cambridge, Mass., 1972), 2:167–68, 175–76, 207–8.

39. Klein, ed., *Independent Reflector*, p. 26; William Livingston, *Address to Sir Charles Hardy* (New York, 1755), pp. vii–viii.

40. "Remarks on the Quebec Bill," in *Hamilton Papers*, 1:169–70.

Rhode Island, maintained exclusive establishments of the Congregational church. Anyone holding this view does not know or understand that multiple establishments were legally permissible and that dual establishments existed in fact.

Massachusetts, the major and archetypal New England colony, proclaimed no establishment of the Congregational church by name after 1692. The General Court's act of that year provided for an establishment of religion on a town basis by simply requiring every town to maintain an "able, learned and orthodox" minister, to be chosen by the voters of the town and supported by a tax levied on all taxpayers.[41] As a matter of law it was theoretically possible for several different denominations to benefit from the establishment.

Because the Congregationalists were the overwhelming majority in nearly every town, they reaped the benefits of the establishment of religion, except in Boston. The act of 1692 exempted Boston because voluntary contributions there had successfully maintained the Congregational churches, making the compulsion of law unnecessary. As a result, non-Congregationalists, chiefly Episcopalians, Baptists, and Quakers, did not face taxation for the benefit of religion in Boston; like the Congregationalists, they were left alone to support their churches as they wished. Except in Boston, the law operated to make Congregationalism the privileged church, which unquestionably was the law's purpose. Non-Congregationalists outside of Boston were taxed for the support of Congregational ministers and buildings.

An extraordinary situation, however, existed in the town of Swansea, settled and dominated by Baptists long before the 1692 statute. By 1693, Swansea, in southern Massachusetts, had two Baptist churches, and they became the official town churches, supported by public taxation. The Baptist ministers received the taxes for the public support of public worship. The exclusive Baptist establishment of religion in little Swansea was undoubtedly unique anywhere in the world. And, like any orthodoxy that had the law on its side as well as an overwhelming majority vote, the Baptist establishment mistreated the local religious minority.

41. Jacob C. Meyer, *Church and State in Massachusetts, 1740 to 1833* (Cleveland, 1930), p. 10.

The Congregationalists, who almost everywhere else in Massachusetts constituted the "standing order," found the tables turned in Swansea. Baptist ministers refused to baptize Congregational infants. Consequently the small Congregational minority presented the town of Swansea to the county court of general sessions for violation of the 1692 act, on the grounds that Swansea did not maintain an "orthodox learned minister." In 1708 the court ruled that religious taxes raised in Swansea must be divided equally between the two denominations, a victory for the Congregationalists that created another unique legal situation. From the time of that decision, Swansea possessed a dual establishment of religion: public taxation supported the churches of the two denominations, at least until 1717. In that year the Congregationalists, who continued to complain of religious persecution by the Baptists, received additional relief from an act of the General Court incorporating the Congregational section of town into the adjoining town of Barrington, where the standing order prevailed. Swansea then reverted to its exclusive Baptist establishment of religion, which lasted until 1727, when the General Court enacted a statute exempting Baptists from the payment of taxes for the support of religion.[42]

In a few towns, where Baptists or Quakers, or the two together, constituted a majority, they successfully refused, on conscientious grounds, to pay the religious taxes. Neither Baptists nor Quakers maintained a learned ministry, and both believed that the state had no jurisdiction over religion, which should be left to voluntary support of believers. In the towns of Tiverton and Dartmouth in Bristol County, people simply defied court orders year after year, even after the governor and council in Boston commanded the imprisonment of the towns' recalcitrant tax assessors. The Quakers of Tiverton appealed directly to England on the grounds that the Massachusetts charter of 1691 guaranteed liberty of conscience to all Protestants. The General Court yielded by agreeing to pay out of the provincial treasury for the

---

42. McLoughlin, *New England Dissent*, 1:136–48, 160; Susan Martha Reed, *Church and State in Massachusetts* (Urbana, Ill., 1914), pp. 70–73. Curry, *First Freedoms*, p. 108, having ignored the case of Swansea, repudiates the reality of multiple establishment and calls it a "theory" that served as a "smokescreen" for Congregationalism.

support of Congregational ministers in the two towns to do missionary work; but sporadic Congregational preaching failed to convert the obdurate dissenters, who controlled the towns and refused to pay taxes for the support of any town ministers. In 1717 Cotton Mather spoke hopefully of "Gospellizing the paganizing Tiverton," but not even his efforts succeeded. Six years later the authorities in Boston again assessed Tiverton for the support of a Congregational minister. The Quakers then challenged the system of an establishment of religion in Massachusetts by arguing before the authorities in London that the Toleration Act of 1689, the provincial charter of 1691, and the Massachusetts act of 1692, which allowed a majority of the town to choose its own minister, had established equality among all Protestants and a liberty of conscience unburdened by compulsory taxation for the support of religion. The Privy Council ruled that the ministerial taxes in Tiverton and Dartmouth were illegal and ought not be imposed by Congregationalists where they did not comprise a majority. During the entire colonial period the two towns paid no taxes under the establishment act of 1692.[43]

Unlike the Baptists and Quakers, the Anglicans (Episcopalians) did not dominate any Massachusetts towns. Scattered groups of them lived in many towns, but in 1727, when they received an exemption from supporting Congregationalist town churches, the Anglicans had only five churches and ministers of their own. Two were in Boston, the others in Newbury, Marblehead, and Bristol. Except in Boston, Anglicans had to pay a pro rata share for Congregational churches and ministers until 1727, or be jailed, and many were. Not surprisingly they sought relief by appealing to London. Some even contended that the true established church in Massachusetts was their own, by virtue of the fact that the church of the mother country was the church of any English colony. Some Congregationalists matched that absurd argument with one of their own, namely, that they, as the minister of Roxbury said in 1724, were "the Original Established Church of England, who do not live in England."[44]

---

43. McLoughlin, *New England Dissent*, 1:165–99; Reed, *Church and State*, pp. 77–78.

44. McLoughlin, *New England Dissent*, 1:217.

The struggle of Anglicans and Congregationalists to define themselves in connection with an establishment of religion led to a concession by some Congregationalists that theirs was not the sole established church in Massachusetts. Two of the preeminent Congregational ministers acknowledged in the 1720s that the act of 1692 commanding public worship at taxpayer expense allowed any denomination to become the established church of a town. Benjamin Colman of the Brattle Street Church in Boston, who declined the presidency of Harvard College, declared in 1725 that "here the Legal Establishment" consisted of the Congregational churches, but "if any Town shall chuse a Gentleman of the Church of England for their Pastor . . . he is their Minister by the Laws of our Province as much as any Congregational Minister among us is so."[45]

That formidable spokesman for Massachusetts orthodoxy, Cotton Mather, made a similar point the following year when he observed that whoever got elected by the majority was "the Minister of the Place," so that "the King's Minister" in any particular locality, the one entitled to tax support, was the people's choice, Christ's, and the king's. "If," Mather added, "the Most of the Inhabitants in a Plantation are Episcopalians, they will have a Minister of their own Persuasion; and the Dissenters if there be any in the place, must pay their proportion of the Tax for the Support of this Legal Minister."[46] Colman and Mather, whose remarks seem calculated to thwart a decision by the Privy Council or the king's attorney general that might harm Congregational interests, accurately interpreted the act of 1692. When the archbishop of Canterbury inquired of the royal governor of Massachusetts "Whether Independency [Congregationalism] be the Establishment of this Country?" Governor Jonathan Belcher replied: "I don't apprehend it is, but that the Church of England is as much established by the laws of this Province as that of the Independents, Presbyterians, or Baptists, and shou'd any town or parish in the Province elect a clergyman of the Church of England to be their minister, and he qualify'd as the law

---

45. Ebenezer Turall, *The Life and Character of Benjamin Colman* (Boston, 1749; Evans, *Early American Imprints*, no. 6434, microcard), p. 138.

46. Cotton Mather, *Ratio Disciplinae* (Boston, 1726; Evans, *Early American Imprints*, no. 2775, microcard), p. 20.

directs, altho' %20 of such parish shoul'd be Dissenters, yet by the laws of the Province they wou'd be oblig'd to pay the maintenance of such minister."[47] Nearer the end of the colonial period, Jonathan Mayhew, the prominent liberal preacher of Boston, explicitly stated that Massachusetts did not establish a single church but rather "protestant churches of various denominations." He understood that "an hundred churches, all of different denominations . . . might be established in the same . . . colony, as well as one, two, or three."[48] Mayhew's interpretation of the establishment of religion in Massachusetts showed that even after the Baptists and Quakers received an exemption from religious taxes in 1728, the law still permitted a multiple establishment and did not fix on an exclusive establishment. If a multiple establishment did not in fact exist, demographic forces, not the law, provided the reason. Few towns had non-Congregational majorities in the prerevolutionary period (Swansea was exceptional), although the growing number of dissenters forced concessions.

The act of 1727 resulted from Anglican pressure to break the Congregationalists' control of their tax monies for religion. While authorities in England considered Anglican claims, Governor William Dummer of Massachusetts urged the General Court to accept his compromise proposal "that the taxes of those belonging to the Church of England be paid by the collectors to the Ministers of the Church of England to whom they belong."[49] In 1727 the Anglicans won a major victory against the standing order, thereby beginning what eventually became a slow but steady trend. From 1727 to 1833 the Congregational church was obliged to retreat "until the other denominations in the Commonwealth were on an equal footing with it."[50] The retreat began in 1727 when the Anglicans won the statutory right of having their religious taxes turned over for the support of their own churches.[51]

47. McLoughlin, *New England Dissent*, 1:218.
48. Jonathan Mayhew, *A Defense of Observations* (Boston, 1763; Evans, *Early American Imprints*, no. 9442, microcard), pp. 46–47.
49. McLoughlin, *New England Dissent*, 1:221.
50. Meyer, *Church and State*, pp. 13–14.
51. Ibid., pp. 14, 16–17, 71–72; Reed, *Church and State*, p. 180; McLoughlin, *New England Dissent*, 1:221. Curry, *First Freedoms*, pp. 112–23, fails to cope with the dual establishment in Massachusetts and Connecticut after 1727.

Town treasurers after that date had a legal obligation to give to Anglican churches the monies paid by Anglicans into the town treasuries for the support of public worship, on condition that the taxpayers regularly attended Anglican services within five miles of their homes.

In 1728 Massachusetts exempted Quakers and Baptists from all taxes for the payment of ministerial salaries; then in 1731 and 1735 each denomination received an exemption from sharing the taxes for building new town churches.[52] After those dates, the General Court periodically renewed tax exemption statutes on behalf of Baptists and Quakers so that members of these denominations would not have to pay religious taxes for the benefit of Congregational churches or of their own. As a result of a variety of complicated legal technicalities, as well as outright illegal action by Congregational town officials, frequent abuses occurred under the system of tax exemption; many Quakers and Baptists were unconscionably forced to pay for the support of Congregationalist churches. Even Anglicans who lived too far from a church of their own denomination to attend its services were taxed for the support of the Congregational churches. But these abuses of both the letter and the spirit of the law do not alter the basic fact that after 1727 an establishment of religion in Massachusetts meant government support of religion and financial aid to two churches, Congregationalist and Episcopalian, without preference to either, indeed, without preference to any.

Church-state relationships in Connecticut closely paralleled those of Massachusetts, except that Congregationalism dominated Connecticut to an even greater degree. In the seventeenth century few towns had any dissenters, let alone a majority of them. The basic law governing Connecticut's establishment in the eighteenth century dated from 1697. It continued the town option system and required the collection of taxes from everyone, even in towns without a settled minister. No one was exempt. The first statute concerning "Dissenters from the Established Order," enacted in 1708, was actually a toleration act passed soon after the founding of the first Anglican church, in Stratford, and the first Baptist church, in Groton. The act guaranteed "full

52. Meyer, *Church and State*, p. 15; McLoughlin, *New England Dissent*, 1:225–43.

liberty of worship" yet required the payment of town ecclesiastical taxes for the benefit of existing Congregational churches. In the same year, 1708, Connecticut's legislature adopted the Saybrook Platform for the governance of its Congregational churches, although it did not mention them by name. The legislation declared that every church united in the platform would be acknowledged "as established by law," although any church or religious society that differed or dissented might exercise worship and discipline "in their own way, according to conscience."[53]

Less than a score of years later, however, the Anglicans of Connecticut enjoyed a de facto establishment of religion. In 1724 the bishop of London requested of Governor Joseph Talcott of Connecticut to indulge members of the Church of England so that they "may not be constrained to contribute to the Independent minister." (In England, the government indulged Independents or Congregationalists by allowing them to worship freely but did not exempt them from religious tithes for the Church of England.) Governor Talcott replied that Connecticut had only one Anglican minister, in Stratford, and that "His people are under no restraint to the support of any other ministers."[54] On the other hand, as the governor conceded, Connecticut towns did not exempt from religious assessments those who failed to attend the Church of England regularly and "pretended" to be a communicant just "to escape a small tax." That meant that any Anglican who did not live in or close to Stratford had to pay for the support of the standing order. When Fairfield imprisoned several of its Anglicans for refusing to pay their rates, they appealed directly to the provincial legislature for relief and got it in "An Act for the Ease of such as soberly Dissent." This act of 1727, which preceded a similar one enacted by Massachusetts in the same year, required Anglicans to continue to pay town taxes for religion but authorized that their taxes be rebated to their own ministers, if ordained according to the canons of the Church of England and if they lived "near" a church they could attend. That helped

53. Cobb, *Rise of Religious Liberty*, pp. 266–67; McLoughlin, *New England Dissent*, 1:247–62; Williston Walker, *The Creeds and Platforms of Congregationalism* (New York, 1893), p. 507.

54. Cobb, *Rise of Religious Liberty*, p. 269.

only Anglicans close enough to a church of their own. Within twenty years Connecticut had fourteen Anglican congregations, so the act of 1727 created a significant dual establishment of religion. No Connecticut authority, civil or religious, ever recognized the Church of England as an established church in the province, but short of recognition as such, that church received by government authority the same kind of financial assistance as the standing order. Officially the government acted neutrally toward Anglicans and Congregationalists; they had to attend worship regularly and pay taxes for the support of church buildings and a ministry, but the government was indifferent toward the denominational choice made by individual citizens. In that sense the Church of England enjoyed a parity with the standing order. Both had the seal of approval backed by coercive taxation and laws compelling church attendance.[55]

Few Quakers lived in Connecticut; by the middle of the eighteenth century no regular Quaker meetinghouse existed yet in the province. By then there were several Baptist churches, and their numbers rapidly increased during the Great Awakening. Regardless of their numbers, Quakers and Baptists, on seeing Anglicans receive exemption in 1727 from supporting local parish churches, also sought relief. Perhaps because the dissenters were so few and deported themselves so peaceably, unlike the fanatical Rogerine sect, tolerant Connecticut authorities supported their petitions for exemption. In 1729 the legislature enacted measures that offered Baptists and Quakers complete exemption from ecclesiastical assessments on condition that they could prove to town authorities that they regularly attended a congregation of their own sect.[56] Many, of course, could not produce certificates entitling them to exemption, because they did not live close enough to a church of their choice, and the Congregational churches as the churches chosen by the majority of the town's freeholders mulcted the dissenters. Nevertheless, Connecticut after 1729 maintained by law a dual establishment of religion, with substantial freedom of worship for dissenters.

55. M. Louise Greene, *The Development of Religious Liberty in Connecticut* (Boston, 1905), pp. 192–202; McLoughlin, *New England Dissent*, 1:263–65.

56. Greene, *Religious Liberty in Connecticut*, pp. 216–17; McLoughlin, *New England Dissent*, 1:265–77.

The situation did not fundamentally differ in New Hampshire, which had no official church. An act of 1693, adopted at a time when New Hampshire had only five churches, all Congregationalist, authorized the freeholders of every town to select and contract for a minister, and also required constables to collect assessments for his support. No one of a different religious persuasion received exemption unless he or she regularly attended a different church. Any Protestant group that won a town election could become the establishment. Thus, New Hampshire's basic law on the subject, at least in legal theory, allowed a multiple establishment of religion. Nevertheless, the town system of establishment actually operated to benefit the Congregational churches exclusively well into the eighteenth century, simply because of the absence or scarcity of dissenters. Although their numbers increased, New Hampshire did not systematically require the payment of rates by dissenters nor always concern itself with the support of their ministers. Quakers, Anglicans, Presbyterians, and Baptists who attended their own churches were exempt from supporting the local established church, which, because of Congregational dominance in town after town, was Congregationalist.[57]

When Presbyterians settled Londonderry in 1719, the situation changed. Presbyterians always dominated that town before the Revolution, and their church was the town's officially established church. As time passed, Anglicans in New Hampshire as well as Presbyterians and even Separate Baptists received authorization to establish their own parishes in towns dominated by Congregationalists and to use town authority to collect taxes for their own churches. The pattern of establishment had become bewilderingly diverse by the eve of the Revolution. Bedford, as well as Londonderry, had an exclusive Presbyterian establishment, although in Pembrooke and Hampton Falls the Presbyterian church and the Congregational church were both established. In Holderness, Anglicans enjoyed an exclusive establishment but shared a dual establishment in Portsmouth. In most towns on the eve of the Revolution, the Congregational church remained the only publicly sup-

57. Charles B. Kinney, *Church and State: The Struggle for Separation in New Hampshire, 1630–1900* (New York, 1955), pp. 36–43, 58–64, 72–82; McLoughlin, *New England Dissent,* 2:833–40; Cobb, *Rise of Religious Liberty,* p. 298.

ported church, although non-Congregationalists in such towns were supposed to have an exemption from religious taxes if they had no church of their own. Some towns had a dual establishment, and the province as a whole had a multiple establishment, with free exercise for dissenters.[58]

Thus, throughout New England there was no single provincial establishment supported by all, and the law of each colony allowed the possibility of multiple establishments. Americans of the colonial period thought of an establishment of religion mainly in terms of the classic establishment of the mother country, as Thomas Curry has shown,[59] but little congruence existed between thought and law or between thought and reality in some New England towns.

58. Kinney, *Church and State*, pp. 72–84; McLoughlin, *New England Dissent*, 2:840–43.

59. Curry, *First Freedoms*, p. 133.

2

State Establishments of Religion: New England

The Revolution triggered a long pent-up movement for disestablishment of religion in several of the states, and condemnations of establishments in three states that had never experienced an establishment of any kind during the colonial period. A fourth state that had never had an establishment, Rhode Island, did not adopt a state constitution and therefore had no provision on the subject.

New Jersey provided in its constitution of 1776 that no person should "ever be obliged to pay tithes, taxes, or any other rates, for the purpose of building or repairing any other church or churches, place or places of worship, or for the maintenance of any minister or ministry, contrary to what he believes to be right, or has deliberately or voluntarily engaged himself to perform."[1] Pennsylvania's provision in its constitution of 1776 was equally broad: ". . . no man ought or of right can be compelled to attend any religious worship, or erect or support any place of worship, or maintain any ministry, contrary to, or against, his own free will and consent."[2] But Delaware, another of the states that in their colonial experience had never had even the semblance of an establishment, used narrow language in its constitution of 1776: "There shall be no establishment of any one religious sect in this State in preference to another."[3] In 1792, however, Delaware adopted a new constitution and substituted the much broader language used by Pennsylvania.[4]

In New York, where a multiple establishment had been maintained in New York City and three adjoining counties, the long history of insistence by the Church of England that it was rightfully the only established church influenced the writing of the clause against establishments in the constitution of 1777. The system of multiple establishments of religion was ended by the following words, reflecting the stubborn determination of non-Episcopalians never to admit, even by implication, that there had ever been an exclusive or preferential establishment of the Church of England: "That all such parts of the said common law, and all such of the said statutes and acts aforesaid, or parts thereof, as may be construed to establish or maintain any particular denomination of Christians or their ministers . . . be, and they hereby are, abrogated and rejected."[5]

In six states proestablishment parties were forced to make concessions to the growing sentiment against any establishments. In those six states, the concessions took the form of a compromise: four states replaced single or exclusive establishments by authorizing multiple es-

1. Francis Newton Thorpe, ed., *The Federal and State Constitutions, Colonial Charters, and Other Organic Laws,* 7 vols. (Washington, 1909), 5:2597.
2. Ibid., 5:082.
3. Ibid., 1:567.
4. Ibid., 1:570.
5. Ibid., 5:2636.

tablishments, while two states substituted multiple establishments for dual ones. The evidence relating to each of the six proves that after the American Revolution an establishment of religion was not restricted in meaning to a state church or to a system of public support of one sect alone; instead, an establishment of religion also meant public support of several or all churches, with preference to none.[6]

Three of these six states were in New England. Massachusetts adopted its constitution in 1780. Article III of its Declaration of Rights commanded the legislature to authorize the "several towns, parishes, precincts, and other bodies politic, or religious societies, to take suitable provision, at their own expense, of the institution of the public worship of God, and for the support and maintenance of public Protestant teachers of piety, religion, and morality." In 1780 religion in Massachusetts was still synonymous with Protestantism, or, rather, Protestantism signified the religions that actually existed in Massachusetts; it had no synagogues or Roman Catholic churches, and the few Jews and Catholics, like the unchurched, were lawfully subject to taxation for the support of the town church. Clause 2 of Article III empowered the legislature to make church attendance compulsory. Clause 3 provided that the towns, parishes, and religious societies should have the right of electing their ministers. Clause 4 created a multiple establishment of all Protestant churches, because it provided that taxpayers could designate the Protestant church of their choice that would receive their enforced contribution: "And all moneys paid by the subject to the support of public worship, and all the public teachers aforesaid, shall, if he require it, be uniformly applied to the support of the public teacher or teachers of his own religious sect or denomination, provided there be any on whose instructions he attends; otherwise it may be paid towards the support of the teacher or teachers of the parish or precinct in which the

---

6. Thomas Curry, *The First Freedoms* (New York, 1986), is an excellent book that advances a different interpretation. We agree on major First Amendment issues, especially on the point that nonpreferential government aid to religion violates the First Amendment, but disagree about multiple establishments. Curry believes that the concept of a preferential establishment dominated American thinking even as late as the framing of the First Amendment (see p. 209).

said moneys are raised." A fifth clause additionally provided that "no subordination of any one sect or denomination to the other shall ever be established by law."[7] In the context of Article III this clause against preference proves that in a constitutional sense, no church had a legal status subordinate to the Congregational church, and the various churches of the establishment were constitutionally equal, no one preferred over others. To state that the "theory of establishment by town disappeared in revolutionary America" ignores the Massachusetts experience, as well as that of New Hampshire, Connecticut, and Vermont.[8]

Several Massachusetts towns whose voters supported the voluntary maintenance of religion opposed ratification of Article III yet endorsed its fifth clause against subordination. They regarded the private support of religion as compatible with the principle of nonpreference or no subordination; that principle signified to those towns that religion should not receive government tax support. For example, Charlton, in Worcester County, rejected taxation for the support of religion as "coercive" and declared that every town should choose its minister "in a manner most agreeable to the dictates of their own Conscience; but no Person Shall be compelled thereto by Law. And . . . no subordination of one Sect or Denomination to another Shall ever be Established by Law."[9] Thus, nonpreferential establishments showed that preference was not necessarily the core of an establishment of religion; and people who subscribed to nonpreference could be voluntarists or disestablishmentarians.

Massachusetts embodied in its fundamental law the principle of government aid to religion (Protestantism) without preference. Article III defined a system that allowed every town, and every parish and body politic within a town, to have an establishment of religion on a

---

7. Thorpe, ed., *Constitutions*, 3:1890–91.

8. Curry, *First Freedoms*, p. 210.

9. Oscar Handlin and Mary Handlin, eds., *The Popular Sources of Political Authority* (Cambridge, Mass., 1966), p. 819, for the town of Charlton. See also pp. 618–19 (West Springfield), p. 674 (Sherborn), pp. 727–28 (Berwick), p. 785 (Medway), and p. 855 (Petersham). Article III is on pp. 442–43.

local option basis. As a matter of law and theory, Baptist taxpayers who lived in a Congregational parish should have had their taxes for religion remitted to the nearest Baptist church they he attended.[10] Moreover, as William G. McLoughlin has written, "a Baptist, Quaker, or Episcopalian church could become the established or Standing Church in a parish and the Congregationalists would then be 'the dissenters' who would have to provide certificates if they did not wish their religious taxes to go to the support of the parish majority."[11]

Although its constitution of 1780 expanded the principle of non-preferential aid to religion on a compulsory basis, Massachusetts was the only state whose laws failed to broaden religious liberty. Indeed, Massachusetts regressed, because Article III made no exceptions. Baptists and Quakers, who previously had enjoyed an exemption from religious taxes, came within the revised system, against their conscientious objections. They were forced to pay taxes for the support of their own worship. Congregationalists, who in most towns administered the system for rebating non-Congregational monies to non-Congregational churches, resorted to various tricks and technicalities to fleece them out of their share of the taxes. The multiple establishment in Massachusetts, though nonpreferential as a matter of constitutional law, was actually preferential in the sense that it favored Congregationalism as a matter of practice, which was the reason for the establishment's existence. But the fact remains that Baptist, Quaker, Episcopalian, Methodist, Unitarian, and even Universalist churches received public tax support under the establishment of 1780, as well as Congregational churches. As a writer in a Boston newspaper stated, in 1811, in the course of presenting the Baptist position on church and state, the "third article of the Constitution as effectively enacts a civil establishment of religion as any political constitution in existence." Because the majority in any parish could establish any form of Protestant worship

---

10. Jacob C. Meyer, *Church and State in Massachusetts, 1740 to 1833* (Cleveland, 1930), pp. 107–10.

11. William G. McLoughlin, "The Balcomb Case (1782) and the Pietistic Theory of Separation of Church and State," *William and Mary Quarterly*, 3d ser., 24 (Apr. 1967): 268–69.

that it pleased, "In one parish the Arian religion may be established, in another the Calvinistic, in a third that of the Universalists, &c., &c."[12] Clearly, establishment in Massachusetts meant government promotion of religion generally, that is, of several different Protestant churches.

However, most Congregationalist supporters of Article III probably did not understand it to create an establishment of religion, let alone a multiple establishment. Article III lacked some of the crucial features of the establishment in England or of any conventional European establishment, such as a prescribed religious creed or the supremacy of one denomination over others. The purpose of Article III was secular, not sectarian, in character; the government promoted religion not to further a true faith or protect the gates of salvation but to make good citizens, or, in the words of the article, to benefit "the happiness of the people" and "the good order and preservation of their government." Article II, cheek by jowl with Article III, guaranteed religious liberty, unlike a conventional establishment of religion, which merely tolerated dissenters. Indeed, those who believed in voluntarism in religious matters censured Article III for creating an establishment that conflicted with Article II.[13] In their view religious liberty assumed that in matters of conscience and worship, the law, like God, made no distinctions among people, while toleration assumed that one denomination, possessing infallible truths, is superior to others. For the sake of public tranquility, toleration indulged the open worship by other denominations, granting them that which religious liberty asserted they have as a right. Article III, to its opponents, intruded coercion where private judgment should be sovereign, contrary to the free exercise of religion but consistent with an establishment of religion. As a writer in the *Boston Gazette* said, during the debate over ratification of the Massachusetts constitution, "The third article is repugnant to and destructive of

12. "Berean," *Independent Chronicle* (Boston), quoted in William G. Mc-Loughlin, *New England Dissent, 1630–1833: The Baptists and the Separation of Church and State*, 2 vols. (Cambridge, Mass., 1971), 2:1092.

13. For statements by town meetings, see Handlin and Handlin, eds., *Popular Sources*, pp. 482, 505, 510, 557–58, 597, 618–19, 633–34, 645–48, 672, 674, 682–83, 728, 785, 819, 855.

the second. The second says the people shall be free, the third says they shall not be free."[14] Supporters of Article III answered that it explicitly repudiated the superiority or preferred status of any denomination and so little resembled an establishment that it allowed for the probability that some parish might elect a Baptist minister who would then receive the taxes of the congregation.[15]

Article III not only allowed for that possibility; it happened. In several towns the Baptists increased so rapidly that they attained a majority and took control, with the result that those self-professed enemies of an establishment of religion became the establishment and their ministers received their salaries from the town treasuries. In still other towns the Baptist churches also became the official churches after the Baptists ganged up on the Congregationalists by allying with other dissenters and even with dissatisfied Congregationalists.[16] The Reverend John Leland, the great Baptist leader who was the only person to fight against establishments of religion in three states, Virginia, Massachusetts, and Connecticut, declared in 1794, "It is true that one sect of Protestant Christians has as fair an opportunity to be incorporated as another"; furthermore, all Protestant sects, if incorporated, might choose their own ministers, contract for the cost of their maintenance, and "assess it upon all within their respective precincts." In towns where Baptists formed a majority, wrote Leland, they might "tax all in the town or precincts to part with their money for religious uses." Leland added that to do so would violate Baptist principles.[17] Some Baptist towns, including Swansea and Rehoboth, had considerable experience violating Baptist principles. The "ultimate irony," according to William G. McLoughlin, occurred where the official town churches were Baptist and "even paid their salaries out of town funds."[18]

14. McLoughlin, *New England Dissent*, 1:623; also see chap. 33, "The Debate over the New Definition of an Establishment of Religion, 1778–1783," pp. 613–35.

15. Ibid., pp. 616–17.

16. Ibid., p. 675.

17. John Leland, "The Yankee Spy" (1794), in *The Writings of John Leland*, edited by L. F. Greene (reprint, New York, 1969), pp. 225, 227.

18. McLoughlin, *New England Dissent*, 1:680, also see p. 690.

As a matter of fact, the ultimate irony, from the standpoint of orthodox Congregationalists, who espoused the doctrine of the Trinity, occurred when parish majorities elected Unitarian ministers even though majorities of church members were orthodox Congregationalists. Of course, on a town basis whatever denomination was supported by a majority became the exclusive establishment of that town, whether Baptist, Unitarian, or Congregationalist—at least until the creation of poll parishes in 1823, which allowed ten or more voters to establish a poll parish within the territorial parish and to pay taxes only for the support of the church of the poll parish (discussed below).

In towns where Baptists composed a minority, complained Leland, they "must either part with their money to support a religion that they do not believe . . . or get a certificate to draw it out of the treasurer's hands." Some had to resort "to the last mode, as being the best alternative" available.[19] Leland meant that in order for Baptists to ensure that their taxes for religion went to their own church, they had to violate their conscientious belief that government had no jurisdiction over religion and had to comply with the laws controlling the demonstration of proof that one regularly attended a church other than the locally established church.

Article III made no reference to a need on the part of anyone to certify regular attendance at a church other than the church of the denomination preferred by a town or parish majority; yet court decisions upheld town authorities, invariably Congregationalists, who demanded such proof. They merely assumed that the old certification system of prerevolutionary days persisted, in harmony with Article III. Baptists and others who refused to obtain certificates lost their lawsuits challenging the certificate system. They found it discriminatory, as did other sectarians, including Shakers, Methodists, and Quakers, but they lived with it.

Baptist ministers, moreover, like other dissenting ministers, even of the deistic Universalists, sued for the recovery of ecclesiastical taxes paid into the town treasuries by their parishioners.[20] Although Article

19. Leland, "Yankee Spy," p. 227.
20. John D. Cushing, "Notes on Disestablishment in Massachusetts, 1780–

III made no distinction between incorporated and unincorporated religious societies, the state supreme court made one. In 1785 it ruled that only ministers of incorporated religious societies were entitled to rebates of taxes paid for religion, but the decision of that year settled little; suits raising the same issue arose intermittently in the state's courts, involving various dissenter churches, during the next fifteen years, without any consistency of judicial interpretation of Article III. A lawyer who opposed the necessity of incorporation for a church to receive the taxes of its members declared that in "many instances" members of unincorporated religious societies collected ministerial salaries from town assessments. That gave the system more of the character of a functioning, rather than a merely theoretical, multiple establishment. "And in cases where this has been refused," wrote the lawyer, "actions have been instituted and maintained on the simple grounds of the Constitution. These cases are too well known as well as too numerous to be detailed."[21] Baptists divided on the question of whether to seek incorporation of each of their churches to qualify for tax rebates; but forty-one Baptist churches sought and received incorporation enactments from the state legislature between 1790 and 1810.[22] Fifty Baptist churches remained unincorporated in 1810 when the issue was still being litigated. Universalist, Shaker, Methodist, Separate Baptists, and other Protestant churches also received the advantage of incorporation by the state legislature, but itinerant clergy, including Roman Catholic priests and Methodist ministers, were denied the taxes of their scattered flocks because those clergy did not serve incorporated societies.[23]

Incredibly, some incorporated Baptist churches, contrary to their conscientious opposition to coercive taxation for religion, "sued their

---

1833," *William and Mary Quarterly*, 3d ser., 26 (Apr. 1969): 169–90, covers the principal Universalist lawsuit, *Murray v. Gloucester* (1785).

21. *Independent Chronicle*, June 13, 1811, quoted in McLoughlin, *New England Dissent*, 2:1094,

22. McLoughlin, *New England Dissent*, 1:644; 2:1088, 1094.

23. Cushing, "Notes on Disestablishment," pp. 182–83. Edward Buck, *Massachusetts Ecclesiastical Law* (Boston, 1866), p. 41.

own members in court," McLoughlin found, "and distrained their goods for failing to pay their duly assessed share of the minister's salary."[24] Distraining negligent or refractory congregants meant seizing their property to enforce payment of taxes and selling it at public auction if necessary to secure the cash value of assessments. Dissenters also squabbled with Congregationalists to win their rightful share of the ownership or use of town meetinghouses and the income from ministerial lands.[25] If an establishment of religion meant government promotion of religion chiefly by financial assistance to religious institutions, Baptists and other non-Congregationalists received that assistance in a variety of ways sanctioned by law after 1780.

A state supreme court decision of 1811 reaffirmed the 1785 ruling against the constitutional right of unincorporated religious societies to secure the rebate of members' taxes.[26] That decision could have had the effect of enhancing significantly the Congregational advantage over the numerous unincorporated non-Congregational churches. A Universalist minister sued the parish of Falmouth in Maine (then part of Massachusetts) for the monies paid by members of his unincorporated congregation. The Supreme Judicial Court sustained the claim of the parish that the state constitution authorized only the ministers of incorporated religious societies to obtain tax rebates. As a result, outraged opponents of the decision, whose churches were rapidly increasing in number, orchestrated a public campaign for relief; they fashioned an alliance with the Republican (Jeffersonian) party to defeat the Federalists, who backed the courts, in the state elections of 1811. The Religious Freedom Act of that year, which was the result, authorized any religious society, whether incorporated or not, to receive the taxes of its members.[27] The 1811 statute in effect confirmed Article III as it was originally understood, without any of the discriminatory refine-

24. William G. McLoughlin, "Isaac Backus and the Separation of Church and State," *American Historical Review* 73 (June 1968):1410.

25. McLoughlin, *New England Dissent*, 1:685–93.

26. *Barnes v. Parish of Falmouth*, 6 Mass. 401 (1810). See Cushing, "Notes on Disestablishment," pp. 184–85; McLoughlin, *New England Dissent*, 2:1086–88.

27. Meyer, *Church and State*, pp. 155–56; Cushing, "Notes on Disestablishment," pp. 185–87; McLoughlin, *New England Dissent*, 2:1088–1106.

ments and catches that had subsequently accrued to the benefit of Congregationalists. After 1811 the basic law of the state again created a multiple establishment of religion without preference to any denomination.

By 1820, when Massachusetts held a new constitutional convention that reconsidered church-state relationships, the mushrooming growth of the non-Congregationalists and a schism within Congregationalism foreshadowed the unviability of Article III. Awkward questions were being asked: "If," for example, "it is necessary to the support of good order in society and to the security of property that Religious establishments should be maintained," why were the cities of Boston, Salem, and Newburyport exempted from compulsory taxation for religion?[28] A Baptist periodical urged the election to the state convention of delegates who would end the establishment with its religious taxes and religious tests; in its place the periodical recommended an equivalent to the establishment clause of the First Amendment.[29] At the convention the Congregationalists staved off radical changes in Article III, even as fundamental differences cleaved them in two when old enemies did not unite them. The convention recommended modest changes in Article III: the use of "Christian" instead of "Protestant"—a concession to a growing Roman Catholic population; abolition of the requirement of compulsory public worship—already a dead letter; and constitutional recognition of the Religious Freedom Act of 1811—adding nothing to the existing rights of unincorporated religious societies. Resentful voters overwhelmingly withheld ratification, leaving Article III unchanged.[30] But a decision by the state's high court in early 1821 produced unforeseen results that transformed church-state relationships.

Baker v. Fales (1821) became notorious as "the Dedham case," by which a Unitarian court assisted the Unitarians in "plundering" the old

28. *Independent Chronicle,* Nov. 18, 1820, quoted in McLoughlin, *New England Dissent,* 2:1149.

29. *Christian Watchman,* Aug. 12, 1820, p. 3, quoted in McLoughlin, *New England Dissent,* pp. 1151.

30. Meyer, *Church and State,* pp. 184–200; McLoughlin, *New England Dissent,* 2:1160–85.

Congregational churches.[31] The case resulted from the burgeoning of Unitarianism in eastern Massachusetts. It spread quickly and captured the venerable Pilgrim church in Plymouth in 1800 and within eight years the Harvard divinity department and all of Boston's colonial churches excepting one. The bitter controversy between Congregationalists divided them into two warring parties, Unitarian and Trinitarian. The Unitarians, who rejected the doctrine of the Trinity as unscriptural, believed that Jesus performed a divine mission but was a mere human being, not at all divine in his person. A legal question worsened profound religious hostilities: Which body constituted the true church when divided loyalties resulted in schism? The question was passionately contested because the victor's prize included the name, records, and property of many a wealthy "first" church. The controversy affected political control of the state and its establishment of religion. And the controversy drew the judiciary into the fray. When Chief Justice Isaac Parker of the Supreme Judicial Court responded to Trinitarian animadversions against his Dedham decision, he indiscreetly published his vindication of the court in the official Unitarian periodical.[32]

The Dedham decision established a precedent that the judiciary maintained against furious Trinitarian assaults. Schism had ruptured the First Congregational Church in Dedham parish. A majority of the parish had become Unitarian. The orthodox majority of the members of the church had seceded when the parish implemented its changed religious views by electing a Unitarian minister. Two bodies within the parish claimed title as the true church in Dedham and to the property rights of that church.

The state's high court held unanimously that the exclusive constitu-

31. The Dedham controversy may be followed in Erastus Worthington, *The History of Dedham . . . to 1827* (Boston, 1827), pp. 112–15; "Letters on the Introduction and Progress of Unitarians in New England," *Spirit of the Pilgrims* (Boston) 3 (Oct. 1830): 507–9; *Christian Disciple* (Boston) 2 (July–Aug. 1829): 257–80 passim. A good secondary account is Charles Warren, *Jacobin and Junto* (Cambridge, Mass., 1931), pp. 286–311.

32. Isaac Parker, "Reply to the Reverend Parsons Cooke," *Christian Examiner* (Boston) 5 (July–Aug. 1828): 277–83.

tional right of the parish to elect its religious teacher created an organic relationship between parish and church. "A church," declared Chief Justice Parker, "cannot subsist but in connection with some corporate parish or religious society." Unconnected to some society, a church had no "legal qualities" and could not control property that it might have held in trust for the society or parish to which it had formerly been attached. Hence, when the Trinitarian majority of the members of a Congregational church separated from the parish, the remaining members of the church, even if a minority of Unitarians, constituted the church in that parish and retained the rights and property belonging to it.[33]

The Dedham decision, which aggravated the clashes among the Congregationalists, resulted in an unprecedented political alliance between the orthodox Congregationalists, who had previously voted Federalist, and the non-Congregational denominations, who usually favored Democrats. With religion as a prominent issue in the state election of 1823, Unitarian-supported Federalist candidates lost to candidates supported by "Calvinists and Republicans" (Trinitarian Congregationalists and Democrats), newly allied. Thus, the orthodox descendants of the Puritans seceded from their churches and from the religious bloc that formerly bolstered the Federalist party. Because Unitarian victories depended on the relationship of a church to its territorial parish, the new reform legislature in 1823 provided that any ten or more legal voters might form a "poll" parish within a territorial parish and be relieved of the burden of supporting the territorial parish church. By a Unitarian estimate in 1830, nine-tenths of the parishes in the state were of the poll parish type, a grossly exaggerated figure.[34]

33. *Baker v. Fales*, 16 Mass. 487, 505 (1820). An interminable semantic, historical, and legal exegesis of the case may be followed in sectarian debates. See "The Congregational Churches of Massachusetts," *Spirit of the Pilgrims* 1 (Feb. 1828): 57–74, and 1 (Mar. 1828): 113–40; the reply in "Review of the 'Vindication of the Rights of the Churches . . . ,'" *Christian Examiner* 5 (May–June 1828): 298–316, and 5 (Nov.–Dec. 1828): 478–505; and the counterreply in "Review of the Rights of the Congregational Churches," *Spirit of the Pilgrims* 2 (July 1829): 370–403.

34. *Christian Examiner* 9 (Sept. 1830): 4–5. My count of the special statutes

The poll parish system made the operation of the multiple establishment of religion in Massachusetts as nonpreferential as it could be in practice. But it did not relieve the Trinitarian Congregationalists who lost their churches. By their own count, they lost eighty-one churches.[35] A writer in the *Puritan Recorder* charged Unitarians with legalized theft. He wrote, "Church after church was plundered of its property, even to its communion furniture and records."[36]

Old-line Congregationalists began to realize that Baptists were also Calvinist and Trinitarian, and, like evangelicals, the orthodox began to regard Unitarians as little better than free-thinking oppressive infidels. Eventually those who had created the establishment of religion in Massachusetts and had long denied that it was an establishment in law or fact came to see it as the non-Congregationalists did. In 1828 the Reverend William Cogswell, the orthodox Congregationalist minister of South Dedham, opposed an alliance between church and state and declared that by having "a civil or ecclesiastical establishment in matters of faith" Massachusetts violated the genius of American government.[37]

Ten years after the Dedham decision, the state's supreme court decided the Brookfield case, *Stebbins v. Jennings* (1830). During the preceding decade there had been at least thirty Congregational schisms, always resulting from Trinitarian secession; in most of the cases the seceders constituted the overwhelming preponderance of the church

---

creating poll parishes showed the incorporation of only sixty, twenty-seven of which were Trinitarian Congregationalist, one Unitarian, and the rest divided among non-Congregationalists.

35. "The Exiled Churches of Massachusetts," *Congregational Quarterly* (Boston) 5 (July 1863): 216–40. Although the number of the Trinitarian Congregational churches that became Unitarian varies with the study, George Punchard, *History of Congregationalism from about A.D. 250 to the Present Time,* 5 vols. (Boston, 1881), 5:686, gave the number as 126, and Albert Dunning, *Congregationalists in America* (Boston, 1894), p. 302, agreed. Dunning stated that of the 361 Congregational (orthodox) churches in Massachusetts in 1810, the meetinghouses and other property of 126 became Unitarian.

36. Quoted in George Ellis, *A Half-Century of the Unitarian Controversy* (Boston, 1857), p. 415.

37. William Cogswell, *Religious Liberty* (Boston, 1828), p. 17.

membership, and without exception they lost the properties of the churches involved. In 1830, with a new chief justice at the head of the court, the entire issue was reargued and redecided. Chief Justice Lemuel Shaw, like Parker a Unitarian, reduced the church to a mere appendage of the parish and reaffirmed the principle of the Dedham decision.[38] Because the parish, territorial or poll, was a public corporation empowered to levy and collect taxes for public worship, it was a "body politic," a subdivision of the state; consequently, the subordination of church to parish in effect produced the closest amalgamation of church and state. Yet the Dedham and Brookfield decisions also had the inadvertent effect of advancing the cause of political and religious liberty even as they subordinated church to body politic. If the decisions had gone the other way, the losers would have been the parish majority who paid most of the taxes for the church yet were not even admitted as members. In a sense the democratic principle of congregationalism had fulfilled itself when the majority of parishioners had the power to govern the local church and be not merely attendants on it but members of it.

With local option prevailing and Unitarianism in control of the east, the Trinitarians finally understood that Article III worked against them. Shortly after the Brookfield decision they abandoned their historic position and united against any establishment of religion; the one that existed suddenly seemed Unitarian. In 1831 the Reverend Parsons Cooke of Ware, an orthodox stalwart among the Congregationalists, published a vehement *Remonstrance Against an Established Religion in Massachusetts*, excoriating Unitarianism as the "state religion." The ballot, he advised, remained a citizen's only way of securing religious liberty and equal rights.[39] *The Spirit of the Pilgrims*, which had been founded to explain the orthodox position among Congregationalists, arrived for the first time at a most belated conclusion. Isaac Backus and his Baptist arguments for disestablishment had been correct. The editor, writing

38. 10 Pickering 172 (1830). For details, see my article "Chief Justice Shaw and the Church Property Controversy in Massachusetts," *Boston University Law Review*, 30 (Apr. 1950): 219–35.

39. Parsons Cooke, *Remonstrance Against an Established Religion in Massachusetts* (Boston, 1831), pp. 20, 23–24.

on "The Third Article in the Declaration of Rights," discovered that it created "a legal, religious establishment" that was "repugnant . . . to the rights of conscience." He was not clear whether the establishment was a Unitarian one, a Protestant one, or a general Christian one, but he believed that it secularized true religion. The Congregationalists then threw their support on the side of overthrowing the "whole system of taxation, by which our laws require religion to be supported."[40]

Although Calvin's progeny had finally adopted the reasoning of the Baptists and Quakers, even of Locke and Madison, a Unitarian writer correctly stated, "It was only when church property was given by the courts to the parish in preference to the church and when the 'standing order' churches had been repeatedly foiled in their effort to retain the old prerogatives, that a majority could be secured for religious freedom."[41] The alliance between the Congregationalists and the non-Congregationalists against the Unitarians jelled in a widespread popular front movement for repeal of Article III. Public opinion favored a system of private voluntary support of religion, as in Boston, where such a system had always prevailed. On November 11, 1833, the voters, by a ten-to-one majority, ratified an amendment to the state constitution by which religion was disengaged as an engine of the state. Massachusetts was the last state to end its establishment of religion.

New Hampshire's establishment of religion after the Revolution differed from the one in Massachusetts but not significantly. New Hampshire entered the Revolution with a crazy-quilt pattern of public support for religion. In the words of Charles B. Kinney, Jr., the historian of the struggle for separation in New Hampshire: "One can find in some towns a pattern of church-state relations to substantiate almost any form he might approve. There were some towns in which there was a single establishment with free exercise for dissenters and not for others. There were some towns in which there was a multiple establishment with free exercise for dissenters. There were some towns in which there was a multiple establishment without free exercise for dissenters. There were some towns in which there was a single establishment other

---

40. *Spirit of the Pilgrims* 4 (Dec. 1831): 630–31, 635.

41. George W. Cooke, *Unitarianism in America* (Boston, 1902), p. 121.

than the predominant one, the Congregational."[42] The New Hampshire experience, like that of Massachusetts, scotches the view that an establishment necessarily prefers one church over others and that aid to all would not constitute an establishment of religion.

The New Hampshire establishment, which lasted until 1819, had been perpetuated by the state constitution of 1784. Its Declaration of Rights, by Article VI, implicitly created a multiple establishment on a local option basis, with a guarantee, in law if not in fact, that no sect or denomination should be subordinated to another. Unlike Massachusetts, New Hampshire did not by its constitution provide that the taxpayers might designate the church that should receive their religious taxes; but the provision that no one should have to pay for the support of a minister not of one's choice allowed the compulsory support of a minister of the taxpayer's choice if the majority of a town voted for such a minister or if the taxpayer belonged to a recognized religious society that had been incorporated. The New Hampshire constitution merely authorized but did not require towns, parishes, or religious societies to maintain Protestant worship. The constitution seems not to have altered the existing system. Indeed, when the legislature got around to exercising its discretionary authority in 1791, it merely reenacted the statute of 1719 that had governed the establishment before the Revolution. That statute, like Article VI of the state's Declaration of Rights, allowed each town to decide for itself whether to enact religious taxes, how to regulate their collection, and how to provide for exemptions so that dissenters from the locally established church would not have to contribute to its support.

In 1803 Chief Justice Jedediah Smith of New Hampshire, a Congregationalist (Unitarian), declared that the state had no union of church and state because "No one sect is invested with any political power much less with a monopoly of civil privileges and civil offices." According to Smith, "A religious establishment is where the State prescribes a formulary of faith and worship," which New Hampshire did not have. Although Smith referred to the fact that the state permitted

---

42. Charles B. Kinney, *Church and State: The Struggle for Separation in New Hampshire, 1630–1900* (New York, 1955), p. 79.

the existence of an Episcopalian town church, he was cloaking the fact that his own denomination benefited most from the system of public support of religion. He preferred to think of an establishment of religion exclusively in the European sense of a single state church, though he inconsistently condemned any New Hampshire citizen who sought to evade the obligation to pay taxes for religion. So long as the law preferred no particular denomination, Smith comprehended no establishment and so, like his counterparts in Massachusetts and Connecticut, he denied, in effect, that Congregationalism was the established church of his state. He was right in the sense that it was not the only established church of the state and in the sense that the law allowed each town or parish to choose its religion "at the expense of the whole" under terms that extended the same privilege "to all denominations" on the grounds that the state saw "all as equally good for the purposes of civil society." "All," according to Article VI, extended to mainline or conventional Protestant groups and, the court declared, to any new sects that might arise, though not to Deists or atheists. In some towns, however, the local establishment refused to exempt members of new sects, with the result that the Free Will Baptists, Shakers, Methodists, and Universalists, among others, had to seek legislative intervention on their behalf.[43]

New Hampshire's Baptists, among other non-Congregationalists, sometimes sought the incorporation of their churches, as in Massachusetts, to ensure tax exemption of the congregants from a local Congregational church. But, says William G. McLoughlin, most of the petitions to incorporate "seemed to originate from the Baptists' desire to enable their congregations to levy religious taxes on their own members which could be binding in law," and Baptists as well as other non-Congregationalists also accepted from the state ministerial lands regardless of the demands of some of them for a separation of church and state.[44]

---

43. *Muzzy v. Wilkins*, 1 New Hampshire Reports, 1–38 (1803).

44. McLoughlin, *New England Dissent*, 2:874, 886. Earlier McLoughlin made statements misconstruing Article VI. He thought that the omission of a clause entitling taxpayers to designate the church to receive their religious taxes "seems clearly to grant to dissenters the right of exemption from paying re-

The establishment of religion in New Hampshire fell victim to state politics, not to the drive to separate church and state. Democrats found that the path to power ran across the corpse of an establishment favored by the state's Federalists even as they denied its existence. Voters, increasingly non-Congregationalist, rallied around the Democrats' condemnation of the tax system as having promoted an establishment of religion that supposedly favored the prevailing denomination at the expense of the religious liberty of others. After the Democrats won the state, they passed a Toleration Act in 1819 that ended the system of tax support for religion. At that date half the towns in the state had already ended all taxation for religion. The demise of compulsory taxation for public worship received the applause of those who had condemned a union of church and state, even though the state's wall of separation did not eliminate a religious test for office; that did not occur until 1876.[45]

Almost until the time of the adoption of the First Amendment, Connecticut was the state that most seemed to maintain a preferential establishment of religion. In effect, its state church was the Congregational church, although after 1784 Connecticut law did not name that church or in any way prescribe doctrines of belief or a mode of worship. Indeed, the law made possible a multiple establishment, if only in theory, because every town could choose its own minister and some might vote in favor of Baptists, other for Rogerines, still others for Methodists. But Congregationalists composed an even greater percentage of the population in Connecticut than in Massachusetts or New Hampshire. Before the Revolution, Connecticut had also ex-

---

ligious taxes at all" (p. 846). Yet he noted that William Plumer, "unquestionably the most significant figure in the religious history of New Hampshire from 1780 to 1820," who favored separation of church and state (pp. 850–51), in 1791 had proposed a constitutional amendment to clarify Article VI by allowing people to certify their dissent from the town church in order to receive exemption from its support (p. 853). Plumer would not have proposed that amendment, which the voters failed to ratify, if Article VI "clearly guaranteed exemption" from the payment of religious taxes to dissenters from paying religious taxes at all. Nor would Baptists have sought the incorporation of their churches in order to receive the taxes of Baptists.

45. Ibid., 2:888, 899, 905, 907–8, 910; Kinney, *Church and State*, pp. 93–108; Curry, *First Freedoms*, pp. 185–88.

empted Quakers and Baptists from its compulsory tax for religion but required Anglicans to pay it for the benefit of their own church. A dual establishment had existed in the colony as a matter of law, though the sheer weight of numbers made Congregationalists the real beneficiaries of the system, which was the reason for its existence.

In 1784 Connecticut abandoned the Saybrook Platform; its comprehensive Toleration Act of the same year benefited "all denominations of Christians differing in their religious sentiments from the people of the established societies in this State." No one doubted that "the established societies" were Congregational, but the statute did not name the denomination that was established. It did, however, name Episcopalians, "Congregationalists called Separatists," Baptists, and Quakers as among those Christians who might publicly worship "in a way agreeable to their consciences" and be exempted from taxes for the town church if they produced certificates proving membership in their own churches and proving that they supported those churches. The administration of the certificate system produced bitter protests about religious persecution. Moreover, some Protestants believed that government had no right to prescribe laws governing religion or compel anything in religious matters, while nonchurchgoing Christians resented having to pay for the support of the local established church. So long as the establishment remained in force, nonchurchgoers received no relief, but Connecticut liberalized the certificate system for the benefit of churchgoers. In 1791 a new law required a justice of the peace to examine and then certify the claims of persons who dissented from a locally established church, attended a different church, and paid their share for its support.[46] Although Congregationalists defended the law as a way to trap tax evaders among inconstant Congregationalists and nonchurchgoers, it inconvenienced conscientious adherents to different denominations. Worse still, non-Congregationalists, especially Baptists, vehemently objected that government had no legitimate authority to inquire into matters of religious belief. Consequently, a tolerant Connecticut legislature passed a new law allowing nonconformists

46. Greene, *Religious Liberty in Connecticut*, p. 372; McLoughlin, *New England Dissent*, 2:926. The statute said "contributed," not "paid," but "contribute" did not then have the connotation of a voluntary donation.

to write their own certificates attesting membership in a different religious society which they supported, thus exempting them from the support of the town church.[47] John Leland, in a tract describing the evils of an establishment of religion, did not doubt that Connecticut had one, even though one's contribution to religion went to the church whose worship one attended.[48]

Connecticut's leading jurist, Zephaniah Swift, a Unitarian Congregationalist, denied that his state maintained an establishment of religion, which he associated with exclusiveness rather than the comprehensiveness characteristic of Connecticut's support of religion. The abandonment of the Saybrook Platform in 1784 meant that Congregationalism had no preference in law, and Connecticut had neither a prescribed mode of worship nor an official creed. The law so respected religious liberty that a "Jew, a Mehomatan, or a Brahmin" could worship with impunity, although non-Christians had to pay religious taxes to the town church. "Every Christian," Swift proudly wrote, "may believe, worship, and support in such manner as he thinks right, and if he does not feel disposed to join public worship he may stay at home as he pleases without any inconvenience but the payment of his taxes to support public worship in the located society where he lives."[49] Swift sensed no contradiction between religious liberty and the compulsory support of public worship. He believed that everyone should support religion because it bulwarked state and society. Connecticut's law recognized the equality of all Christians, he contended; a town church, even if Congregationalist, received no legal favors because its members were dissenters in relation to a poll parish that maintained a church of some other denomination.[50] Because Swift could not conceive of a multiple establishment of religion, he denied that Connecticut main-

47. Greene, *Religious Liberty in Connecticut*, pp. 373–76; McLoughlin, *New England Dissent*, 2:937.

48. John Leland, "The Rights of Conscience Inalienable," in *Writings of John Leland*, p. 186. See Curry, *First Freedoms*, pp. 178–84, for another treatment of Connecticut.

49. Zephaniah Swift, *System of the Law of Connecticut*, 2 vols. (Windham, Conn., 1791–96), 1:146.

50. Ibid., 1:144–45.

tained any establishment whatever. His view was probably the predominant one in the four New England states that maintained establishments of religion. In a legal sense, they were nonpreferentialist but in fact preferred the Congregational church, which professed not to be established by law.

Even anticlerical Congregationalists of Connecticut as well as advocates of separation of church and state saw an establishment of religion in a bill to pay clerical salaries from state funds. The Western Lands Bill of 1793 proposed to divide proportionately among all religious societies the interest on the principal of $1,200,000 from the sale of public land, on condition that the money be used for ministerial support. One argument advanced to defeat this bill was that state aid to religion, even if on a nonpreferential basis, constituted an establishment of religion that violated religious liberty.[51] The state used the money to support its public school system.

In 1802 the Baptists in Connecticut petitioned the legislature to repeal the system of compulsory religious taxes. The legislature rejected that petition on the grounds that religion, like schools and courts, deserved every taxpayer's support; therefore the state could tax everyone.[52] A statewide Baptist convention then remonstrated against Connecticut's establishment because it favored the Congregationalists, and also because religion should be left to voluntary support. In 1804 a Baptist petition complained that the General Assembly had "fixed the laws so that no man can be taxed by the Baptists or Episcopalians &c. until he has said in a certificate that he belongs" to the taxing body.[53] The Baptists concluded that a Congregational society could not fairly tax anyone until the person produced a certificate proving he or she was a Congregationalist. If Connecticut's Baptists made any consistent argument it was that the existing church-state relationship preferred Congregationalism, despite Congregational denials, and that private donations should be the only source of support to religion, despite Baptist participation in the establishment's largesse.

In 1816, for example, when Connecticut expected a windfall repayment from the United States of state costs incurred during the War of 1812, the state legislature passed "An Act for the Support of Religion and Literature." The act divided the money among the major denominations in proportion to their numbers, after reserving one-seventh to Yale. Even the Baptists, despite protests, accepted their share, proof again that state aid to religion in Connecticut showed the existence of a multiple establishment of religion.[54] In 1818 the Hartford Baptists announced that candor required recognition of the fact that in Connecticut "Religion is established and supported by law," but Baptists believed that one denomination enjoyed dominance. Voluntarism would protect religious liberty, a position conformable to that of the state's Toleration or Democratic party and to that of most non-Congregationalists, who were growing faster than the Congregationalists. A constitutional convention of 1818 scrapped the old charter of 1662 as revised during the American Revolution and wrote the state's first constitution. It disestablished church and state by providing that no one could be compelled to support any religious society, yet allowed any religious society to tax itself and privately collect the assessment from each member.[55]

Vermont became the fourteenth state in 1791, and its vote was counted to determine whether enough states had ratified the Bill of Rights. Therefore its brief history with an establishment of religion merits notice. Vermont's constitution of 1777 guaranteed the free exercise of religion including the right of every person not to be compelled to support any place of worship or minister against his or her conscience, but inconsistently provided too that every sect or denomination of Christians "ought to . . . support some sort of religious worship . . . agreeable to the revealed will of God."[56] In 1783 the legislature enacted a statute described by William G. McLoughlin as "an elaborate

54. Greene, *Religious Liberty in Connecticut*, pp. 467–71; J. Hammond Trumbull, *Historical Notes of the Constitutions of Connecticut, 1639 to 1818, and Progress of the Movement which resulted in the Convention of 1818* (Hartford, Conn., 1901), pp. 35–36.

55. Richard Purcell, *Connecticut in Transition* (Washington, D.C., 1918), pp. 384–85, 400–403; Greene, *Religious Liberty in Connecticut*, pp. 423–96; Trumbull, *Historical Notes*, pp. 46–62; McLoughlin, *New England Dissent*, 2:1006–62.

56. Thorpe, ed., *Constitutions*, 7:3740.

attempt to create a general establishment of religion without giving preference to any particular group of believers and without obliging anyone who conscientiously objected to it to support the establishment."[57]

As elsewhere in New England, the local option system prevailed. A two-thirds majority of voters in a town decided which church should be its established church, but anyone attending a different church could be exempted from paying a tax for religion. As a matter of law Baptists could benefit from the establishment in one town, Quakers in the next, and so on. Because the demography of Vermont favored Congregationalism, so did the establishment as a matter of practice, although non-Congregationalists dominated west of the Green Mountains. In 1786 Vermont adopted a new constitution that omitted a religious test for office, referred to "people" rather than "Christians," and also omitted the words "and support" from the clause obligating every sect in the matter of public worship. In the following year the legislature provided that whenever a religious society agreed to hire a minister or build a church, it could assess its members for costs and appoint collectors who should have the same powers as town tax collectors. Never did law create a more liberal establishment, aiding every religion in the state.

Baptists, however, pledged themselves to assess no rates and maintain their preachers and churches with free contributions only. A Baptist elder preached before the state assembly in 1792 on the theme that "religious establishment by law" damaged both church and state. He insisted that religion was always a private matter between God and individuals, yet he favored "friendly aids" to religion such as compulsory attendance, not enforced in Vermont, and Sabbath laws. An establishment, in his opinion, seemed to mean taxation for religion and any means used by government to enforce taxes for religion, such as certificate laws.[58] Baptists conscientiously opposed Vermont's certificate laws, although they were as liberal as possible; after 1794 dissenters from a town church could write their own certificates exempting them

57. McLoughlin, *New England Dissent*, 2:800.
58. Ibid., 2:803.

from support of that church. In 1807, when the Jeffersonians controlled state politics and a Baptist was speaker of the house, Vermont repealed all laws concerning taxation for religion, thus separating church and state.[59]

59. Ibid., 2:789–832, is the best treatment of Vermont's establishment.

3

State Establishments of Religion: The South

In the five southern states, where the Church of England had benefited from an exclusive establishment in each colony, the Revolution spurred pent-up opposition.[1] Every one of the five states disestablished the Anglican church, but only North Carolina showed no temptation to create a general establishment that taxed people only for the church of their choice. By its constitution of 1776

1. Thomas Curry, *The First Freedoms: Church and State in America to the Passage of the First Amendment* (New York, 1986), pp. 134–58, covers disestablishment in the southern states during the revolutionary period.

North Carolina became the first southern state to separate church and state. Indeed, North Carolina did so easily, in contrast to the other southern states. Disestablishmentarians in Virginia, Maryland, South Carolina, and Georgia quickly broke the Anglican monopoly on religious privileges but needed at least a decade more to muster the necessary votes against nonpreferential state aid to religion. In North Carolina the Anglicans maintained what one historian called "the most unhealthily established church in the American colonies."[2] They had fewer than ten churches in 1776, still fewer ministers, and they suffered chronically from weakness and public hostility. In the generation before independence the population of North Carolina swelled in the central and western counties, where the nearly nonexistent Church of England confronted Scotch Presbyterians, German Moravians, English Quakers, a variety of evangelical sects, and possibly a majority of nonchurchgoers, if not nonbelievers. The governor of the colony during the controversy with Britain remarked, "Every sect of religion abounds here except the Roman Catholic," the only one more unpopular than the Anglican. Mecklenburg County, when adopting resolutions to instruct its delegates to a revolutionary provincial meeting, prefigured the shape of church-state relationships when demanding religious freedom and equality for all Protestants as well as severance of any union between church and state.[3]

A year later, in 1776, the new state constitution banned the "establishment of any one religious church or denomination in this state, in preference to any other." This language, which seemed directed against an exclusive establishment only, applied to even a nonpreferential one, because the next clause of the same section provided that "neither shall any person, on any pretence whatsoever, be compelled to attend any place of worship, contrary to his own faith or judgment, nor be obliged

2. Gary Freeze, "Like a House Built on Sand: The Anglican Church and Establishment in North Carolina," *Historical Magazine of the Protestant Episcopal Church* 48 (1979): 405, 430.

3. A. Roger Ekrich, *Poor Carolina: Politics and Society in Colonial North Carolina, 1729–1776* (Chapel Hill, N.C., 1981), pp. 30, 44; "Instructions for the Delegates of Mecklenburg County Proposed to the Consideration of the County," in *The Colonial Records of North Carolina*, edited by William L. Saunders, 10 vols. (Raleigh, N.C., 1886–90), 10:241.

to pay, for the purchase of any glebe, or the building of any house of worship, or for the maintenance of any minister or ministry, contrary to what he believes right, or has voluntarily and personally engaged to perform; but all persons shall be at liberty to exercise their own mode of worship."[4] The phrasing against preference reflected the state's colonial experience with an exclusive establishment, not an authorization to support religion nonpreferentially. North Carolina never granted financial aid to religion after 1776.

In Maryland, Georgia, and South Carolina "an establishment of religion" as a matter of law meant very much what it did in the New England states that maintained multiple establishments. However, those three southern states merely permitted but did not create establishments. Maryland's constitution of 1776 provided that no person could be compelled "to maintain any particular place of worship, or any particular ministry," thus ending the former supremacy of the Episcopalian church, which had enjoyed an exclusive establishment in the colonial period. But that did not separate church and state because the same constitution provided for a new establishment of religion by a special enabling clause: "yet the Legislature may, in their discretion, lay a general and equal tax, for the support of the Christian religion; leaving to each individual the power of appointing the payment of the money, collected from him, to the support of any particular place of worship or minister."[5] "Christian" rather than "Protestant" was used in Maryland because of the presence of a large Roman Catholic population, thus ensuring nonpreferential support of all churches existing in the state. The enabling clause showed that a constitutional provision against a "particular" or preferential establishment did not by itself empower the legislature to create a multiple establishment or to grant financial aid to all churches or denominations on a nondiscriminatory basis.

A proposal of 1780 to impose an "equal assessment and Tax" for the benefit of religion got nowhere. In 1783 the governor urged a measure

---

4. Francis Newton Thorpe, ed., *The Federal and State Constitutions, Colonial Charters, and Other Organic Laws*, 7 vols. (Washington, D.C., 1909), 5:2793, sec. 34.

5. Ibid., 3:1689, Article 33.

"placing every branch of the Christian Church upon the most equal and respectable footing."[6] In 1784 another such bill proposed a tax for the aid of all Christian churches with preference to none; the bill exempted from the tax anyone professing to be a "Jew or Mohometan, or [declaring] that he does not believe in Christian religion."[7] A Baltimore newspaper, seeing the "camel's nose" under the tent, censured the proposal as the reintroduction of an establishment. The legislature favored the bill but decided to leave its fate to the voters in their selection of representatives to the next legislative session. A blizzard of newspaper articles and petitions condemned the bill as a new establishment of religion and a violation of the Christian spirit, asserted that establishments harmed religion, and darkly warned about an Episcopalian conspiracy to regain supremacy. Opponents of the bill also argued that compulsory support of religion violated religious freedom.[8] The voters chose a legislature strongly opposed to a general assessment, because additional taxation for any purpose triggered public hostility. In 1785 the bill was voted down by a two-to-one majority.[9] Maryland never did implement its constitutional authorization for a multiple establishment of religion. In 1810 the power to enact a multiple establishment was taken from the legislature by a constitutional amendment that outlawed "an equal and general tax or any other tax . . . for the support of any religion."[10]

Georgia's constitution of 1777 tersely effected the disestablishment

6. Albert W. Werline, *Problems of Church and State in Seventeenth and Eighteenth Century Maryland* (S. Lancaster, Mass., 1948), p. 175.

7. Quoted in Curry, *First Freedoms*, p. 155. On Maryland, I have also used John C. Rainbolt, "The Struggle to Define Religious Liberty in Maryland, 1776–1785," *Journal of Church and State* 17 (1975): 445–58; Werline, *Problems of Church and State*, pp. 143–208.

8. Allan Nevins, *The American States during and after the Revolution* (New York, 1924), p. 431; Werline, *Problems of Church and State*, pp. 169–86; Rainbolt, "The Struggle to Define Religious Liberty," p. 448. Rainbolt said that the proposed measure would have inaugurated a "plural establishment" (p. 447).

9. The newspaper, cited by Werline, Rainbolt, and Curry, was the *Maryland Gazette or Baltimore General Advertiser*. See issues of Jan. 28, Mar. 4, and Mar. 25, 1785.

10. Thorpe, ed., *Constitutions*, 3:1705.

of the Church of England while permitting a multiple establishment of all churches without exception: "All persons whatever shall have the free exercise of their religion; . . . and shall not, unless by consent, support any teacher or teachers except of their own profession."[11] "This, of course, left the way open for taxation for the support of one's own religion," says one historian of eighteenth-century church-state relationships in Georgia, "and such a law was passed in 1785," although similar bills had failed in 1782 and 1784.[12] According to the general assessment act of 1785, all Christian sects and denominations were to receive tax support in proportion to the amount of property owned by their respective church members, but it is not clear whether this measure ever went into operation. What is clear is that an establishment of religion meant government tax support of all churches, with preference for none.

The state constitution in force at the time of the framing of the Bill of Rights was adopted in 1789. Its relevant provision declared that no persons should be obliged "to contribute to the support of any religious professions but their own," thereby permitting a multiple establishment as before. In the state constitution adopted in 1798, however, Georgia finally separated church and state in law as well as in fact by a guarantee that no person should be "obliged to pay tithes, taxes, or any other rate, for . . . any place of worship, or for the maintenance of any minister or ministry, contrary to what he believes to be right, or hath voluntarily engaged." The very next sentence redundantly prohibited the establishment of any religious society in preference over another, showing that a constitutional policy of no preference did not imply the constitutionality of nonpreferential measures in favor of religion generally. No preference in 1798 signified the abandonment of Georgia's previous constitutional regime of nonpreference.[13]

At the time of the framing of the First Amendment, South Carolina's constitution also permitted a nonpreferential or multiple establishment of churches. The temporary constitution of 1776 had left church-

11. Ibid., 2:784.

12. Reba D. Strickland, *Religion and the State in Georgia in the Eighteenth Century* (New York, 1939), p. 164; see also p. 166.

13. Thorpe, ed., *Constitutions*, 2:801, sec. 9.

state relationships unaffected, with the result that dissenters, who out-numbered Anglicans by a four-to-one majority, organized to obtain the disestablishment of the Church of England. In 1771 the Reverend William Tennent, a Presbyterian who framed "The Petition of the Dis-senters," addressed the South Carolina General Assembly on the theme that "all religious establishments are an infringement of re-ligious liberty" and that all Protestants should enjoy equal privileges, religious as well as civil. Tennent had heard of a proposal "to establish all denominations by law and pay them all equally," but the idea struck him as absurd, on the supposition that the establishment of all religions would contradict the idea of an establishment. Tennent could not grasp the concept of the multiple establishment because he thought in terms of the Anglican establishment in South Carolina; "only the Church of England is legal," he complained, "only its Ministers may perform legal marriages, only it has legal contracts."[14]

Charles Cotesworth Pinckney, a future member of the Philadelphia Constitutional Convention, introduced a plan for an establishment of all Protestant churches in South Carolina, but without mandatory tax support. Tennent, reversing himself, announced his "pleasure to find that a *general establishment*, or rather incorporation of all denominations is now thought of, and likely to be adopted." Pinckney's proposal, Ten-nent continued, "opens the door to the equal incorporation of all de-nominations, while not one sect of Christians in preference to all others but Christianity itself is the established religion of the state."[15] Ten-nent's use of "general establishment" shows how quickly he grasped the distinction between an exclusive establishment and a multiple one.

Pinckney's proposal became the basis of Article XXXVIII of the South Carolina constitution of 1778, which blueprinted a "general es-tablishment," in Tennent's phrase, of the "Christian Protestant reli-gion" as the replacement of the former exclusive establishment of An-glicanism. Every Protestant denomination received a guarantee of equality. Any religious society of a Protestant denomination might

14. John Wesley Brinsfield, *Religion and Politics in South Carolina* (Easky, S.C., 1983), pp. 115–18. For Tennent's remarks, see above, chap. 1, text connected with note 13.

15. Ibid., pp. 121–22; emphasis added.

therefore be incorporated and become "a church of the established religion of this State" on condition of subscribing to the articles of faith: a belief in God, a promise to worship Him publicly, profession of Christianity as "the true religion," and reliance on the Scriptures as divinely inspired. No person was obligated to pay toward the maintenance and support of a religious worship that he or she did "not freely join . . . or has not voluntarily engaged to support." Pursuant to these constitutional provisions, Protestant societies qualified as established churches.[16] Never before had an establishment been known that did not exact religious assessments and could not constitutionally do so. Although the legislature incorporated churches of various denominations, it did not enact a tax to support religion, despite proposals to that effect. In 1790 South Carolina adopted a new constitution that omitted the previous provisions for an establishment of religion and guaranteed the free exercise of religion—for Roman Catholics and Jews as well as for Protestants.[17]

The Virginia constitution of 1776 avoided the issue of an establishment of religion, although it guaranteed to every person equality in the "free exercise of religion," thanks to the efforts of young James Madison.[18] Madison failed, however, to win acceptance for his proposal, which would have ended any union of church and state, that no one "ought on account of religion to be invested with peculiar emoluments or privileges."[19] Baptists were disappointed with the inadequacy of the

16. Thorpe, ed., *Constitutions*, 6:3253–57.

17. Ibid., 6:3664.

18. Virginia Declaration of Rights, sec. 16, in ibid., 7:3814; William T. Hutchinson et al., eds., *The Papers of James Madison*, ser. in progress (Chicago, 1962–), 1:173–75.

19. *Madison Papers*, 1:174; Thomas E. Buckley, *Church and State in Revolutionary Virginia 1776–1787* (Charlottesville, Va., 1977), p. 19. James McClellan, "The Making and the Unmaking of the Establishment Clause," in *A Blueprint for Judicial Reform*, edited by Patrick B. McGuigan and R. R. Rader (Washington, D.C., 1981), p. 305, wrongly states that Madison's motion passed. McClellan's essay is littered with errors, great and small, some of them howlers. He grossly distorts history, gets nuances wrong, and says silly things. He scarcely understands what an establishment of religion is. He thinks Protestants had a preferred status over Dissenters, not knowing that Dissenters were Protestants,

new state constitution, which did not make religion "stand upon its own merits." They petitioned for freedom from the compulsion of having to support any clergy but their own, and they wanted to be free also from having to pay other clergy in order to "be married, buried, and the like."[20] Caleb Wallace, a Presbyterian clergyman who was a member of the General Assembly, declared that 10,000 freeholders signed that Baptist petition.[21] Baptists also demanded that the legislature should guarantee "equal privileges to all ordained ministers of every denomination" in order to break the Anglican monopoly on the administration of the sacraments, especially the rites of marriage.[22]

The Hanover Presbytery, in an imperishable document of October 1776, remonstrated against the establishment and advocated the separation of church and state in language remarkably like that of Madison and Jefferson. Caleb Wallace, for the Hanover Presbytery, regarded an establishment of religion as a violation of the free-exercise clause of the Virginia Declaration of Rights, of the natural rights of mankind, and of "freedom of enquiry and private judgment." Every argument favoring the establishment of Christianity, Wallace reasoned, was comparable to arguments favoring the establishment of the "tenets of Mahomet by those who believe the Alkoran." No magistrate could judge the "right of preference among the various sects which profess the Christian faith, without erecting a chair of infallibility, which would lead us back to the Church of Rome." Establishments, he argued, greatly injured "the temporal interests" of any community. And, because the kingdom of God was not of this world, the gospel needed only spiritual aid, none from state power. The only proper object of civil government was the protection of natural rights. The duty one owed to God and the manner of discharging it could only be directed by reason or conviction "and is nowhere cognizable but at the tribunal of the Universal Judge."

and he thinks too that every state but Rhode Island rejected separation of church and state.

20. Charles F. James, *Documentary History of the Struggle for Religious Liberty in Virginia* (Lynchburg, Va., 1900), p. 66.

21. H. J. Eckenrode, *Separation of Church and State in Virginia* (Richmond, Va., 1910), p. 51.

22. Albert Henry Newman, *A History of the Baptist Church in the United States* (New York, 1915), p. 368.

Therefore, concluded the memorial of the Hanover Presbytery, "we ask no ecclesiastical establishment for ourselves, neither can we approve of them and grant it to others." The sole support of any church should derive from the "private choice or voluntary obligation" of its supporters.[23]

Evangelical demands for the separation of church and state, supported principally by Baptists and Presbyterians, ultimately prevailed in Virginia. But the disproportionate influence in the General Assembly of tidewater conservatives, who were greatly overrepresented, and the widespread belief that government and society could not flourish without subsidized religion as a prop, prevented decisive action except to relieve dissenters. As 1776 ended, the legislature repealed almost every statute that bulwarked the establishment of the Church of England. The repealed statutes had criminalized religious opinions that subverted Anglicanism, penalized failure to attend church, and discriminated against any but the Anglican mode of worship. The Anglican clergy still monopolized the administration of certain sacraments, particularly marriage rites. But the statute passed at the close of 1776 also provided that "dissenters from the church established by law" should be exempt from taxes for its support and suspended the collection of taxes even from members of the established church. An indecisive legislature expressly reserved for future decision the great question of whether to separate church and state or to create a general establishment by taxing everyone on a nonpreferential basis for the support of the churches of their choice: "And whereas great variety of opinions has arisen, touching the propriety of general assessments, or whether every religious society should be left to voluntary contributions . . . it is thought most prudent to defer this matter."[24] Subsequent events proved that the act terminated the union of the government with the

---

23. William Addison Blakely, ed., *American State Papers Bearing on Sunday Legislation*, revised and enlarged by W. A. Colcard (Washington, D.C., 1911), pp. 91–95, reprints the document under the heading "Dissenters' Petition."

24. "An Act for Exempting the Different Societies of Dissenters," in *The Statutes At Large . . . of Virginia*, edited by William Waller Hening, 13 vols. (Richmond, Va., 1809–28), 9:164–67.

"church established by law," because it received no government support after 1776. In 1777 and again in 1778 the legislature renewed the suspension of religious taxes even for Anglicans, and in 1779 it repealed the old colonial statute levying those taxes.

In 1779 two conflicting bills were introduced in the legislature. Jefferson's "Bill for Religious Freedom" provided in part "that no man shall be compelled to frequent or support any religious worship, place, or ministry whatsoever."[25] The principle underlying this provision was the belief that religion, as a personal matter between God and an individual, was not rightfully subject to the jurisdiction of the civil government. By contrast, "A Bill concerning Religion," which proposed a general assessment, declared the Christian religion to be the "established Religion" of Virginia and provided articles of faith to which church members had to subscribe in order to be incorporated as an established church. These articles were modeled on the comparable provision of the South Carolina constitution of 1778.[26] Each established church and its minister were to have their share of the tax proceeds assessed on tithable personal property collected by county sheriffs. All persons could designate the church of their choice as the recipient of their taxes; money collected from anyone who did not designate membership was to be divided proportionately among all the churches of the county.[27] Neither this bill nor Jefferson's could muster a majority in the legislature for several years. Then the Presbyterian clergy, attracted by the prospect of state support for their own church, reversed their position and endorsed the principle of a general assessment.

In 1784 Patrick Henry, who had a substantial Presbyterian constituency, introduced a new general assessment bill, entitled "A Bill Establishing a Provision for Teachers of the Christian Religion," whose purpose was to carry into effect a house resolution in favor of requiring a

25. Julian Boyd et al., eds., *Papers of Thomas Jefferson*, ser. in progress (Princeton, N.J., 1950–), 2:546. Hereafter cited as *Jefferson Papers*.

26. See above, this chapter, text connected with note 16.

27. Buckley, *Church and State*, pp. 47–62. Buckley reprints the general assessment bill of 1779 on pp. 185–88.

"moderate tax or contribution annually for the support of the Christian religion, or of some Christian church, denomination or communion of Christians, or for some form of Christian worship."[28] It retained the idea of a multiple establishment but was a far more secular version than the one of 1779. The bill declared the "liberal principle" that all Christian sects and denominations were equal before the law, none preferred over others. It did not speak of the "established religion" of the state, contained no articles of faith, and purported to be based on non-religious considerations only—the furtherance of public peace and morality rather than of Christ's kingdom on earth or the encouragement of religion.[29]

The more secularized version of the general assessment, sponsored by the most popular and powerful man in the legislature and backed by Episcopalians, Methodists, and Presbyterians, commanded a majority in the legislature. Richard Henry Lee, who supported the bill, told Madison, "I fully agree with the Presbyterians, that true freedom embraces the Mahomitan and Gentoo [Hindus] as well as the Christian religion."[30] But Madison, who had earlier noted that the Presbyterian clergy favored "a more comprehensive establishm[en]t," angrily wrote to James Monroe that the Presbyterians "seem as ready to set up an establishmt. which is to take them in as they were to pull down that which shut them out."[31] Madison cleverly helped to get Patrick Henry out of the legislature by supporting his election as governor, thus depriving the general assessment forces of their charismatic leader. The bill passed to its third and last reading, however. The notes of Madison's speech in opposition show that he argued that the "true question" was not whether religion was necessary but "are Religs. Estabts. nec-

28. See Eckenrode, *Separation of Church and State*, p. 86, for the resolution.

29. Buckley, *Church and State*, reprints the bill on pp. 189–91. Michael J. Malbin, *Religion and Politics: The Intention of the Authors of the First Amendment* (Washington, D.C., 1978), p. 23, purporting to describe the 1784 bill, confuses it with the 1779 bill.

30. Richard Henry Lee to James Madison, Nov. 26, 1784, in *Madison Papers*, 8:149.

31. James Madison to James Monroe, Nov. 14, 1784, and Apr. 12, 1785, in ibid., 8:137, 261. On the position of the Presbyterian clergy, see Buckley, *Church and State*, pp. 92–96.

essy. for Religion? no."[32] Madison won a postponement of the final vote until the next session of the legislature a year later so that the members could test public opinion on the issue. His opposition confidently agreed to the delay; they relished the prospect that public opinion would back the election of the general assessment supporters who would favor a "more comprehensive establishment."

In 1785 Madison took to the people his case against an establishment of religion—any establishment of religion. He wrote his famous "Memorial and Remonstrance against Religious Assessments," in which he argued that religion is a private, voluntary affair not subject to government in any way. Madison assumed, as had the Hanover Presbytery in 1776 and all other opponents of tax aids to religion, that a general assessment was in fact an establishment of religion. Any establishment, he contended, violated the free exercise of religion and threatened public liberty. The principle that government could create an establishment must be denied, Madison wrote; he did not care how mild or comprehensive an establishment of religion might be, because the same authority that created it might create a preferential one, favoring one sect over others. To Madison, religion was simply not an "engine of civil policy," and Christianity did not stand in need of government support, nor did the government need the support of religion. Establishments produced bigotry and persecution, defiled religion, corrupted government, and ended in spiritual and political tyranny. The proposed establishment, he declared, differed from the Inquisition "only in degree," not in principle.[33]

Many others also wrote against the general assessment. Over one hundred petitions and memorials, signed by over 11,000 Virginians, deluged the legislature when it met in the fall of 1785, and nine out of ten condemned the proposal. Some of the remonstrances against the assessment spoke for religious denominations—Presbyterians, Baptists, and Quakers. But a petition by an unknown author garnered the

32. Dec. 23–24, 1784, in *Madison Papers*, 8:198. For Madison's outline of the speech, see 8:195–99.

33. "Memorial and Remonstrance against Religious Assessments," June 20, 1785, in ibid., 8:298–304. For further discussion of the "Memorial," see chap. 4, below.

greatest number of signatories. It reflected the views of "evangelical Christians believing deeply in the principle of voluntary support."[34] The author of this petition was an active Christian who believed that the general assessment bill would not thwart the spread of Deism, despite arguments to the contrary by the bill's supporters. Its opponents relied mainly on religious arguments to buttress their position.[35] Yet the evangelicals' arguments did not substantially differ from those of the rationalists whom Madison represented. Rationalists and evangelicals differed in style and emphasis; the rationalists took a somewhat more secular view by stressing the harmful effects of an establishment on society and on government, while the evangelicals gave prime consideration to the effect on religion. Almost everyone who condemned an establishment, including the mild one proposed, found it hostile to the best interests of the gospel and violative of natural rights, especially of religious freedom.[36]

In one variant of a popular evangelical petition against the general assessment bill, inhabitants of Cumberland County declared "that the blessed author of the Christian religion not only maintained and supported his gospel in the world for several hundred years without the aid of civil power, but against all the powers of the earth," and, they added, because of the purity of the gospel, it succeeded against all opposition. However, after Constantine established Christianity as the official religion of the Roman Empire, the church suffered from superstition and error. History showed that "religious establishment has never been a means of prospering the gospel."[37] Another variant of the same peti-

34. Buckley, *Church and State*, p. 149.

35. "Editorial Note on Madison's Memorial," in *Madison Papers*, 8:298; Curry, *First Freedoms*, p. 147.

36. Buckley, *Church and State*, pp. 149–51, and Curry, *First Freedoms*, pp. 143–47, analyze the various manuscript petitions, which are available on microfilm from the Virginia State Library, Richmond, in a collection entitled "Religious Petitions, 1774–1802, Presented to the General Assembly of Virginia." Curry made a typescript of the collection through 1787 and generously gave me a copy.

37. "Religious Petitions," Petition of Cumberland County, Oct. 26, 1785. The original capitalizes almost every noun. In quoting from these petitions I

tion urged that the Virginia legislature should leave people "inti in matters of religion and the manner of supporting it."[38]

A petition from the Presbyterian churches of Virginia, whicl switched allegiance, argued that Christianity is most effective when left alone under God, "free from the intrusive hand of the civil magistrate." God did not think it necessary to render religion dependent on government, "and experience has shown that this dependence, where it has been effected, has been an injury rather than an aid." Religion and morality, the Presbyterians asserted, "can be promoted only by the internal conviction of the mind and its voluntary choice which such establishments cannot effect." Therefore, the subjects of Jesus Christ opposed the attempt of civil rulers to regulate or promote religious matter.[39] Evangelicals of Rockingham County agreed. They explained that the basis for opposing aid by government to religion derived from the separate spheres of the two: "Any legislative body that takes upon themselves the power of governing religion by human laws assumes a power that never was committed to them by God nor can be by man." The government's jurisdiction reached only "civil concernments." Exceptions to that principle were dangerous, because "if you can do any thing in religion by human laws you can do everything." The "pernicious consequences" of establishments of religion supplied the proof; persecution and denials of religious liberty invariably attended establishments. Consequently, governments should restrict themselves to "affairs of state." As for "the Church of Christ, be content to let it stand on its own gospel foundations regulated by its own laws."[40]

The foundation of this edifice of reasoning received expression in a petition against the general assessment by Virginia's Baptist associations: "As the Church of the Kingdom of Christ 'is not of this world' as himself declares; it appears an evident impropriety, to intrust in the

---

have modernized capitalization but have retained the original spelling and punctuation.

38. Ibid., Nansemond County, Oct. 27, 1785.

39. Ibid., Miscellaneous Petition of the Ministers and Lay Representatives of the Presbyterian Church, Nov. 2, 1785.

40. Ibid., Rockingham County, Nov. 2, 1784.

management of any of its proper interests offices which relate wholly to secular matters. And cannot therefore have any proper connection with a spiritual body." Thus, to compel support of the Christian religion even from the faithful "is inconsistent both with the generous and independent spirit of the Christian religion, and the custom of the primitive Church."[41] So too another fundamentalist petition declared, "But religion and all its duties being of divine origin and of a nature wholly distinct from the secular affairs of the public society ought not to be made the object of human legislation. For the discharge of the duties of religion every man is to account for himself as an individual in a future state and ought not to be under the direct of influence of any human laws."[42] Chesterfield County's various Christians agreed with the Baptists that because Christ had declared that his kingdom is not of this world, to legislate for his subjects in religious matters violates "his Kingly prerogative."[43] A Quaker memorial construed state aid to religion exacted from its believers to be "directly contrary to the doctrine of our Saviour."[44]

An evangelical petition contended that the general assessment bill, which its defenders advocated as a public support of religion, was "calculated to destroy religion."[45] Still another petition insisted that "Christ the head of the Church has left plain directions concerning religion, and the manner of supporting its teachers, which should be by free contributions" rather than by the "heavy yoke" imposed by a general assessment for religion.[46] And Washington County added that the general assessment bill was "big with empending danger" and "highly improper" because in the same way that civil policy "can never make us Christians, neither can Christianity be benefitted by the laws of the commonwealth but only by the constitutions of Christ."[47]

41. Ibid., Remonstrance and Petition of the Committees of Several Baptist Associations in Virginia Assembled in Powhatan County, Aug. 13, 1785, received by the Assembly on Nov. 3, 1785.

42. Ibid., Rockbridge County, Nov. 2, 1785.

43. Ibid., Chesterfield County, Nov. 12, 1785.

44. Ibid., Miscellaneous Petition, Nov. 14, 1785.

45. Ibid., Rockbridge County, Dec. 1, 1785.

46. Ibid., Westmoreland County, Nov. 2, 1785.

47. Ibid., Washington County, Dec. 10, 1785.

A petition from Dinwiddie County, populated mainly by Episcopalians and Methodists who previously had supported the general assessment bill, opposed it "as a measure injurious to the liberties of the people [and] destructive to the true religion."[48] Similarly, Amherst County, also dominated by Episcopalians and Methodists, switched its position by condemning the "General Establishment" bill because it threatened religious liberty and because Christianity "disclaims any dependence on human laws."[49] Seen in its context then, Madison's "Memorial and Remonstrance" more reflected public opinion than shaped it when he argued that religion must be left to private conscience, is exempt from civil governance, and would be damaged by the proposed establishment. He struck responsive chords when declaring that Christianity did not need civil support and that such support contradicted the Christian religion.[50]

Virginia's intensive and prolonged debate on whether to adopt a general establishment or leave religion to private conscience produced an upheaval in public opinion. Among religious bodies, only the Episcopal Church and the Methodists continued to endorse the general assessment, although their congregations divided on the issue. The rank and file of Presbyterians, unlike their clergy, probably never had abandoned their loyalty to private conscience and voluntary support; and their clergy during 1785 returned to the principles of the Hanover Presbytery of 1776. Madison surmised that the clergy feared the wrath of the laity and the possibility of an Episcopalian resurgence.[51] Presbyterian counties censured the general assessment bill and elected deputies who opposed it, while the Hanover Presbytery endorsed the enactment of Jefferson's bill for religious liberty, which provided for separation of church and state. Madison exulted that the "steps taken throughout the Country to defeat the General Assessment had produced all the effect that could have been wished."[52]

48. Ibid., Dinwiddie County, Nov. 28, 1785.

49. Ibid., Amherst County, Dec. 10, 1785.

50. "Editorial Note on Madison's Memorial," in *Madison Papers*, 8:298; Curry, *First Freedoms*, p. 147.

51. James Madison to Thomas Jefferson, Aug. 20, 1785, in *Madison Papers*, 8:345.

52. James Madison to Thomas Jefferson, Jan. 22, 1786, in ibid., 8:473. On

George Washington's reaction suggested the turnabout in opinion. He had originally supported the general assessment bill, and still found nothing alarming, he wrote, in making people pay for "the support of that which they profess, if of the denominations of Christians," so long as Jews, Mohammedans, and other professed non-Christians obtained proper relief. Yet the issue was so divisive that Washington regretted it had ever arisen. When George Mason sent him a copy of Madison's "Memorial" and asked Washington to subscribe, he replied, "As the matter now stands, I wish an assessment had never been agitated—and as it has gone so far, that the bill could die an easy death; because I think it will be productive of more quiet to the State, than by enacting it into a Law; which in my opinion, would be impolitic, admitting there is a decided majority for it, to the disgust of a respectable minority. In the first case the matter will soon subside; in the latter it will rankle, and perhaps convulse the State."[53]

The state elections of 1785 produced a legislature whose membership overwhelmingly opposed a general establishment of religion. The legislature, which let the assessment bill die unnoticed, by a vote of 60 to 27 enacted Jefferson's great emancipating bill instead. At the time, Jefferson represented the United States in Paris. Madison, then the most influential member of the state legislature, presented Jefferson's bill and managed the defeat of a motion to restrict its protections to Christians only. The Virginia Statute for Religious Freedom declared in its preface that to compel anyone to support religious opinions he did not share was tyrannical and "that even the forcing him to support this or that teacher of his own religious persuasion, is depriving him of the comfortable liberty" of giving his money as he pleased. The enabling provisions stated "that no man shall be compelled to frequent or support any religious worship, place, or ministry whatsoever." The significance of the statute is not just that it broadened freedom of worship or

---

the Presbyterians, see the memorial adopted at Bethel, Aug. 1785, in James, *Documentary History*, p. 240.

53. George Washington to George Mason, Oct. 3, 1785, in *The Papers of George Mason*, edited by Robert Rutland, 3 vols. (Chapel Hill, N.C., 1970), 2:831–32.

of opinion in matters of religion but that it separated church and state in the context of protecting religious liberty.

At the same time as Madison chaperoned Jefferson's bill for religious freedom through the Virginia legislature, Madison also introduced other measures proposed by Jefferson's committee on the revision of the laws. They recommended a bill to protect the property of the Anglican church; a bill to punish anyone who disturbed public worship and to punish violators of the Christian sabbath; and a bill for fixing a date of fasting and prayer, which was not enacted. Accordingly, at this date and at a state level, Jefferson and Madison were by no means absolutists on the question of separation of government and religion. On the other hand it is preposterous to regard the bill for the protection of church property as a bill that "advantaged a single sect," given the fact that "sect" was being disestablished. Jefferson had supported disestablishment as early as June 1776 when he drafted three versions of a state constitution, each including a clause guaranteeing that no person should be compelled "to frequent or maintain" any religious service or institution.[54] Moreover, the engine behind the bill to punish disturbers of the religious peace was the protection of religious liberty. Sunday laws were common throughout the country; and Jefferson himself, as wartime governor of Virginia, had proclaimed a day of fasting and prayer. In 1802, in his address to the Danbury Baptists, when he urged a "wall of separation between Church and State," he relied on the establishment clause to justify his refusal as president to recommend a day of thanksgiving prayers.[55] By then his views seemed to support separation more consistently even at a state level.

---

54. *Jefferson Papers*, 1:344, 353, 363.

55. Daniel L. Dreisbach, *Real Shadow and Mere Threat: Religious Liberty and the First Amendment* (Westchester, Ill., 1987), pp. 119–26, surveys Jefferson's views, although Dreisbach twists the data to support his nonpreferential beliefs, as when referring to the bill that advantaged one sect only. He insists that the other bills provide a context for the great Virginia Statute of Religious Freedom, but he ignores entirely the context of widespread evangelical support for a wall of separation that divided the spiritual and secular dimensions, discussed in this chapter, and he ignores Jefferson's "Query VII on Religion," in

Supporters of government aid to religion have contended that Jefferson advocated the use of public funds in Virginia for a school of theology for the training of clergymen; that he approved of elaborate arrangements for the students of private theological schools to share the facilities of the University of Virginia; that he recommended that a room in the university be used for worship; and that he did not protest against the use by Virginia of tax monies on behalf of education. The contention, in other words, is that Jefferson did not apply his own principle of separation in the field of education in Virginia.[56]

In matters of education, however, Jefferson was a secularist, compared with others of his time. In 1778 he submitted, in a "Bill for the More General Diffusion of Knowledge," a comprehensive plan for public education at the primary and secondary levels.[57] Religious instruction was completely absent from Jefferson's proposed curriculum at a time when it was a prominent feature in schools everywhere else. The omission was deliberate. Jefferson wrote in his *Notes on Virginia*: "Instead therefore of putting the Bible and Testament into the hands of children, at an age when their judgments are not sufficiently matured for religious enquiries, their memories may here be stored with the most useful facts from Grecian, Roman, European and American history."[58] Religion was also conspicuous by its absence from Jefferson's plan of 1817; his "Bill for Establishing a System of Public Education" enumerated only secular subjects. In an effort to eliminate possible religious influence in the public schools, Jefferson specified that ministers should not serve as "visitors" or supervisors, and provided that "no religious reading, instruction, or exercise, shall be prescribed or practised" in violation of the tenets of any sect or denomination.[59]

Jefferson's *Notes on Virginia*, edited by William Peden (Chapel Hill, N.C., 1955), pp. 157–612. Dreisbach also slants the data on Jefferson and education, pp. 131–32, discussed below.

56. See, for example, James M. O'Neill, *Religion and Education under the Constitution* (New York, 1949), pp. 76–77, 205–6.

57. *Jefferson Papers*, 2:526–35.

58. Jefferson, *Notes on Virginia*, p. 147.

59. *The Writings of Thomas Jefferson*, edited by Andrew A. Lipscomb and Albert Ellery Bergh, 20 vols. (Washington, D.C., 1903–4), 17:425. Hereafter cited as *Jefferson's Writings*.

Clearly Jefferson opposed the use of public funds for the teaching of religion in public schools.

Jefferson made his first proposal on higher education in 1779. His "Bill for the Amending of the Constitution of the College of William and Mary" stated that the college consisted of "one school of sacred theology, with two professorships therein, to wit, one for teaching the Hebrew tongue, and expounding the holy scriptures; and the other for explaining the commonplaces of divinity, and controversies with heretics." There were six other professorships divided among a school of philosophy, one of classical languages, and another for teaching Indians reading, writing, and "the catechism and the principles of the Christian religion." Jefferson proposed to abolish both the school of theology with its professorships of religion and the school for teaching Indians. In place of the school for Indians, he proposed that a missionary be selected by a newly constituted faculty who would not teach religion but investigate Indian "laws, customs, religions, traditions, and more particularly their languages." Jefferson's missionary was to be an anthropologist charged with reporting his findings to the faculty and preserving his reports in the college library. In place of the school of theology and the professorships of religion, Jefferson proposed simply a professorship of "moral philosophy" and another "of history, civil and ecclesiastical."[60]

Jefferson's proposed bill of 1779 failed because of Episcopalian (Anglican) opposition. However, in the same year he and Madison as visitors of the college instituted such changes as could be made by executive authority without legislative approval. In 1821 he summarized those changes by writing: "When I was a visitor, in 1779, I got the two professorships of Divinity . . . put down, and others of law and police, of medicine, anatomy, and chemistry, and of modern languages substituted."[61] A comparable statement appeared in his *Notes on the State of Virginia* where he remarked that the school of divinity was "excluded."[62]

60. *Jefferson Papers*, 2:535–42.

61. Thomas Jefferson to Joseph C. Cabell, Feb. 22, 1821, in *Early History of the University of Virginia*, edited by Nathaniel F. Cabell (Richmond, Va., 1856), p. 207.

62. Jefferson, *Notes on Virginia*, p. 151.

Jefferson was never satisfied with the education offered by the College of William and Mary. Failing to achieve adequate reform of the college, he turned to the establishment of a new state university. He also attempted in 1814 to transform Albemarle Academy, a small private school. He wanted an enlarged institution offering instruction from the primary grades through college and postgraduate training that would be supported by public funds. At no point in the entire curriculum before the professional level was there any provision for religious education. However, one of the "professional schools" was to be devoted to "Theology and Ecclesiastical History," to which would come the "ecclesiatic" as would the "lawyer to the school of law."[63] Here is an inconsistency, indicating Jefferson's support of the use of tax monies on behalf of religious education, although only at the graduate level. Albemarle, though privately established and endowed, was to be aided by public funds. More to the point, Jefferson never renewed the proposal, which failed.

In 1818, for instance, his academic plan for the newly authorized state university included ten professorships and thirty-four subjects, none of them relating to religion. This curriculum, which was adopted, was laid out in a report, written by Jefferson as chairman of the commissioners for the University of Virginia, which stated: "In conformity with the principles of our Constitution, which places all sects of religion on an equal footing . . . we have proposed no professor of divinity. . . . Proceeding thus far without offence to the Constitution, we have thought it proper at this point to leave every sect to provide, as they think fittest, the means of further instruction in their own peculiar tenets." The report also stated: "It is probable, that a building . . . may be called for in time, in which may be rooms for religious worship . . . for public examinations, for a library."[64]

The conditional phrasing of this sentence suggests that Jefferson

63. Thomas Jefferson to Peter Carr, Sept. 7, 1814, in *Jefferson's Writings*, 19:212–21. See also Roy J. Honeywell, *The Educational Work of Thomas Jefferson* (Cambridge, Mass.), pp. 15–16, 39–42; the letter to Carr is reprinted in Appendix E.

64. Report of the Commissioners, in *Educational Work of Jefferson*, Appendix J, pp. 256, 249.

was seeking to fend off an anticipated barrage of criticism against the university as a "godless" institution. In fact he was under constant pressure from church groups to make suitable provisions for theological training and religious worship at the university. The "supposed probable" room that might in time be a place for worship was a concession to those who, as Jefferson reported in a letter to Dr. Thomas Cooper, used the absence of a professorship of divinity to spread the idea that the university was "not merely of no religion, but against all religion."[65]

Although he provided for no professor of divinity or theology, Jefferson expected the professor of ethics to treat "the proofs of the being of a God, the creator, preserver, and supreme ruler of the university, the author of all the relations of morality."[66] A good deist, Jefferson believed that the natural rights of mankind derived from God. He was not hostile to theism, despite his anticlericalism and distaste for formal Christianity. However, opposition to the secular character of the university resulted in a postponement of instruction, forcing additional concessions to religious interests. In 1822 Jefferson, as rector of the university, and the Board of Visitors, among them Madison, reluctantly proposed to accept suggestions "by some pious individuals . . . to establish their religious schools on the confines of the University, so as to give their students ready and convenient access and attendance on the scientific lectures of the University." This report noted also that the religious schools would offer places where regular students of the university could worship as they pleased, "But always understanding that these schools shall be independent of the University and of each other." The report concluded that if the legislature questioned "what here is suggested, the idea will be relinquished on any surmise of disapprobation which they might think proper to express."[67]

Jefferson explained that in order to silence the calumny that the

65. Thomas Jefferson to Thomas Cooper, Nov. 2, 1822, in *Jefferson's Writings*, 15:405.

66. Philip Alexander Bruce, *History of the University of Virginia*, 4 vols. (New York, 1920), 2:366, 369.

67. Minutes of the Board of Visitors, Oct. 7, 1822, in *Jefferson's Writings*, 19:414–16.

university was atheistic, "In our annual report to the legislature, after stating the constitutional reasons against a public establishment of any religious instruction, we suggest the expediency of encouraging the different religions to establish, each for itself, a professorship of their own tenets, on the confines of the University."[68] In 1824, shortly before the first classes, Jefferson and the Board of Visitors adopted formal regulations that provided that the "religious sects of this State" might "establish within, or adjacent to, the precincts of the University" schools for instruction in their own religion. Students of the university were "free, and expected to attend religious worship" at the "establishment" of their choice on condition that they did so in the mornings before classes, which began at half past seven. The same regulations also provided for the use of one of the university's rooms for worship as well as for other purposes, although the students were enjoined by the regulation of the previous paragraph to attend services in the theological seminaries surrounding the university.[69]

No part of the regular school day was set aside for religious worship. Possibly the proposal that a room belonging to the university be used for worship was intended originally as a makeshift arrangement until the various sects established their own schools of theology. Although none in fact did so for several decades, Jefferson did not permit the room belonging to the university to be used for religious purposes. In 1825 he rejected a proposal to hold Sunday services on university property. The Board of Visitors, he wrote, had already turned down an application to permit a sermon to be preached in one of the rooms on the grounds that "the buildings of the Univ. belong to the state, that they were erected for the purposes of an Univ., and that the Visitors, to whose care they are commd [commanded or committed] for those purposes, have no right to permit their application to any other." His position was that the legislature had failed to sanction a proposal to use university facilities for worship and that, consequently, an alternative plan had been adopted "*superseding* the 1st idea of permitting a room in the Rotunda to be used for religious worship."[70] The alternative plan

68. Jefferson to Cooper, Nov. 2, 1822, in ibid., 15:405.

69. Minutes of the Board of Visitors, Oct. 4, 1824, in ibid., 19:449.

70. Thomas Jefferson to A. S. Brockenbrough, Apr. 21, 1825, quoted in R.

was the one permitting the different sects to establish their own divinity schools, without public aid, independently of the university.

The university did not even appoint a chaplain while Jefferson was its rector. "At a time when, in most colleges and universities of the country, ministers were presidents and common members of boards of control, daily chapel attendance was compulsory, courses in religion were required, and professors of theology and doctors of divinity had a prominent place on the faculties, the University of Virginia stood out sharply in contrast with its loyalty to the principle of separation of church and state."[71]

The struggle for separation of church and state in Virginia often dominates in accounts of the history of separation of church and state in America. No doubt historians focus their attention on the Virginia story because the sources are uniquely ample,[72] the struggle was important and dramatic, and the opinions of Madison, the principal framer of the First Amendment, and of Jefferson were fully elicited. As a result, the details of no other state controversy over church-state relationships are so familiar. If, however, the object is to understand what was meant by "an establishment of religion" at the time of the framing of the Bill or Rights, the histories of the other states are equally important, notwithstanding the stature and influence of Jefferson and Madison as individuals. Indeed, the abortive effort in Virginia to enact Patrick Henry's assessment bill is less important than the fact that five states actually had constitutional provisions authorizing general assessments for religion, and a sixth (Connecticut) provided for the same by statute. Had the general assessment bill in Virginia been enacted, it would simply have increased the number of states authorizing multiple establishments of religion from six to seven.

In no state or colony, of course, was there ever an establishment of religion that included every religion without exception. Judaism, Bud-

---

Freeman Butts, *The American Tradition in Religion and Education* (Boston, 1950), p. 129.

71. Ibid., p. 130.

72. In 1785, the same year the general assessment bill was debated in Virginia, both Maryland and Georgia, as noted above, also considered general assessment bills; little is known about their history.

dhism, Mohammedanism, or any religion but a Christian one was never established in America. In 1791, when the First Amendment was ratified, the addition of Vermont to the Union brought the number of states authorizing establishments of religion to seven. All seven authorized multiple establishments. In four of the seven, Protestantism was the established religion; in the other half, Christianity was. It may therefore be argued that the concept of a multiple establishment is fallacious and that every state establishment of religion was an exclusive one. Such a statement would be true so far as it goes, but alone it is a misleading half-truth.

In each of the seven states where multiple establishments existed, the establishment included the churches of every denomination and sect with a sufficient number of adherents to form a church. In general, where Protestantism was established, it was synonymous with religion, because there were no Jews and Roman Catholics or too few of them to make a difference; and where Christianity was established, as in Maryland, which had many Catholics, Jews were scarcely known. Where Jewish congregations existed, as in Savannah and Charleston, state law reflected obliviousness to their presence rather than deliberate discrimination, and no evidence exists to show that Jews were actually taxed to support Christianity.

Clearly, the provisions of these seven states show that to understand the American meaning of "an establishment of religion" one cannot adopt a definition based on European experience. In European precedents of an establishment, the religion established was that of a single church. Many different churches, or the religion held in common by all of them, that is, Christianity or Protestantism, were never simultaneously established by any European nation—excepting Transylvania. Establishments in America, on the other hand, both in the colonial and the early state periods, were not limited in nature or in meaning to state support of one church. An establishment of religion in America at the time of the framing and ratification of the Bill of Rights meant government aid and sponsorship of religion, principally by impartial tax support of the institutions of religion, all the churches.

Not one of the seven American states maintaining or authorizing establishments of religion at that time preferred one church to others in their constitutional law. Even in New England, where the Congregational church was dominant as a result of numerical superiority, constitutional and legal guarantees censured subordination or preference. Such an establishment can hardly be called an exclusive or preferential one, as in the case where only one church, as in the European precedents, was the beneficiary. The uniqueness of the American experience justifies defining an establishment of religion as any support, especially financial support, of religion by government, whether the support be to religion in general, to all churches, some churches, or one church.

On the other hand, the American multiple establishments were nonpreferential in law and theory but not necessarily in fact. In the four New England states that maintained establishments, the Congregationalists dominated overwhelmingly, as was expected when they adopted the system of tax-supported nonpreferential aid.

Moreover, most states, and not just those that had establishments, provided a variety of aids to religion that were not financial in character. All but two had religious tests for office, disqualifying Jews, Unitarians, and agnostics. Some states even refused to enfranchise them, so they could not vote. In some states, anyone refusing to swear or affirm the existence of God could not testify at a trial. Generally, anyone who rejected the doctrine of the Trinity suffered civil disabilities. Christianity was regarded by state jurists as part and parcel of the law of the land. Thus, to protect Christianity, the states punished both profanity and blasphemy. Profanity consisted of a statement calling upon God to damn or curse someone, or a statement taking the name of the Lord in vain by invoking his name in a situation not requiring it as a matter of law. Blasphemy consisted of any verbal comment aspersing or reproaching, even denying, Christianity, the Trinity, Jesus Christ, or the Bible. Prosecutions for profanity were common in all the states; prosecutions for blasphemy were unusual but they existed even in states that never had an establishment of religion, such as Pennsylvania and Delaware. The penalties actually administered, however, never approached the draconian punishments stipulated by the law on the books. Religion was also supported by laws enforcing the Christian sabbath, and prosecutions were fairly common. In schools, which were for the most part run by religious organizations, prayer and religious services were daily affairs. Finally, nontheists suffered legal discriminations that disallowed them from holding or conveying property in trust; accordingly, they could not bequeath monies to orphanages, hospitals, or schools devoted to propagation of their beliefs. All these aids to religion were preferential in character.[73]

Nonpreferentialism existed only as a matter of law and theory with respect to financial aid for churches and clergymen. But nonpreferentialism as a matter of law and theory was a profoundly developed American characteristic. By contrast, as to nonfinancial aids to religion, Americans reacted reflexively, not having made an effort to explore the significance or implications of the principle of separation. Spending tax monies for religion was an old and controversial issue that inspired considerable thought; other aids for religion had not been the subject of controversy in the colonies or states and tended to be taken for granted.

73. On civil disabilities, see Morton Borden, *Jews, Turks, and Infidels* (Chapel Hill, N.C., 1984). On Christianity as part and parcel of the law of the land and on prosecutions for blasphemy and for disabilities relating to trusts and conveyances, see Leonard W. Levy, *Blasphemy: Verbal Offense against the Sacred, from Moses to Salman Rushdie* (New York, 1993). My characterizations of prosecutions for Sabbath breaking and profanity are impressionistic, based on extensive research in legal records when looking for blasphemy cases. On Sunday laws, see also the historical data in the opinion by Frankfurter in *McGowan v. Maryland*, 366 U.S. 420, 484–95, 543–59 (1961).

4

The
Constitution
and
Religion

The Constitutional Convention of 1787, which
framed the Constitution of the United States, gave only slight attention
to the subject of a bill of rights and even less to the subject of religion.
In contrast to the Declaration of Independence and to many acts of the
Continental Congress, the Constitution contains no references to God;
the convention did not even invoke divine guidance for its deliberations. Its finished product made no reference to religion except to pro-

hibit a religious test as a qualification for federal officeholders.[1] On August 20 Charles Pinckney proposed that "no religious test or qualification shall ever be annexed to any oath of office under the authority of the U.S."[2] The proposal was referred to the Committee of Detail without debate or consideration by the convention. When the committee reported ten days later, it ignored Pinckney's proposal. From the floor of the convention he moved it again. The chairman of the committee, Roger Sherman of Connecticut, stated that such a provision was "unnecessary, the prevailing liberality being a sufficient security against such tests."[3] However, two delegates, in unreported speeches, "approved the motion" by Pinckney, and when it was put to a vote, it passed without further debate.[4] The Committee on Style rephrased it and incorporated it into Article VI, clause 3, of the Constitution; ". . . no religious test shall ever be required as a qualification to any office or public trust under the United States."

This clause "went far," according to one scholar, "in thwarting any

1. Several scholars declare that the germ of the establishment clause derived from a proposal allegedly advanced by Charles Pinckney of South Carolina on May 29: "The legislature of the United States shall pass no law on the subject of religion. . . ." See Leo Pfeffer, *Church, State and Freedom* (Boston, 1953), pp. 110, 145; Anson Phelps Stokes, *Church and State in the United States*, 3 vols. (New York, 1950), 1:526–27. Pinckney's proposal appears in Madison's *Notes on the Debates* as part of the comprehensive plan of union submitted to the convention by Pinckney. See also Jonathan Elliot, ed., *The Debates in the Several State Conventions on the Adoption of the Federal Constitution . . . In Five Volumes* (Philadelphia, 1941), 5:131. However, the Pinckney plan has been revealed to be spurious. Neither it nor the proposal banning laws on religion was ever presented to the convention. See Charles Warren, *The Making of the Constitution* (Boston, 1928), pp. 142–43. Pfeffer's *Church, State, and Freedom*, revised in 1967, is the most authoritative constitutional history of America's experience with the double-faceted principle of religious liberty and separation of government and religion under the First Amendment. He reviewed the contemporary constitutional law of the subject in *Religion, State, and the Burger Court* (Buffalo, N.Y., 1984).

2. Elliot, ed., *Debates*, 5:446.

3. Ibid., 5:498.

4. Ibid.

State Church" in the United States.[5] His reasoning is that in the absence of the clause Congress might have had the power to require an oath or subscription to the articles of faith of some particular church,[6] or to Protestantism, or to Christianity generally. But no one at the time defined the scope of the protection; that is, the implied ban against an establishment of religion is no aid in explaining the meaning of such an establishment. Moreover, all but two states had religious tests for office, including Rhode Island, Pennsylvania, Delaware, and New Jersey, which never had any kind of establishment of religion.[7] The ban on religious tests for office, therefore, did not extend to a ban on establishments.

There are no other references to the subject of religion at the Constitutional Convention, except for Benjamin Franklin's speech at a critical juncture of the proceedings on the reason that prayer should open its session. Former president Ronald Reagan, who sometimes reinvented history, mistakenly declared that as a result of Franklin's motion, "From that day on they opened all the constitutional meetings with a prayer." Practical considerations—an unwillingness to let the public think the convention was in trouble, lack of money to pay a minister, and deference to Philadelphia's Quakers—resulted in the death of the Franklin motion. The convention, he noted, "except three or four persons, thought prayers unnecessary."[8]

When George Mason of Virginia expressed a wish that the new constitution "had been prefaced with a Bill of Rights," he offered no suggestions as to the contents of such a bill. Nor did Elbridge Gerry of

5. Stokes, *Church and State*, 1:527. See also Pfeffer, *Church, State, and Freedom*, p. 110.

6. See James Madison to Edmund Randolph, Apr. 10, 1788, in William T. Hutchinson et al., eds., *The Papers of James Madison*, ser. in progress (Chicago, 1962–), 11:19.

7. Morton Borden, *Jews, Turks, and Infidels* (Chapel Hill, N.C., 1984), pp. 11–12; Thomas J. Curry, *The First Freedoms: Church and State in America to the Passage of the First Amendment* (New York, 1986).

8. Warren, *Making of the Constitution*, pp. 250–51. Reagan's remarks of Oct. 13, 1983, to leaders of Christian religious organizations are in *Weekly Compilation of Presidential Documents* (Washington, D.C., 1983), p. 1427.

Massachusetts who, agreeing with Mason, moved for a committee to prepare a bill of rights. This motion aroused opposition on the grounds that the state bills of rights "being in force are sufficient." Mason rejoined, "The Laws of the U.S. are to be paramount to state Bills of Rights," but without further debate the motion that a bill of rights be prepared was put to a vote. It was defeated 10 to 0, the delegates voting as state units.[9] Thus, the record of the Constitutional Convention is no guide in discerning the understanding of the framers as to an establishment of religion.

On the other hand, the failure of the convention to provide for a bill of rights should not be misunderstood. The members of the convention did not oppose personal liberties; in the main they simply regarded a bill of rights as superfluous. They reasoned that the new national government possessed only expressly enumerated powers, and no power had been granted to legislate on any of the subjects that would be the concern of a bill of rights. Because no such power existed, none could be exercised or abused, and therefore all provisions against that possibility were unnecessary. Of the many statements of this argument,[10] the most widely publicized was that of Hamilton in *The Federalist* where he concluded simply: "For why declare that things shall not be done which there is no power to do? Why, for instance, should it be said that the liberty of the press shall not be restrained, when no power is given by which restrictions may be imposed?"[11]

9. Max Farrand, ed., *The Records of the Federal Convention*, 3 vols. (New York, 1911), 2:587–88.

10. For example, see Elliot, ed., *Debates*, 3:203–4, 450, 600 (Randolph and Nicholas in Virginia), 4:149 (Iredell in North Carolina), 4:315–16 (C. C. Pinckney in South Carolina), and 2:78 (Varnum in Massachusetts). For the very influential statements by Wilson of Pennsylvania, see 2:436, 453. See also John Bach McMaster and Frederick D. Stone, eds., *Pennsylvania and the Federal Constitution, 1787–1788* (Lancaster, Pa., 1888), pp. 313–14. See also McKean in ibid., p. 337; Ellsworth in Paul L. Ford, ed., *Essays on the Constitution of the United States* (Brooklyn, N.Y., 1892), pp. 163–64; Williamson, "Remarks," ibid., p. 398 (North Carolina); and Hanson, "Remarks on the Proposed Plan," in *Pamphlets on the Constitution of the United States*, edited by Paul L. Ford, ed.(Brooklyn, N.Y., 1888), pp. 241–42 (Maryland).

11. *The Federalist*, edited by Jacob E. Cooke (Middletown, Conn., 1961), no.

The reasoning here is of the utmost significance in defining the powers of Congress in regard to establishments of religion. Abundant evidence shows the belief of the framers that Congress was bereft of any authority over the subject of religion. The whole concept of a federal system of distributed powers, with the national government possessing only limited, delegated powers, forms the principal evidence. In addition, consider the following specific comments by framers, which are illustrative rather than exhaustive. James Wilson of Pennsylvania, in response to the allegation that there was no security for the rights of conscience, asserted: "I ask the honorable gentlemen, what part of this system puts it in the power of Congress to attack those rights? When there is no power to attack, it is idle to prepare the means of defense."[12] Edmund Randolph of Virginia declared that "no power is given expressly to Congress over religion" and added that only powers "constitutionally given" could be exercised.[13] Madison said, "There is not a shadow of right in the general government to intermeddle with religion."[14] Richard Dobbs Spaight of North Carolina maintained: "As to the subject of religion . . . [n]o power is given to the general government to interfere with it at all. Any act of Congress on this subject would be a usurpation."[15] Wilson, Randolph, Madison, and Spaight had attended the Constitutional Convention. Their remarks show that Congress was powerless, *even in the absence of the First Amendment*, to enact laws that benefited one religion or church in particular or all of them equally and impartially.

From late 1787 through the following year, the proposed constitution engrossed the political attention of the country. The Congress of the Confederation submitted the document to state conventions for ratification. Men for and against ratification sought election as delegates. A torrent of speeches, essays, articles, and pamphlets poured

---

84, pp. 579–80. For an analytical discussion of the Constitutional Convention's failure to include a bill of rights, see Leonard W. Levy, *Emergence of a Free Press* (New York, 1985), pp. 220–36.

12. Elliot, ed., *Debates*, 2:455.

13. Ibid., 3:204; see also 3:469.

14. Ibid., 3:330.

15. Ibid., 4:208.

forth from partisans on both sides. Opponents of ratification feared most of all that the centralizing tendencies of a consolidated national government would extinguish the rights of states and individuals. The failure of the new instrument to provide for a bill of rights constituted the most important single objection, and the Constitution would probably not have received the requisite number of state votes for ratification had not some Federalist leaders like Madison pledged themselves to seek amendments constituting a bill of rights as soon as the new government went into operation. Indeed, six of the thirteen original states accompanied their instruments of ratification with recommendations for amendments, some of which would have secured specified fundamental personal liberties.[16]

Accordingly, it is astonishing to discover that the debate on a bill of rights occurred on a level of abstraction so vague as to convey the impression that Americans of 1787–88 had only the most nebulous conception of the meanings of the particular rights they sought to ensure. The insistent demands for the "rights of conscience" or "trial by jury" or "liberty of the press" by the principal advocates of a bill of rights were not accompanied by a reasoned analysis of what these rights meant, how far they extended, and in what circumstances they might be limited. Many opponents of ratification discovered that to denounce the omission of a bill of rights was a politically effective tactic, one that provided a useful mask for less elevating, perhaps even sordid, objections relating to such matters as taxation and commerce.[17]

One cannot assume that there was no necessity for careful definition on the grounds that the meanings of specific rights were widely known and agreed to by all. They were not. Not even trial by jury, which was protected by more state constitutions than any other right, had the same meaning and scope from state to state.[18] Moreover, there were

16. Massachusetts, New Hampshire, Virginia, New York, North Carolina, and Rhode Island.

17. For a thorough discussion, see Levy, *Emergence of a Free Press*, chap. 8.

18. See Elliot, ed., *Debates*, 2:112, 114 (Gore and Davis in Massachusetts), 3:468 (Randolph in Virginia), 4:145, 150 (Iredell and Johnston in North Carolina); for Wilson of Pennsylvania, see McMaster and Stone, eds., *Pennsylvania and the Constitution*, pp. 309, 353, 406. On the variety of early state procedures

substantial differences in the character and number of the rights guaranteed by the various states.[19] Several state conventions, in ratifying the Constitution, even recommended amendments to protect rights not known in their own constitutions.[20] Whatever the explanation, the fact is that from the tens of thousands of words exchanged during the ratification controversy on the subject of a bill of rights no illumination can be gained as to the understanding and content attached at that time to particular rights.

This generalization applies to the subject of establishments of religion. An awareness of the need for analytical precision in discussions of the subject might have been expected, considering the variety of historical experiences with establishments before and after independence and considering the diversity of relevant state constitutional and statutory provisions. At the very least, one would expect frequent expressions of fear and concern on the subject. Yet the startling fact is that it was rarely mentioned at all and then only very briefly. One searches in vain for a definition in the rhetorical effusions of leading

---

concerning the rights of accused persons, see generally Charles Fairman, "The Supreme Court and Constitutional Limitations on State Government Authority," *University of Chicago Law Review* 21 (Autumn 1951): 40–78 passim. Charles Warren, in *Congress, the Constitution and the Supreme Court* (Boston, 1925), p. 81, pointed out that, in civil cases, the citizens of four states had been deprived of jury trial in the seven-year period before the Constitution was framed.

19. For example, only seven of the thirteen states had separate bills of rights in their constitutions; six states allowed establishments of religion, which were prohibited by others; six states did not constitutionally provide for the right to the writ of habeas corpus. See generally Francis Newton Thorpe, *The Constitutional History of the United States*, 3 vols. (Chicago, 1901), 2:199–211, for a table on state precedents for the federal Bill of Rights; Edward Dumbauld, "State Precedents for the Bill of Rights," *Journal of Public Law* 7 (1958): 323–44; Levy, *Emergence of a Free Press*, pp. 226–27.

20. For example, Massachusetts recommended the right to indictment by grand jury but did not provide for it in its own constitution; Virginia and North Carolina recommended constitutional protection for freedom of speech, which they did not protect in their respective constitutions; and New York recommended protections against compulsory self-incrimination and double jeopardy, neither of which New York constitutionally protected.

advocates of a bill of rights and in the debates of the state ratifying conventions.[21]

The debates of the ratifying conventions of Delaware, New Jersey, and Georgia are nonexistent. Moreover, each ratified unconditionally and without proposing any amendments. Nothing, therefore, can be said of opinion in those states.[22]

In Connecticut, which also ratified without recommendations for amendments, the fragmentary record of the debates shows only that Oliver Wolcott, briefly mentioning the value of the clause against test oaths, said: "Knowledge and liberty are so prevalent in this country, that I do not believe that the United States would ever be disposed to establish one religious sect, and lay all others under legal disabilities."[23] Similarly, Oliver Ellsworth, writing in a tract, referred to the fact that religious tests for office were always found in European nations where one church is established as the state church.[24] Neither Ellsworth nor

21. Elliot, ed., *Debates*, reports in detail the debates of five states (Massachusetts, New York, Virginia, North Carolina, and South Carolina) and in very fragmentary fashion the debates of three others (Maryland, Pennsylvania, and Connecticut). McMaster and Stone, *Pennsylvania and the Constitution*, collects extant Pennsylvania debates together with pamphlets and essays from that state, while Ford, *Essays*, and Ford, *Pamphlets*, collect important essays and pamphlets from all the states. Modern collections of primary sources will, when completed, supersede earlier works. Herbert Storing, ed., *The Complete Anti-Federalist*, 7 vols. (Chicago, 1981), seems definitive but in time will give way to Merrill Jensen et al., eds., *The Documentary History of the Ratification of the Constitution*, ser. in progress (Madison, Wisc., 1976–). Eight volumes are completed to date. Vol. 1 covers the period 1776–87, before the framing of the Constitution; vol. 2 replaces McMaster and Stone on Pennsylvania; vol. 3 covers the ratification in Delaware, New Jersey, Georgia, and Connecticut; vol. 8 (edited by John P. Kaminski and Gaspar J. Saladino) covers Virginia. Kaminski and Saladino, eds., *Commentaries on the Constitution: Public and Private*, vols. 13–16, cover Feb. 21, 1787, to Mar. 16, 1788.

22. Jensen et al., eds., *Documentary History*, vol. 3, includes every scrap of information concerning the ratification of the Constitution by these states without referring to religious liberty, let alone establishments of religion.

23. Ibid., 3:558.

24. Ford, ed., *Essays*, p. 168.

Wolcott, both Federalists, believed the Congress could legislate on the subject of religion.

In Pennsylvania, which had never experienced an establishment of religion, the state convention ratified unconditionally after voting against a series of amendments, constituting a bill of rights, proposed by the Anti-Federalist minority. These defeated amendments, while protecting the "rights of conscience," contained no provision respecting an establishment of religion, although John Smilie, an Anti-Federalist, had expressed the fear that "Congress may establish any religion," and an "Old Whig" lamented that nothing could prevent Congress from enacting an "establishment of a national church."[25] Tench Coxe, a Federalist tract writer, used the words "established church" when pointing out that only members of the Church of England could hold office in Great Britain.[26] Opponents of ratification from the town of Carlisle proposed that "none should be compelled contrary to his principles or inclination to hear or support the clergy of any one established religion."[27] "Centinel," who also recommended a bill of rights, proposed more broadly in the language of the Pennsylvania constitution that "no man ought, or of right can be compelled to attend any religious worship, or erect or support any place of worship, or maintain any ministry, contrary to or against his own free will and consent."[28]

Massachusetts, which maintained an establishment of religion at the time of ratification, was the first state to ratify with amendments, but the amendments had nothing to do with religion. The delegates to the state convention included over twenty Baptists, among them the Reverend Isaac Backus. He described the Constitution as a door "opened for the establishment of righteous government, and for securing of equal liberty, as never before opened to any people on earth."[29] No

---

25. Jensen et al., eds., *Documentary History*, 2:623, 592; see also Storing, ed., *Complete Anti-Federalist*, 2:37, 179, for "Old Deliberator" warning that Congress might "establish an uniformity in religion throughout the United States."

26. Ford, ed., *Pamphlets*, p. 146.

27. McMaster and Stone, *Pennsylvania and the Constitution*, p. 502.

28. Ibid., p. 589. "Centinel" was probably Samuel Bryan.

29. Elliot, ed., *Debates*, 2:236.

person in the state convention or in antiratificationist tracts alluded to an establishment of religion, which the Baptists vehemently opposed. None even mentioned religious liberty. This would be an astonishing fact, considering the hostility within the state to the establishment there existing, unless there was an undisputed understanding that Congress had no power over religion.[30]

Maryland ratified without amendments,[31] although fifteen had been recommended, including a proposal "that there be no national religion established by law; but that all persons be equally entitled to protection in their religious liberty."[32] Maryland's own constitution permitted an establishment of religion, though none existed. All fifteen of the defeated amendments had aimed chiefly at protecting state governments from infringement by the national government.[33] They failed not because the Federalist-dominated convention of Maryland disagreed with them but because it wished to ratify unconditionally for the purpose of demonstrating confidence in the new system of government.[34] The same may be said of Pennsylvania and all other states that ratified without recommending amendments.

In South Carolina the Reverend Francis Cummins made the only reference to an establishment of religion when he condemned "religious establishments; or the states giving preference to any religious denomination."[35] The convention's recommendations for amendments, however, mentioned nothing about a bill of rights.[36] At the time,

---

30. Charles C. Tansill, ed., *Documents Illustrative of the Formation of the Union of the American States* (Washington, D.C., 1927), pp. 1018–20; William G. McLoughlin, *New England Dissent, 1630–1833: The Baptists and the Separation of Church and State*, 2 vols. (Cambridge, Mass., 1971), 2:780–83.

31. Tansill, ed., *Documents*, pp. 1021–22.

32. Elliot, ed., *Debates*, 2:553.

33. Philip A. Crowl, *Maryland during and after the Revolution* (Baltimore, Md., 1943), p. 156; Werline, *Problems of Church and State*, pp. 143–68.

34. Werline, *Problems of Church and State*, chap. 6.

35. Chester J. Antieau, Arthur T. Downey, and Edward C. Roberts, *Freedom from Federal Establishment: Formation and Early History of the First Amendment Religion Clauses* (Milwaukee, Wisc., 1964), p. 106, quoting *City Gazette or Daily Advertiser of Charleston*, May 26, 1788.

36. Tansill, ed., *Documents*, pp. 1022–24.

South Carolina proclaimed the "Christian Protestant . . . religion to be the established religion of this state." No churches received public financial support, but those that accepted a prescribed creed were "considered as established."[37]

New Hampshire's debates do not exist. Although the state maintained an establishment, its instrument of ratification included among recommendations for amendments the following: "Congress shall make no laws touching Religion, or to infringe the rights of Conscience."[38]

In Virginia, where the most crucial struggle against establishments of religion had ended in victory just three years before the state ratifying convention met, only two speakers during the course of the lengthy debates alluded to an establishment. Edmund Randolph, defending the Constitution against Patrick Henry's allegation that it endangered religious liberty, pointed out that Congress had no power over religion and that the exclusion of religious tests for federal officeholders meant that "they are not bound to support one mode of worship, or to adhere to one particular sect." He added that there were so many different sects in the United States that "they will prevent the establishment of any one sect, in prejudice to the rest, and forever oppose all attempts to infringe religious liberty."[39] Madison, also addressing himself to Henry's general and unsupported accusation, argued at this time that a "multiplicity of sects" would secure freedom of religion, but that a bill of rights would not. He pointed out that the Virginia Declaration of Rights (which guaranteed "the free exercise of religion, according to the dictates of conscience") would not have exempted people "from paying for the support of one particular sect, if such sect were exclusively established by law." If a majority were of one sect, liberty would be poorly protected by a bill of rights. "Fortunately for this commonwealth," he added, "a majority of the people are decidedly against any exclusive establishment. I believe it to be so in the other states. There is not a shadow of right in the general government to intermeddle with

---

37. Thorpe, ed., *Constitutions*, 6:3255; John Wesley Brinsfield, *Religion and Politics in South Carolina* (Easly, S.C., 1983), pp. 122–27.

38. Thorpe, ed., *Constitutions*, 6:1026.

39. Elliot, ed., *Debates*, 3:204.

religion. Its least interference with it would be a most flagrant usurpation. . . . A particular state might concur in one religious project. But the United States abound in such a variety of sects, that it is a strong security against religious persecution; and it is sufficient to authorize a conclusion that no one sect will ever be able to outnumber or depress the rest."[40]

Nonetheless, Madison and his party could not muster sufficient votes to secure Virginia's ratification of the Constitution without accepting a recommendation for amendments that were first submitted by Patrick Henry. Henry's amendments, including a Declaration of Rights, were read before the convention but not reported in its record of proceedings; the reporter states that they "were nearly the same as those ultimately proposed by the Convention"[41] after perfunctory endorsement by a committee on amendments. Among the recommended amendments was a provision that "no particular religious sect or society ought to be favored or established, by law, in preference to others."[42]

In New York, Thomas Tredwell, an antiratificationist, made the only reported reference to an establishment in his speech favoring a bill of rights: "I could have wished also that sufficient caution had been used to secure to us our religious liberties, and to have prevented the general government from tyrannizing over our consciences by a religious establishment—a tyranny of all others most dreadful, and which will assuredly be exercised whenever it shall be thought necessary for the promotion and support of their political measures."[43] The New York debates were fully reported until just before the closing days of the convention when John Lansing, an antiratificationist leader, introduced a bill of rights to be prefixed to the Constitution. Although debate began on this subject on July 19, 1788, and continued intermittently through July 25 when the convention adopted Lansing's bill of

40. Ibid., 3:330. See also the similar statement by Zachariah Johnson, 3:645–46.

41. Ibid., 3:593.

42. Ibid., 3:659; Tansill, ed., *Documents*, p. 1031.

43. Elliot, ed., *Debates*, 2:399.

rights, not a word of debate is reported.[44] Thus there is no indication of the meaning attached by the convention to its recommendation that "no Religious Sect or Society ought to be favored or established by Law in preference of others."[45] This language was similar to that used in the state constitution of 1777, which disestablished the Church of England even as it alleged that the church had never been established.

North Carolina, which had ended its establishment in 1776, recommended an amendment like that of Virginia and New York.[46] The subject first arose in the state ratification convention when a delegate, Henry Abbot, expressing concern about the possibility of the general government's infringing religious liberty, asserted that "some people" feared that a treaty might be made with foreign powers to adopt the Roman Catholic religion in the United States. "Many wish to know what religion shall be established," he added. He was "against any exclusive establishment; but if there were any, I would prefer the Episcopal." In the next breath, he expressed a belief that the exclusion of religious tests was "dangerous," because congressmen "might be all pagans."[47]

James Iredell, the state's leading Federalist, answered Abbott's fears by pointing out that the exclusion of a religious test indicated an intent to establish religious liberty. Congress was powerless to enact "the establishment of any religion whatsoever; and I am astonished that any gentleman should conceive they have. Is there any power given to Congress in matters of religion? . . . If any future Congress should pass an act concerning the religion of the country, it would be an act which they are not authorized to pass, by the Constitution, and which the people would not obey."[48] Governor Samuel Johnston agreed with Iredell and concluded: "I hope, therefore, that gentlemen will see there is no cause of fear that any one religion shall be exclusively established."[49] The

44. Ibid., 2:410–12.
45. Tansill, ed., *Documents*, p. 1035.
46. Ibid., p. 1047; Elliot, ed., *Debates*, 4:244.
47. Elliot, ed., *Debates*, 4:191–92.
48. Ibid., 4:194.
49. Ibid., 4:198–99.

Reverend David Caldwell, a Presbyterian minister, then spoke in favor of a religious test that would eliminate "Jews and pagans of every kind."[50] Samuel Spencer, the leading Anti-Federalist, took Caldwell's statement as endorsing the establishment of "one particular religion," which Spencer feared would lead to persecution. He believed that religion should stand on its own "without any connection with temporal authority."[51] William Lenoir agreed with Spencer but warned that federal ecclesiastical courts might be erected and they "may make any establishment they think proper."[52] Richard Dobbs Spaight, who had been a delegate to the Federal Convention, answered: "As to the subject of religion, I thought what had been said [by Iredell] would fully satisfy that gentleman and every other. No power is given to the general government to interfere with it at all. Any act of Congress on this subject would be a usurpation."[53]

When Rhode Island's convention tardily met to ratify the Constitution, eight states had already ratified the Bill of Rights. Accordingly, Rhode Island's recommendation for an amendment against an establishment,[54] modeled after those of New York, Virginia, and North Carolina, was a superfluous flourish that had no effect on the framing of the First Amendment.

What conclusions do these scant facts, drawn from the ratification controversy, yield? No state or person favored an establishment of religion by Congress. On the few occasions when convention delegates or contemporary writers mentioned an establishment, they spoke against its desirability or against the likelihood that there would be one. The evidence does not permit a generalization as to what was meant by an establishment of religion. To be sure, most of the few references to an establishment expressly or in context referred to the preference of one church or sect or religion above others. This fact taken by itself proves little. For example, Coxe of Pennsylvania had merely said that in England, where there was an "established church," only its members could hold office. From this statement we can conclude only that Coxe

50. Ibid., 4:199.
51. Ibid., 4:200.
52. Ibid., 4:203.
53. Ibid., 4:208.
54. Tansill, ed., *Documents*, p. 1053.

thought that the exclusive support of one church or denomination by the government, such as the Episcopal Church enjoyed in England, constituted an established church. There is no argument about that, but did he distinguish between an established church and an establishment of religion? Did he understand an establishment of religion to be government support of all church denominations or of one only? Coxe's brief statement provides no answers to these questions, and the same may be said of the statements by the other speakers on the subject. Madison, for example, was simply saying to those who believed that religious liberty was endangered by the proposed national government, "Not even your worst fear shall come to pass."

The recommendations for amendments by Virginia, New York, North Carolina, and Rhode Island, which used nonpreferential language, are not clarifying; they do not even necessarily indicate that preference of one denomination over others was all that was comprehended by an establishment of religion. They do indicate that preference of one denomination over others was something so feared that a political necessity existed to assuage that fear by specifically making it groundless. Viewed in context, the recommendations by these four states derived from Anti-Federalist fears of the new national government and a desire to limit its powers. All four states, indeed all the states and all factions, agreed with the recommendation of New Hampshire that "Congress shall make no laws touching religion." Rhode Island, which never had an establishment and opposed every sort of one, did not likely use the language of nonpreferentialism as an indirect way of recommending that Congress be empowered to aid religion generally. Still less would Patrick Henry's Virginia forces have insisted on Virginia's similar language in order to aggrandize the authority of the United States. Not a single recommendation for amendment by any state on any subject was intended to enhance or add to national powers.

As at the Constitutional Convention, a widespread understanding existed in the states during the ratification controversy that the new central government would have no power whatever to legislate on the subject of religion. This by itself does not mean that any person or state understood an establishment of religion to mean government aid to any or all religions or churches. It meant rather that religion as a subject of legislation was reserved exclusively to the states.

5

Framing

the

Establishment

Clause

At the first session of the First Congress, Representative Madison on June 8, 1789, proposed for House approval a series of amendments to the Constitution.[1] He accompanied his presentation with a lengthy speech explaining his action and defending the value of a

1. *The Debates and Proceedings in the Congress of the United States, Compiled from Authentic Materials*, edited by Joseph Gales and W. W. Seaton, 42 vols. (Washington, D.C., 1834–56), 1:448–59. This source, commonly known by its bookbinder's title as the *Annals of Congress*, will hereafter be cited as *Annals*.

bill of rights, but he did not discuss the proposal relating to an establishment of religion. The section on religion read: "The civil rights of none shall be abridged on account of religious belief or worship, nor shall any national religion be established, nor shall the full and equal rights of conscience be in any manner, or on any pretext, infringed."[2]

The term "national religion" has ambiguous connotations. It might have meant quite narrowly a nationwide preference for one denomination over others or, more broadly, preference for Christianity, that is, for all Christian denominations over non-Christian religions. Proponents of a narrow interpretation of the establishment clause see in the word "national" proof of their contention that nothing more was intended than a prohibition against the preference for one church or religion over others. Madison did not, at this time or when the proposal was debated, explain what he meant by the clause "nor shall any national religion be established."

Taken in the context of Madison's recommended amendments, it seems likely that "national" in this case signified action by the national government, because his next recommendation proposed a restriction upon the powers of the states: "No State shall violate the equal rights of conscience, or the freedom of the press, or the trial by jury in criminal cases."[3]

In other words, the term "national" signified that the prohibition against an establishment of religion—whatever that meant—applied to Congress only and not to the states. That is, Congress had no power to enact an establishment of religion or to interfere with state establishments. Perhaps the word "national" was superfluous, but Madison aimed at allaying apprehensions on the part of those states that maintained their own establishments of religion. In any case, if there is any validity to the argument that "national" signified the intention to prohibit only the establishment of a single religion or sect, the fact remains that the word "national" was deleted and does not appear in the final version of the amendment, thereby indicating that Congress rejected that intention and meant something broader by its ban on an establishment of religion.

2. Ibid., 1:451.
3. Ibid., 1:452.

Without debate, Madison's recommendations for amendments were referred for consideration to a select committee of the House, composed of one member from each state, including Madison.[4] Although we know nothing of the committee's deliberations, which took one week, its report to the House shows that Madison was the dominating figure because his proposed amendments remained intact with but slight changes in phraseology in the interest of brevity. From the proposal on religion the committee deleted the clause on civil rights and the word "national." The proposed amendment then read: "No religion shall be established by law, nor shall the equal rights of conscience be infringed."[5] The report of the select committee to the House merely recommended a redrafting of the original proposals; no explanation of the changes was included.

The House, sitting as a Committee of the Whole, began and ended its debate on the amendment on August 15. Our only account of the debate, in the *Annals of Congress*, is more in the nature of a condensed and paraphrased version than it is a verbatim report.[6] The account is brief enough to be given here in full:

Saturday, August 15

AMENDMENTS TO THE CONSTITUTION

The House again went into a Committee of the Whole on the proposed amendments to the constitution, Mr. Boudinot in the chair.

The fourth proposition being under consideration, as follows:

Article I. Section 9. Between paragraphs two and three insert "no religion shall be established by law, nor shall the equal rights of conscience be infringed."

Mr. Sylvester had some doubts of the propriety of the mode of

---

4. In addition to Madison, the committee included three other signers of the Constitution: Abraham Baldwin of Georgia, Roger Sherman of Connecticut, and George Clymer of Pennsylvania. Also on the committee were Aedanus Burke of South Carolina, the only Anti-Federalist; Nicholas Gilman of New Hampshire; Egbert Benson of New York; Benjamin Goodhue of Massachusetts; Elias Boudinot of New Jersey; and John Vining of Delaware, who was chairman. Ibid., 1:691.

5. Ibid., 1:757.

6. See Appendix.

expression used in this paragraph. He apprehended that it was liable to a construction different from what had been made by the committee. He feared it might be thought to have a tendency to abolish religion altogether.

Mr. Vining suggested the propriety of transposing the two members of the sentence.

Mr. Gerry said it would read better if it was, that no religious doctrine shall be established by law.

Mr. Sherman thought the amendment altogether unnecessary, inasmuch as Congress had no authority whatever delegated to them by the constitution to make religious establishments; he would, therefore, move to have it struck out.

Mr. Carroll—As the rights of conscience are, in their nature, of peculiar delicacy, and will little bear the gentlest touch of governmental hand; and as many sects have concurred in opinion that they are not well secured under the present constitution, he said he was much in favor of adopting the words. He thought it would tend more towards conciliating the minds of the people to the government than almost any other amendment he had heard proposed. He would not contend with gentlemen about the phraseology, his object was to secure the substance in such a manner as to satisfy the wishes of the honest part of the community.

Mr. Madison said, he apprehended the meaning of the words to be, that Congress should not establish a religion, and enforce the legal observation of it by law, nor compel men to worship God in any manner contrary to their conscience. Whether the words are necessary or not, he did not mean to say, but they had been required by some of the State Conventions, who seemed to entertain an opinion that under the clause of the constitution, which gave power to Congress to make all laws necessary and proper to carry into execution the constitution, and the laws made under it, enabled them to make laws of such a nature as might infringe the rights of conscience, and establish a national religion; to prevent these effects he presumed the amendment was intended, and he thought it as well expressed as the nature of the language would admit.

Mr. Huntington said that he feared, with the gentleman first up on this subject, that the words might be taken in such latitude as to be extremely harmful to the cause of religion. He understood the amendment to mean what had been expressed by the gentleman from Virginia; but others might find it convenient to put another construction upon it. The ministers of their congregations to the Eastward were maintained by the contributions of those who belonged to their society; the expense of building meeting-houses was contributed in the same manner. These things were regulated by by-laws. If an action was brought before a Federal Court on any of these cases, the person who had neglected to perform his engagements could not be compelled to do it; for a support of ministers, or building of places of worship might be construed into a religious establishment.

By the charter of Rhode Island, no religion could be established by law; he could give a history of the effects of such a regulation; indeed the people were now enjoying the blessed fruits of it [intended as irony]. He hoped, therefore, the amendment would be made in such a way as to secure the rights of conscience, and a free exercise of the rights of religion, but not to patronize those who professed no religion at all.

Mr. Madison thought, if the word national was inserted before religion, it would satisfy the minds of honorable gentlemen. He believed that the people feared one sect might obtain a preeminence, or two combine together, and establish a religion to which they would compel others to conform. He thought if the word national was introduced, it would point the amendment directly to the object it was intended to prevent.

Mr. Livermore was not satisfied with that amendment; but he did not wish them to dwell long on the subject. He thought it would be better if it was altered, and made to read in this manner, that Congress shall make no laws touching religion, or infringing the rights of conscience.

Mr. Gerry did not like the term national, proposed by the gentleman from Virginia, and he hoped it would not be adopted by the House. It brought to his mind some observations that had taken place in the conventions at the time they were considering the present constitution. It had been insisted upon by those who were called antifederalists, that this form of Government consolidated the Union; the honorable gentleman's motion shows that he considers it in the same light. Those who were called antifederalists at that time complained that they had injustice done them by the title, because they were in favor of a Federal Government, and the others were in favor of a national one; the federalists were for ratifying the constitution as it stood, and the others not until amendments were made. Their names then ought not to have been distinguished by federalists and antifederalists, but rats and antirats.

Mr. Madison withdrew his motion, but observed that the words "no national religion shall be established by law," did not imply that the Government was a national one; the question was then taken on Mr. Livermore's motion, and passed in the affirmative, thirty-one for, and twenty against it.[7]

The debate as unreliably reported was sometimes irrelevant, usually apathetic and unclear. Ambiguity, brevity, and imprecision in thought and expression characterize the comments of the few members who spoke. That the House understood the debate, cared deeply about its outcome, or shared a common understanding of the finished amendment seems doubtful. Only a few members participated. Not even Madison himself, dutifully carrying out his pledge to secure amendments, seems to have troubled to do more than was necessary to get something adopted in order to satisfy the popular clamor for a bill of rights and deflate Anti-Federalist charges that the new national government imperiled liberty. Indeed, Madison agreed with Roger Sherman's statement that the amendment was "altogether unnecessary, inasmuch as Congress had no authority whatever delegated to them by the constitution to make religious establishments." The difficulty, however, lies in the fact that neither Sherman, Madison, nor anyone else except Benjamin Huntington took the trouble to define what he was talking about. What were "religious establishments"? Huntington of Connecticut understood that government support of ministers or of places of worship came within the meaning of the term. But what did the select committee on amendments intend by recommending that

7. *Annals*, 1:757–59.

"no religion shall be established by law"? Madison's statement that the words meant "that Congress should not establish a religion" hardly showed the clarity for which we might have hoped.

On two occasions, however, he commented in such a way as to give some force to the arguments of those who defend a narrow interpretation of the establishment clause. In his answer to Sherman, made after Daniel Carroll's comment, Madison declared that the amendment was intended to satisfy "some of the State Conventions," which feared that Congress "might infringe the rights of conscience, and establish a national religion. . . ." At the time he spoke, he had the recommendations from four states. That of New Hampshire, drafted by the same Samuel Livermore who was present in Congress and took an essential part in the debate, was very much in line with his own thinking. But the recommendations from Virginia, New York, and North Carolina used the language of no preference. If Madison's intent was merely to yield to their requests, whatever may have been his own ideas on the subject, he might have meant by "national religion" that Congress should not prefer one denomination over others.

That such was his intent seems possible in view of his response to Huntington. The reporter present tells us of Madison: "He believed that the people feared one sect might obtain a preeminence, or two combine together, and establish a religion to which they would compel others to conform. He thought that if the word national was introduced, it would point the amendment directly to the object it was intended to prevent." Here Madison himself used the language of no preference or no preeminence. Yet we know from other evidence (reviewed later) that Madison himself did not regard the element of preference as indispensable to the idea of an establishment of religion. If *all* denominations combined together or if the government supported all, giving preference to none, the result would in his mind have been an establishment.

Huntington's ambiguous statement probably referred to the eastern states (contrasted with southern and middle) such as his own, Connecticut, where taxes for religion were euphemistically called "contributions"[8] and were regulated by parish bylaws. Huntington, therefore,

8. Under Connecticut's Toleration Act of 1784, non-Congregationalists

probably expressed a fear that state establishments might be interfered with by Congress. If so, Madison's reply makes sense, because he was saying only that the proposed amendment restricted Congress but not the states. Even his use of the language of no preference makes sense if construed as a reply in kind to Huntington's *ironic* reference to the effects in Rhode Island of the lack of an establishment. That is, Madison may have been saying, in effect, "What the people fear, Mr. Huntington, is not the situation in Rhode Island, which has no establishment of religion, but that in Connecticut, where one sect has obtained a preeminence, or two, the Congregationalists and Episcopalians, have combined together and compel others to conform." If this was what Madison meant, then his use of the language of no preference revealed one intent of the proposed amendment but not its only intent.

Livermore's motion for a change of wording apparently expressed what Madison meant by his use of the word "national" and satisfied the Committee of the Whole. The proposed amendment, adopted by a vote of 31 to 20, then read: "Congress shall make no laws touching religion, or infringing the rights of conscience." But a few days later, on August 20, when the House took up the report of the Committee of the Whole and voted clause by clause on the proposed amendment, an additional change was made. Fisher Ames of Massachusetts moved that the amendment read: "Congress shall make no law establishing religion, or to prevent the free exercise thereof, or to infringe the rights of conscience."[9] Without debate the House adopted Ames's motion by the necessary two-thirds vote. Apparently the House believed that the

---

who wished to be exempt from the tax for the support of the town Congregational Church could pay their tax to the church they regularly attended, after obtaining a certificate proving that they "*contributed* their share and proportion to supporting the public worship and ministry thereof. . . ." See M. Louise Greene, *Development of Religious Liberty in Connecticut* (Boston, 1905), p. 372. The use of "contribution" as a euphemism or synonym for "tax" appeared in other states as well. In Virginia, for example, the resolution of the state legislature designed to carry out a motion for a general assessment for religion provided "That the people . . . ought to pay a moderate tax or *contribution* annually, for the support of the Christian religion. . . ." Quoted in H. J. Eckenrode, *Separation of Church and State in Virginia* (Richmond, Va., 1910), p. 86.

9. *Annals*, 1:796.

draft of the clause based on Livermore's motion might not satisfy the demands of those who wanted something said specifically against establishments of religion. The amendment as submitted to the Senate reflected a stylistic change that gave it the following reading: "Congress shall make no law establishing religion, or prohibiting the free exercise thereof, nor shall the rights of conscience be infringed."

The Senate began debate on the House amendments on September 3 and continued through September 9. The debate was conducted in secrecy, and no record exists but the bare account of motions and votes in the *Senate Journal.* According to the record of September 3, three motions of special interest here were defeated on that day.[10] These motions restricted the ban in the proposed amendment to establishments preferring one sect above others. The first motion would have made the clause in the amendment read: "Congress shall make no law establishing one religious sect or society in preference to others." After the failure of this motion and of another to kill the amendment, a new motion was made to change it to read: "Congress shall not make any law infringing the rights of conscience, or establishing any religious sect or society." The final defeated motion restated the same thought differently: "Congress shall make no law establishing any particular denomination of religion in preference to another." The Senate then adopted the language of the House: "Congress shall make no law establishing religion."

The failure of these three motions, each of which seemed to express a narrow intent, and the Senate's adoption of the House version prove that the Senate intended something broader than merely a ban on preference to one sect. Yet if anything is really clear about the problem of "meaning" and "intent," it is that little is clear; when the Senate returned to the clause six days later, it altered the House amendment to read: "Congress shall make no law establishing articles of faith or a mode of worship, or prohibiting the free exercise of religion." Like the

---

10. *Journal of the First Session of the Senate of the United States* (Washington, D.C., 1820), p. 70. The modern scholarly edition is Linda Grant De Pauw, ed., *Documentary History of the First Federal Congress of the United States of America,* 3 vols. (Baltimore, Md., 1972); see vol. 1, *Senate Legislative Journal,* p. 151; for the House's adamance, see vol. 3, *House of Representatives Journal,* p. 228.

three previously defeated motions, this one had the unmistakable meaning of limiting the ban to acts that prefer one denomination over others or that, to put it simply, establish a single state church.[11]

Appearances can be deceiving, however. A Baptist memorial of 1774 had used similar language: ". . . the magistrate's power extends not to the establishing any articles of faith or forms of worship, by force of laws." Yet the Baptists, who advocated separation of government and religion, opposed nondiscriminatory government aid to all sects— proving once again how misleading language can be.[12] To Baptists, if law did not extend to articles of faith, no establishment of religion was possible. And, as the 1780 returns from Massachusetts towns showed, people who endorsed the principle that no denomination should be subordinated to any other or that no denomination should have preference of any kind favored separation of church and state.[13] In short, nonpreferentialism could signify voluntarism or the private support of religion.

The Senate's wording provoked the House to take action that made *its* intent clear, as the next step in the drafting of the amendment revealed. In voting on the Senate's proposed amendments, the House accepted some and rejected others, including the Senate's article on religion. To resolve the disagreement between the two branches, the House proposed a joint conference committee. The Senate refused to recede from its position but agreed to the proposal for a conference committee. The committee, a strong and distinguished one, consisted of Madison as chairman of the House conferees, joined by Sherman and Vining, and Ellsworth as chairman of the Senate conferees, joined by Paterson and Carroll. Four of the six men had been influential members of the Constitutional Convention. The House members of the conference flatly refused to accept the Senate's version of the amend-

11. *Journal of First Session*, p. 77; De Pauw, ed., *Documentary History*, 1:166.

12. For the Baptist statement in a memorial to the Continental Congress of October 1774, see Alvah Hovey, *The Life and Times of the Reverend Isaac Backus* (Boston, 1858), p. 209; the entire document covers pp. 204–10.

13. See above, chap. 2, note 9 and related text. See also below, chap. 5, notes 53–58 and related text, for additional examples of the language of no preference being used to mean no government aid whatever.

ment on religion, indicating that the House would not be satisfied with merely a ban on preference of one sect or religion over others. The Senate conferees abandoned the Senate's version, and the amendment was redrafted to give it its present phraseology. On September 24, Ellsworth reported to the Senate that the House would accept the Senate's version of the other amendments provided that the amendment on religion "shall read as follows: Congress shall make no laws respecting an establishment of religion, or prohibiting the free exercise thereof."[14] On the same day, the House sent a message to the Senate verifying Ellsworth's report.[15] On the next day, September 25, the Senate by a two-thirds vote accepted the condition laid down by the House.[16] Congress had passed the establishment clause.

The one fact that stands out is that Congress very carefully considered and rejected the wording that seems to imply the narrow interpretation. The House's rejection of the Senate's version of the amendment shows that the House did not intend to frame an amendment that banned only congressional support of one sect, church, denomination, or religion. The Senate three times defeated versions of the amendment embodying that narrow interpretation, on a fourth vote adopted such a version, and finally abandoned it in the face of uncompromising hostility by the House. The amendment's framers definitely intended something broader than the narrow interpretation that some judges and scholars have given it. The amendment reflected the fundamental fact that the framers of the Constitution had not empowered Congress to act in the field of religion. The "great object" of the Bill of Rights, as Madison explicitly said when introducing his draft of amendments to the House, was to "limit and qualify the powers of Government"[17] for the purpose of making certain that the powers granted could not be exercised in forbidden fields, such as religion.

Madison also wanted to limit the state governments. He knew that some states had no bills of rights and others "very defective ones." He believed that the states constituted a greater danger to personal liber-

14. *Journal of the First Session*, p. 86.
15. Ibid., p. 87.
16. Ibid., p. 88; De Pauw, ed., *Documentary History*, 1:186, 189, 192.
17. *Annals*, 1:454.

ties than the new national government. Accordingly, he proposed an amendment that read: "No State shall violate the equal rights of conscience, or the freedom of the press, or the trial by jury in criminal cases." He argued that the states would likely abuse their powers if not controlled by "the general principle, that the laws are unconstitutional which infringe" the people's rights. When a congressman moved to strike the proposed restriction on state powers, Madison carried the House by the necessary two-thirds majority after he argued that this was "the most valuable amendment in the whole list." The amendment was defeated, however, in the Senate. Had the Senate passed it, a constitutional basis would have existed for interpreting the rights of conscience as being contradictory to establishments of religion. Such an interpretation had to wait until long after the Fourteenth Amendment imposed restrictions on the states. In any case, Madison's advocacy of his "most valuable amendment" shows that the principle of federalism was by no means the main force behind what became the First Amendment.[18]

The history of the drafting of the establishment clause does not provide us with an understanding of what was meant by "an establishment of religion." To argue, however, as proponents of a narrow interpretation do, that the amendment permits congressional aid and support to religion in general or to all denominations without discrimination leads to the impossible conclusion that the First Amendment added to Congress's power. Nothing supports such a conclusion. Every bit of evidence goes to prove that the First Amendment, like the others, was intended to restrict Congress to its enumerated powers. Because Congress possessed no power under the Constitution to legislate on matters concerning religion, Congress has no such power even in the absence of the First Amendment. It is therefore unreasonable, even fatuous, to believe that an express prohibition of power—"Congress shall make no law respecting an establishment of religion"—vests or creates the power, previously nonexistent, of supporting religion by aid

18. Madison's speech to the House, June 8, 1789, is conveniently reprinted in *The Bill of Rights: A Documentary History*, edited by Bernard Schwartz, 2 vols. (New York, 1971), 2:1027, 1033, 1113; pp. 1145–58 treat the Bill of Rights in the Senate.

to all religious groups. The Bill of Rights, as Madison said, was not framed "to imply powers not meant to be included in the enumeration."[19]

Little or no new light on the meaning of the establishment clause derives from the deliberations of the state legislatures to which the amendments to the Constitution were submitted for ratification. Records of state debates are nonexistent; private correspondence, newspapers, and tracts provide no help.

The admission of Vermont to the Union made necessary the ratification by eleven states. Nine approved the Bill of Rights within six months. The four recalcitrant states that by mid-1790 had not yet taken action on the proposed amendments were Virginia, Massachusetts, Connecticut, and Georgia; indeed, the last three states took no action until 1939 when, on the sesquicentennial anniversary of the Constitution, they belatedly ratified the Bill of Rights.[20]

Of the three states that failed to ratify the Bill of Rights until 1939, Georgia took the position that amendments were unnecessary until experience under the Constitution showed the need for them.[21] Connecticut's lower house voted to ratify in 1789 and again the following year, but the state senate, apparently in the belief that the Bill of Rights was superfluous, adamantly refused. Yankee Federalists in the state seem to have thought that any suggestion that the Constitution was not perfect would add to the strength of the Anti-Federalists. The same sentiment prevailed in Massachusetts. There Federalist apathy to the Bill of Rights was grounded on satisfaction with the Constitution as it was unamended, while the Anti-Federalists expressed more interest

19. James Madison to Thomas Jefferson, Oct. 17, 1788, in William T. Hutchinson et al., eds., *The Papers of James Madison*, ser. in progress (Chicago, 1962–), 11:297.

20. David M. Matteson, "The Organization of the Government under the Constitution," in *History of the Formation of the Union under the Constitution*, directed by Sol Bloom (Washington, D.C., 1943), pp. 316–19. Robert A. Rutland, *The Birth of the Bill of Rights, 1776–1791* (Chapel Hill, N.C., 1955), pp. 213–18; Bernard Schwartz, ed., *The Bill of Rights: A Documentary History*, 2 vols. (New York, 1971), 2:1171–1203, conveniently collects the primary sources on ratification.

21. Matteson, "Organization of the Government," pp. 325–28.

in amendments that would weaken the national government and strengthen the states than in protecting personal liberties. The Bill of Rights was caught between conflicting party interests, and as a result Massachusetts failed to take final action on the proposed amendments. The lower house adopted most amendments, as did the upper; both approved of what became the First Amendment, the Second through the Seventh, and the Ninth, but a special committee dominated by Anti-Federalists urged that all the amendments that Massachusetts had recommended when ratifying the Constitution should be endorsed again by the state before it finally concurred in the proposals from Congress. Jefferson, the secretary of state, believed that Massachusetts had ratified, bringing the number of ratifying states to the necessary ten, but a Massachusetts official, replying to Jefferson's query, stated, "It does not appear that the Committee ever reported any bill." Thus, because of the inaction of a committee charged with reconciling the measures taken by both houses, Massachusetts failed to approve officially the Bill of Rights.[22]

The circumstances surrounding ratification in Virginia are of particular interest. The state senate held up ratification for nearly two years while Anti-Federalists attacked the amendment as inadequate. The eight state senators who opposed it explained their vote publicly in these words:

> The 3d amendment [the First Amendment] recommended by Congress does not prohibit the rights of conscience from being violated or infringed: and although it goes to restrain Congress from passing laws establishing any national religion, they might, notwithstanding, levy taxes to any amount, for the support of religion or its preachers; and any particular denomination of [C]hristians might be so favored and supported by the General Government, as to give it a decided advantage over others, and in process of time render it as powerful and dangerous as if it was established as the national religion of the country. . . . This amendment then, when

22. Thomas Jefferson to Christopher Gore, Aug. 8, 1791, in *Documentary History of the Constitution of the United States of America, 1786–1870. Derived from Records, Manuscripts and Rolls Deposited in the Bureau of Rolls and Library of the Department of State,* 5 vols. (Washington, D.C., 1894–1905), 5:177.

considered as it relates to any of the rights it is pretended to secure, will be found totally inadequate, and betrays an unreasonable, unjustifiable, but a studied departure from the amendment proposed by Virginia.[23]

Taken out of context and used uncritically, this statement by the eight Virginia senators supposedly proves that the establishment clause had only the narrowest intent of nonpreferentialism, that the Virginia legislators so understood it, and that the state eventually approved of it with only that narrow intent attached. The conclusion is drawn that the amendment did not purport to ban government aid to religion generally or to all denominations without discrimination. However, examination of the intricate party maneuverings and complex motives in the Virginia ratification dispute sheds a different light on the senators' statement.

Virginia's Anti-Federalists, led by Patrick Henry and U.S. senators Richard Henry Lee and William Grayson, had opposed the ratification of the Constitution for a variety of reasons. Chief among these was the belief that the Constitution established too strong a central government at the expense of the states. For example, the Anti-Federalists wanted amendments to the Constitution that would restrict Congress's commerce and tax powers. The same people led the movement for amendments that would protect personal liberties, but many cried out against the absence of a bill of rights more for the purpose of defeating the Constitution than of actually getting such a bill of rights.

---

23. *Journal of the Senate of the Commonwealth of Virginia; Begun and Held in the City of Richmond, on Monday, the 18th Day of October, . . . 1789* [binder's title, *Journal of the Senate, 1785 to 1790*] (Richmond, Va., 1828), p. 62. Quoted by John Courtney Murray, "Law or Prepossessions," and quoted by Edward S. Corwin, "Supreme Court as National School Board," *Law and Contemporary Problems* 14 (Winter 1949): 43, 12, respectively. The statement by the eight Virginia senators was revived and quoted by an advocate of the narrow interpretation of the establishment-of-religion clause in "Brief for Appellees," pp. 51–54, filed in the case of *McCollum v. Board of Education*, 333 U.S. 203 (1948). Both Murray and Corwin, who were wrong, quoted the brief rather than *Journal of the Senate* and drew their conclusions on this matter from the brief alone without investigating the context of the statement by the eight senators.

When Congress had considered amending the Constitution, the Anti-Federalists sought to secure amendments that would aggrandize state powers, but in this effort they failed. In the ratification controversy, therefore, the strategy of Virginia's Anti-Federalists hinged on the defeat of the proposed Bill of Rights in order to force Congress to reconsider the whole subject of amendments. The Federalists, on the other hand, eagerly supported the Bill of Rights in order to prevent additional amendments that might hamstring the national government.

On November 30, 1789, Virginia's lower house, dominated by the Federalists, quickly passed all the amendments proposed by Congress "without debate of any consequence."[24] But the opposition party controlled the state senate. "That body," reported Edmund Randolph to Washington, "will attempt to postpone them [the amendments]; for a majority is unfriendly to the government."[25] As a member of the Virginia lower house reported to Madison, the state senate was inclined to reject the amendments not from dissatisfaction with them but from apprehension "that the adoption of them at this time will be an obstacle to the chief objection of their pursuit, the amendment on the subject of direct taxation."[26] As Randolph had predicted, the senate, by a vote of 8 to 7, did decide to postpone final action on what are now the First, Sixth, Ninth, and Tenth Amendments until the next session of the legislature, thereby allowing time for the electorate to express itself. It was on this occasion that the eight senators in question made their statement on the allegedly weak Bill of Rights by presenting themselves as champions of religious liberty and advocates of separation between government and religion.

Madison remained unworried by this tactic, confidently predicting that the action of the senators would boomerang against them. "The

24. Edmund Randolph to George Washington, Dec. 6, 1789, in *Documentary History . . . Department of State*, 5:222–23.

25. Ibid.

26. Hardin Burnley to James Madison, Dec. 5, 1789, in *Madison Papers*, 12:460. See also James Madison to George Washington, Dec. 5, 1789, in ibid., 12:459; Irving Brant, *James Madison, Father of the Constitution* (Indianapolis, 1950), pp. 286, 491 (n. 15).

miscarriage of the third article [the First Amendment], particularly, will have this effect," he wrote to George Washington.[27] His confidence is explainable on several counts. First, he knew that the First Amendment had the support of the Baptists, the one group most insistent upon demanding a thorough separation between government and religion.[28] Second, he knew that the eight senators did not come before the electorate with clean hands. Like Henry and Lee, who laid down their strategy for them, they had consistently voted against religious liberty and in favor of taxes for religion. Their legislative record on this score was well known. By contrast, the seven senators who favored ratification of the First Amendment had stood with Jefferson and Madison in the fight between 1784 and 1786 against a state establishment of religion and for religious liberty.[29] Finally, Madison reasoned that the statement by the eight senators was an inept piece of propaganda with little chance of convincing anyone because it was so obviously misleading and inaccurate. The eight senators alleged that "any particular denomination of Christians might be so favored and supported by the general government, as to give it a decided advantage over others"—a construction of the First Amendment that not even proponents of the narrow interpretation would accept—and they also asserted that the amendment "does not prohibit the rights of conscience from being violated or infringed"—despite the positive statement in the amendment that Congress shall not abridge the free exercise of religion. It is absurd to argue that "in the search for the intentions of the Founding Fathers as embodied in the First Amendment, the statement of the Virginia Senate is probably the most revealing extant document."[30] It is difficult to believe that those who rejected the establishment clause understood it better than its framers, that the Anti-Federalists knew better than Madison and his cohorts, and that those who supported an

---

27. Matteson, "Organization of the Government," pp. 321–22; James Madison to George Washington, Nov. 20, 1789, in *Madison Papers*, 12:453.

28. *Madison Papers*, 12:453.

29. See Brant, *James Madison*, pp. 286–87, 491 n. 16, for the voting records.

30. Chester J. Antieau, Arthur T. Downey, and Edward C. Roberts, *Freedom from Federal Establishment: Formation and Early History of the First Amendment Religion Clauses* (Milwaukee, Wisc., 1964), p. 145.

establishment of religion in Virginia revealed the criteria for interpreting the limitation on Congress's powers. Moreover, the amendment proposed by Congress banned a law even *respecting* an establishment; the amendment proposed by Virginia and endorsed by the eight senators was framed in nonpreferentialist language—no preference to one sect over others, and was therefore not nearly as protective in its text as the amendment proposed by Congress.

In the end, Madison's confidence proved justified. On December 15, 1791, after a session of inaction on the Bill of Rights, the state senate finally ratified without a recorded vote. In the context of Anti-Federalist maneuverings, there is every reason to believe that Virginia supported the First Amendment with the understanding that it had been misrepresented by the eight senators. There is no reason to believe that Virginia ratified with the understanding that the amendment permitted any government aid to religion.

What conclusions can one come to, then, in connection with ratification of the First Amendment by the states? In Virginia, the one state for which there is some evidence, we can arrive only at a negative conclusion: the narrow interpretation of the establishment clause is insupportable. In nine other states there was perfunctory ratification, with no record of the debates, and in the remaining three states there was inaction. Therefore, it is impossible to state on the basis of ratification alone the general understanding of the establishment clause. But the legislative history of the framing of the clause demonstrates that Congress rejected a narrow or nonpreferentialist intent. And that history, seen in the context of the drive to add a bill of rights to the Constitution in order to restrict the powers of the national government, proves that the framers of the establishment clause meant to make explicit a point on which the entire nation agreed: the United States had no power to legislate on the subject of religion.

6

James Madison versus the Nonpreferentialists

A formidable school of nonpreferentialists—scholars, politicians, publicists, and judges—has developed a plausible but fundamentally defective interpretation of the establishment clause to prove that its framers had no intention of prohibiting government aid to all denominations or to religion on a nonpreferential basis. The nonpreferentialists are innocent of history but quick to rely on a few historical facts that, when yanked out of context, seem to provide a patristic lineage to their views. Sharp logicians, they are adept at parsing the proposals that emerged as the establishment clause. Their view is that the legislative history of the clause and its final phrasing prove an intent to impose upon the national government merely a ban against aiding an exclusive or preferential establishment, which results in their conclusion that government assistance to religion generally, without a hint of discrimination, would not violate the establishment clause.[1] "The legislative history of the establishment clause," we have been misinformed, "shows that the framers accepted nondiscriminatory aid to religion."[2]

Chief Justice William H. Rehnquist, the judicial leader of the non-preferentialists, presented their view in a dissenting opinion of 1985 when he declared, wrongly, that the "well-accepted meaning" of the establishment clause is that it prohibited the establishment of a "national religion," which he defined as the official "designation of any church as a national one." The clause also "forbade preference among religious sects or denominations." But it created no wall of separation between government and religion, not even between church and state. "The Establishment Clause," Rehnquist wrote, "did not require government neutrality between religion and irreligion nor did it prohibit the federal government from providing nondiscriminatory aid to reli-

1. Edward S. Corwin, "The Supreme Court as a National School Board," *Law and Contemporary Problems* 14 (Winter 1949): 3–23; James O'Neill, *Religion and Education under the Constitution* (New York, 1949); Chester J. Antieau, Arthur T. Downey, and Edward C. Roberts, *Freedom from Federal Establishment: Formation and Early History of the First Amendment Religion Clauses* (Milwaukee, Wisc., 1964); Robert G. McCloskey, "Principles, Powers and Values: The Establishment Clause and the Supreme Court," in *1964 Religion and the Public Order*, edited by Donald A. Giannella (Chicago, 1965), pp. 3–33; Walter Berns, *The First Amendment and the Future of American Democracy* (New York, 1976); Michael J. Malbin, *Religion and Politics: The Intentions of the Authors of the First Amendment* (Washington, D.C., 1978); James McClellan, "The Making and the Unmaking of the Establishment Clause," in *A Blueprint for Judicial Reform*, edited by Patrick B. McGuigan and Randall R. Rader (Washington, D.C., 1981), pp. 295–325; Robert L. Cord, *Separation of Church and State: Historical Fact and Current Fiction* (New York, 1982); James Reichley, *Religion in American Public Life* (Washington, D.C., 1985); Richard P. McBrien, *Caesar's Coin: Religion and Politics in America* (New York, 1987); Daniel L. Dreisbach, *Real Threat and Mere Shadow: Religious Liberty and the First Amendment* (Westchester, Ill., 1987).

2. Malbin, *Religion and Politics*, p. 16.

gion."[3] Nonpreferentialists fasten onto every exception to an absolute separation of church and state ("In God We Trust" or Thanksgiving Day), and they convert every exception into a triumphal archway through the wall of separation. They want to bulldoze that wall so that it cannot impede a variety of nonpreferential aids to religion. And, finally, they lambaste the constitutional doctrine by which the Supreme Court applies to the states the First Amendment's ban on establishments.

If, as nonpreferentialists suppose, the views of James Madison, the legislative history of the establishment clause, and its original meaning support the constitutionality of impartial government aid to religion, then the guiding light of history burns incandescently on behalf of nonpreferentialism. But they are wrong in thinking that they have a prop in Madison. They misconstrue the legislative history of the clause. And they mistakenly connect an establishment of religion with only a national church or a national religion. A good nonpreferential scholar, Daniel L. Dreisbach, declared that because the framers sought to "proscribe the establishment of a national church," the conclusion reasonably follows that the national government is "not foreclosed from extending general benefits to religion if administered on an equal basis and in a manner that did not infringe on the free exercise rights of any religious group."[4] Dreisbach even endorsed the view that the Constitution allows "the promotion of a generalized or nondenominational form of Christianity. . . ." Dreisbach failed to indicate which clause of the Constitution empowers Congress to extend general benefits to religion or to Christianity. None does.

Edwin Meese III, attorney general of the United States under President Reagan and a preeminent political leader of the nonpreferentialists, advocated that "the First Amendment forbad the establishment of a particular religion or a particular church. It also precluded the federal government from favoring one church, or one church group over another. That's what the First Amendment did, but it did not go further. It did not, for example, preclude federal aid to religious groups so long

---

3. *Wallace v. Jaffree*, 472 U.S. 38, 98, 99, 106 (1985).

4. Dreisbach, *Real Threat and Mere Shadow*, p. 65; chap. 6 is entitled "The Prohibition of the Establishment of a National Church."

as that assistance furthered a public purpose and so long as it did not discriminate in favor of one religious group against another."[5] Nonpreferentialists simply do not trifle to state what part of the Constitution empowers the government to aid religion nonpreferentially. Even scholars of the nonpreferential persuasion have failed in this regard, although they could show that enumerated powers may be exercised in ways that indirectly benefit religion if the purpose and effect of an enactment is primarily secular in nature. Religiously affiliated universities such as Fordham or Yeshiva, for example, might be the recipients of a federal grant program for the teaching of mathematics. Such legislation, however, is secular in character and does not single out religiously affiliated institutions for special benefits, nor does the legislation rest on a power to regulate religion.

The nonpreferential interpretation seems persuasive if one can ignore or forget the fact that the First Amendment, no matter how parsed or logically analyzed, was framed to deny power, not to vest it. The fundamental defect of the nonpreferential interpretation is that it results in the unhistorical contention that the First Amendment augmented a nonexistent congressional power to legislate in the field of religion. The nonpreferential interpretation also seems persuasive if one can also ignore or forget the fact that neither Christianity nor Protestantism was ever a state church. The nonpreferentialists, having a tin ear for history, call Christianity or Protestantism one religion as if one religion were the equivalent of one church, as in the term "state church." Invariably they end up with "state church" as the definition of an establishment of religion.[6] The nonpreferentialist effort results in the proposition that government aid to religion without hint of discrimination would not violate the establishment clause. Supposedly the legislative history of the establishment clause provides elaborate proof of the nonpreferential thesis.

Although Madison initially proposed "nor shall *any* national religion

---

5. Edwin Meese III, "Address before the Christian Legal Society," San Diego, September 29, 1985 (U.S. Department of Justice, Washington, D.C., transcript), pp. 8–9.

6. Cord, *Separation of Church and State*, pp. 5, 6, 10; Malbin, *Religion and Politics*, p. 14. See also Dreisbach, *Real Threat and Mere Shadow*, p. 65.

be established," in the debate that followed he explained himself by saying that his proposal meant that "Congress shall not establish a religion." The word "a" has great significance for the nonpreferential- ists. They emphasize the fact that in the debate Madison wished to proscribe "*a* national religion," that is, a single or exclusive religion preferred over all others "and nothing else." Similarly, they stress that the term used in the final version of the amendment is "an establish- ment of religion." The use of the singular noun, "an establishment," supposedly has the effect of narrowing the scope of the prohibition.[7] Madison allegedly wanted only to prohibit "discriminatory religious assistance" and "a national church." The climax of this view follows: "At the same time, the phrase 'an establishment' seems to ensure the legality of nondiscriminatory religious aid. Had the framers prohibited '*the* establishment of religion,' which would have emphasized the ge- neric word 'religion,' there might the been some reason for thinking they wanted to prohibit all official preferences of religion over irre- ligion. But by choosing 'an establishment' over 'the establishment,' they were showing that they wanted to prohibit only those official ac- tivities that tended to promote the interests of one or another particu- lar sect."[8] Preferring "religion over irreligion" is a red herring; the ques- tion of such a preference was not an issue. The government possessed no power to aid irreligion or religion.

What shall we say, however, about the interpretation based on the use of the indefinite rather than the definite article? First, we are not interpreting a verbatim record of the debate. The record we have de- rives from unreliable newspaper reports. It is incomplete and does not purport to be a literal transcription of the words of the speakers. Re- porters took notes that they later rephrased and expanded for publica- tion. Any interpretation of the debate that turns on single words or precise nuances of phrasing must be suspect.[9] And any interpretation that turns on the use of the indefinite article rather than the definite article must be utterly rejected, for the simple reason that the reporter who took shorthand notes of the debates on the Bill of Rights omitted

7. Cord, *Separation of Church and State*, p. 5.

8. Malbin, *Religion and Politics*, p. 14.

9. See Appendix.

articles, both definite and indefinite. He recorded the main outlines of speech and later reconstructed those speeches from his memory. He omitted a great deal and sometimes garbled what he included. Madison said, when sending a copy of the reporter's work to Jefferson, it gave "some idea of the discussion," though it showed "the strongest evidences of mutilation & perversion, and of the illiteracy of the Editor." To another correspondent Madison wrote that the reporter "sometimes filled up blanks in his notes from memory or *imagination*" and that he also made drunken reports.[10]

Second, the nonpreferentialists stress the "a" in Madison's recommended amendment without considering that it did not pass the House. The amendment as adopted bans any law "respecting the establishment of religion." It does not refer to "a religion" or "a national religion." The reference is to religion in general. The nonpreferentialist argument is founded on a discarded proposal rather than the constitutional text. Nevertheless, Madison had an interpretation of "national religion," as we shall see, that undoes the nonpreferentialist argument.

Third, "the" is not "generic"; it is specific. Contrary to Robert Cord, Daniel Dreisbach, and the others, the employment of "the" instead of "an" as the article preceding "establishment of religion" would not have broadened the establishment clause. Fourth, "the" can be as singular as "a" or "an." But those are quibbles.

A more important objection to the nonpreferentialist emphasis on the definite article in the establishment clause derives from the attempt to construe it literally or strictly. That which is inherently ambiguous cannot be strictly construed. Worse still, strict construction of the First Amendment, if ever taken seriously, would lead to the destruction of basic rights. Strict construction often leads to narrow-mindedness. Consider the exact language of the amendment: "Congress shall make

---

10. James Madison to Thomas Jefferson, May 9, 1789, in William T. Hutchinson et al., eds., *The Papers of James Madison*, ser. in progress (Chicago, 1962–), 12:142. See Marion Tinling, "Thomas Lloyd's Reports of the First Federal Congress," *William and Mary Quarterly*, 3d ser., 18 (Oct. 1961): 530, on the omission of articles, and pp. 530–38 for contemporary criticism of Lloyd's reporting. Tinling quotes a Madison letter of Jan. 7, 1832, describing the reporter as a "votary of the bottle" who made "too free use of it" (pp. 537–38).

no law respecting the establishment of religion, or prohibiting the free exercise thereof; or abridging the freedom of speech, or of the press." The framers of the amendment deliberately used different verbs in the freedom of religion and freedom of the press clauses. That is a matter of considerably greater semantic importance than the difference between "an" and "the" in the establishment clause. If the framers meant what they said and said what they meant, then Congress may abridge the free exercise of religion so long as Congress does not prohibit it. The point is that contrary to Rehnquist and company, the principles embodied in the First Amendment's clauses, not some misunderstanding based upon a grammarian's niceties, command our constitutional respect.

The still more important fact is that the type of article used in the establishment clause made no difference. The First Amendment does not say that Congress shall not establish a religion or create an establishment of religion. It says Congress shall make no law *respecting* an establishment of religion. Whether "respecting" connotes honoring or concerning, the clause means that Congress shall make no law on that subject. The ban is not just on establishments of religion but on laws respecting them, a fact that allows a law to fall short of creating an establishment yet still be unconstitutional. The entire nonpreferentialist argument reduces to the proposition that, although a law preferring one religion over others would be unconstitutional, government aid to all without preference to any would be constitutional. But if government cannot pass a law on the subject of an establishment of religion, whether the aid is to all without preference or to only one makes no difference. A law of either kind is a law on a forbidden subject and therefore unconstitutional.

Another important fact shows that the type of article, whether definite or indefinite, singular or plural, made no difference for any practical purpose. President Jefferson, for example, when refusing to proclaim a day of national thanksgiving, thought the establishment clause did use "the" instead of "a," for he misquoted it, stating that is said "no law shall be made respecting *the* establishment or free exercise of religion."[11] What is significant is not the misquotation by Jefferson but his

11. Thomas Jefferson to Samuel Miller, Jan. 23, 1808, in *The Writings of*

belief that the ban on an establishment extended to presidentially proclaimed fast and thanksgiving days.

Similarly, President Madison misquoted the establishment clause
but also had an extremely broad view of it. He usually quoted it as if it
outlawed "religious establishments." A "religious establishment" is a
church or some religious institution and carries no implication of government aid to religion or involvement with religion as does an "establishment of religion." That Madison quoted the clause as if it outlawed
religious establishments shows that he understood it to mean that Congress had no authority to legislate on religion or its institutions. President Madison vetoed a land-grant bill intended to remedy the peculiar
situation of a Baptist church that, as a result of a surveying error, had
been built on federal land. Congress had sought to rectify the error by
permitting the church to have the land rather than buy it or be dis-
possessed. Here was no making of broad public policy, yet President
Madison saw a dangerous precedent, and he vetoed the bill on the
grounds that it "comprises a principle and precedent for the appropria-
tion of funds of the United States for the use and support of religious
societies, contrary to the article of the Constitution which declares that
'Congress shall make no law respecting a religious establishment.' "[12]

It is interesting and significant that Madison, the "father" of the
Constitution and of the Bill of Rights, in a formal message to Congress
should have misquoted the First Amendment in the particular way he
did, using "religious establishment" synonymously with "an establishment of religion," although the first, unlike the second, does not imply
an act of the government. The point is, of course, that Madison never
altered his early view, which was widely shared by the other framers of
the Constitution, that Congress had no power to legislate on any matters concerning religion. His use of "religious establishment" instead of
"establishment of religion" shows that he thought of the clause in the
First Amendment as prohibiting Congress from making any law touching or "respecting" religious institutions or religion. He misquoted the

---

Thomas Jefferson, edited by Andrew A. Lipscomb and Albert E. Bergh, 20 vols.
(Washington, D.C., 1903–4), 11:428; emphasis added.

12. James D. Richardson, ed., *A Compilation of the Messages and Papers of the
Presidents*, 10 vols. (Washington, D.C., 1969), 1:490, message of Feb. 28, 1811.

First Amendment in the same way in another veto message against a congressional bill that would have incorporated a church in the District of Columbia,[13] showing that he regarded even simple recognition, without financial support, to be within the ban against an establishment of religion.

As a member of the First Congress, Madison served on the joint committee that created congressional chaplaincies. Contrary to former chief justice Warren E. Burger and the Supreme Court, we do not know that Madison "voted for the bill authorizing payment of chaplains."[14] True, there is no record of that date to indicate his objection to such chaplaincies. Nonpreferentialists assume from the silence of the record that Madison must have supported the chaplaincy bill in 1789, but they ignore his later statement that he disapproved of it. In a letter of 1822 to Edward Livingston he stated that he had not approved at that time or later: "I observe with particular pleasure the view you have taken of the immunity of religion from civil jurisdiction. . . . This has always been a favorite principle with me; and it was *not* with my approbation, that the deviation from it took place in Congress when they appointed Chaplains, to be paid from the National Treasury."[15]

Madison also treated the establishment clause as if it prohibited a national religion and yet construed the clause as if it separated religion and government by erecting between them a high and impregnable wall, just as Jefferson construed the clause. The phrase "national religion" appeared in Madison's first draft of the First Amendment, and

13. Ibid., 1:489, message of Feb. 21, 1811.

14. *Marsh v. Chambers*, 463 U.S. 783, 788, n. 8. Burger cited *Annals of Congress*, 1:891, but nothing on that page is pertinent. In *Annals*, 1:1077, Jan. 7, 1790, not Sept. 25, 1789, as Burger said, we learn that the House resolved that each branch of Congress should appoint a chaplain and that the chaplains should be of different denominations, but the *Annals* does not record the vote or say how any member voted.

15. James Madison to Edward Livingston, July 10, 1822, in *The Writings of James Madison*, edited by Gaillard Hunt, 9 vols. (New York, 1900–1910), 9:100; emphasis added. See Cord, *Separation of Church and State*, p. 23; Antieau, Downey, and Roberts, *Freedom from Federal Establishment*, pp. 180–81, for Madison's alleged support of the bill.

when the House drafting committee dropped the word "national," he suggested in debate that it be restored. Nonpreferentialists construe his use of "national" to mean that he sought merely to prohibit the establishment by Congress of a single state church or congressional preference for one church or religion over others. But the evidence indicates that by his use of the word "national" in 1789 Madison intended to distinguish an act of the national government from that of a state, without regard to the preferential or nonpreferential character of the national act on a matter respecting religion. In the floor debate, he used "national religion" to mean "that Congress should not establish a religion."[16] He discussed the establishment clause as if the word "national" still remained in it, yet he continued to interpret the meaning of the clause with the most extraordinary latitude.

As president, however, Madison had proclaimed several days for fast and thanksgiving, but he found extenuating circumstances in the fact that he was chief executive during the time a war was fought on national soil. And as he pointed out in his letter of 1822 to Livingston, although he "found it necessary" to deviate from "strict principle" by his proclamations, he "was always careful to make the Proclamation absolutely indiscriminate, and merely recommendatory; or, rather mere *designations* of a day on which all who thought proper might unite in consecrating it to religious purposes, according to their own faith and forms" (emphasis in original). Nevertheless, Madison could have followed the example of Jefferson, who, as president refused Congress's requests to declare days of fasting and thanksgiving. Moreover, as president, Madison approved of chaplains for the armed forces, an action that he later thought unconstitutional.[17]

In Madison's "Detached Memoranda," written after he retired from the presidency in 1817, he expressed concern that the "danger of silent accumulations & encroachments by Ecclesiastical Bodies have [*sic*] not sufficiently engaged attention in the U.S."[18] He asked, "Is the appoint-

16. *Annals*, 1:757.
17. Dreisbach, *Real Threat and Mere Shadow*, pp. 152–53.
18. Elizabeth Fleet, ed., "Madison's 'Detached Memoranda,'" *William and Mary Quarterly* 3 (1946): 554.

ment of Chaplains to the two houses of Congress consistent with the Constitution, and with the pure principle of religious freedom?" By way of answer he replied:

> in strictness the answer on both points must be in the negative. The Constitution of the U.S. forbids everything like an establishment of a *national* religion. The law appointing Chaplains establishes a religious worship for the national representatives, to be performed by Ministers of religion, elected by a majority of them; and these are to be paid out of the national taxes. Does not this involve the principle of a national establishment, applicable to a provision for a religious worship for the Constituent as well as of the representative Body, approved by the majority, and conducted by Ministers of religion paid by the entire nation?[19]

Madison continued: "The establishment of the chaplainship to Congress is a palpable violation of equal rights, as well as of Constitutional principles. . . . If Religion consists in voluntary acts of individuals, singly, or voluntarily associated, and it be proper that public functionaries, as well as their Constituents should discharge their religious duties, let them like their Constituents, do so at their own expense."[20] He classified chaplainships for the army and navy "in the same way," as forbidden "establishments" or an "establishment of a *national* religion."[21] Clearly a man who considered unconstitutional the use of public funds for the support of interfaith invocations and benedictions— and nothing could be more nonpreferential or lacking in exclusiveness—would also consider unconstitutional the use of public funds for any other purpose respecting religion. He warned against evil "lurking under plausible disguises, and growing up from small beginnings. Obsta principiis [resist the beginnings]."[22] The Constitution, he said, misquoting again, "forbids everything like an establishment of a *national* religion."[23] He included chaplains for Congress, military and

19. Ibid., p. 558; emphasis added.
20. Ibid., pp. 558–59.
21. Ibid., pp. 559–60; emphasis added.
22. Ibid., p. 558.
23. Ibid.; emphasis added.

naval chaplains, and presidential proclamations "recommending fasts & thanksgivings" as examples "of a *national* religion."[24] Rather than let these examples, which went beyond "the landmarks of power," have the effect of legitimate precedents, he said it was better to apply to them "the legal aphorism of de minimis non curat lex [the law does not bother with trifles]."[25]

Thus, the proposition that Madison meant merely a national church or no preference in the support of religion is groundless, as foolish perhaps as his proposition that the provision of military chaplains was like a national religion. The point, however, is that to Madison "a national religion" broadly covered as much as even the most trifling matters. Chief Justice Rehnquist built most of his opinion favoring the constitutionality of nonpreferential government aid to religion on the baseless reading he gave to "national religion," without considering or knowing that Madison believed that military chaplains or a fast day constituted a national religion.[26] Rehnquist merely read his own values into "national religion" (as did Madison). The views that Madison expressed in 1789 on establishments of religion conformed generally to his views, whether he thought in terms of a general assessment, a religious establishment, or a national religion. In each instance he wanted "perfect separation"[27] between government and religion.

In his "Detached Memoranda" Madison also stated that "Religious proclamations by the Executive recommending thanksgivings and fasts are shoots from the same root with the legislative acts reviewed [the chaplaincies]."[28] Madison made this remarkable judgment about so innocuous an act as a presidential recommendation for a day of thanksgiving, another extreme example of nonpreference on a matter respecting religion. He regarded such recommendations as violating the First Amendment: "They seem" he wrote, "to imply and certainly nourish the erronious [*sic*] idea of a *national* religion."[29]

24. Ibid., pp. 558–60; Madison's emphasis.
25. Ibid., p. 559.
26. *Wallace v. Jaffree*, 472 U.S. 38, 91–114 (1985).
27. Thomas Jefferson to Edward Livingston, July 10, 1822, in *Writings of Madison*, 9:100.
28. Fleet, ed., "Madison's 'Detached Memoranda,'" p. 560.
29. Ibid.; Madison's emphasis.

In the 1822 letter to Livingston, Madison warned that the danger of an "alliance or coalition between Government and Religion . . . cannot be too carefully guarded against. . . . Every new and successful example therefore of a *perfect separation* between ecclesiastical and civil matters is of importance . . . religion and Government will exist in greater purity, without [rather] than with the aid of Government."[30] His stress on a "perfect separation" appears also in his "Detached Memoranda," where he noted: "Strongly guarded as is the separation between Religion and Government in the Constitution of the United States the danger of encroachment by ecclesiastical Bodies, may be illustrated by precedents." One of his illustrations was the "attempt in Kentucky, for example, where it was proposed to exempt Houses of Worship from taxes."[31] Madison believed that any semblance of support to religion by government was unconstitutional. But Madison's "perfect separation" was less than perfect during his presidency, although he seems to have thought that his imperfections were excusable under the *de minimis* doctrine.

Among the evidence that nonpreferentialists have warped to prove that Madison "took the word 'establishment' to mean [only] a governmental religion such as a state church"[32] is Madison's statement at the Virginia ratifying convention of 1788: "Fortunately for this Commonwealth, a majority of the people are decidedly against *any exclusive establishment*—I believe it to be so in other states. *There is not a shadow of right in the general government to intermeddle with religion.* . . . The United States abound in such variety of sects, that it is a strong security against religious persecution, and it is sufficient to authorize a conclusion, that no one sect will ever be able to outnumber or depress the rest."[33] That a nonpreferentialist would italicize the second sentence as a revealing aid to his thesis passes belief. Those words prove that Madison opposed all government support of religion, because government has no power to legislate on the subject. But we are told that Madison simply opposed

30. Jefferson to Livingston, July 10, 1822, in *Writings of Madison*, 9:100–103.

31. Fleet, ed., "Madison's 'Detached Memoranda,' " p. 555.

32. Cord, *Separation of Church and State*, p. 10.

33. Elliot, ed., *Debates*, 3:330, as quoted in Cord, *Separation of Church and State*, p. 8; Cord's emphasis.

"raising one religion above the others."[34] The fact that Madison undoubtedly assailed an exclusive establishment does not prove that he equated every establishment with exclusivity. His statement must be understood in its context.

The immediately preceding speaker, Patrick Henry, had opposed ratification of the Constitution because, in part, it had no bill of rights to protect religious liberty. Madison reminded the delegates of some recent Virginia history, the attempt to enact a general assessment; he was making the then standard Federalist point that a bill of rights was not necessary and would not protect the people. He meant that, although Virginia's constitution of 1776 had a bill of rights that guaranteed the free exercise of religion, it did not secure religious liberty because it did not prevent the attempt to enact a general assessment and would not have prevented an exclusive establishment if one sect had dominated the state. Having a national bill of rights, he argued, would not defend liberty if a majority of the people were of one sect. The country enjoyed religious liberty because of "that multiplicity of sects which pervades America, and which is the best and only security for religious liberty in any society"; the existence of many prevented one from oppressing the others. Fortunately for Virginia, he continued, the people opposed an establishment, and the national government had no authority over religion.

Thus, Madison was not saying that he or the people of Virginia opposed *only* an exclusive establishment. He was saying, rather, that the worst fear, an exclusive establishment, would not materialize even if the proposed constitution had no bill of rights.

Some, however, have transmogrified Madison, turning that principled opponent of all financial assistance by government to religion into an advocate of such aid on condition that it be nonpreferential in nature. They argue that Madison opposed Virginia's general assessment bill only because it "placed Christianity in a preferred religious position."[35] They disagree with the conventional interpretation of Madison's "Memorial and Remonstrance," namely, that it shows that he called for the separation not merely of church and state but of

34. Cord, *Separation of Church and State*, p. 8.
35. Ibid., p. 20.

religion and government.[36] The conventional interpretation is the right one because Madison opposed all types of establishments on grounds of principle.

Madison's "Memorial and Remonstrance" certainly shows that he regarded the general assessment bill as an establishment of religion. He repeatedly referred to "the establishment proposed by the bill," "ecclesiastical establishment," "the establishment in question," "the proposed establishment," and so on.[37] The bill's supporters admitted that it was an establishment of religion, as its very name indicated: "A Bill Establishing a Provision for Teachers of the Christian Religion." In a letter to Monroe, Madison entitled it the "Bill for establishing the Christian Religion in this State."[38]

Proponents of the narrow interpretation emphasize that the bill provided for an exclusive establishment of one religion, Christianity, and therefore that Madison's opposition shows merely that he opposed only government support of one religion.[39] Presumably we are supposed to believe that if the bill taxed Jews for the support of a rabbi and Roman Catholics for the support of a priest, Madison would have supported it. But there were no rabbis or priests in Virginia and no synagogues or Catholic chapels either, although a few Jews and Catholics lived in Virginia, a very few. Religion in Virginia in 1784 was synonymous with Protestant Christianity. Moreover, the fact that the bill discriminated provided the basis of only one of the many reasons Madison opposed it.

Further, to depict the general assessment bill of 1784 as creating an exclusive establishment ignores the fact that it would have established all Christian churches in contrast to the situation before 1776, when the law established only the Church of England. Prerevolutionary law had created an exclusive establishment. To describe the 1784 proposal as exclusive mangles the meaning of the word "exclusive" as well as the

36. Berns, *First Amendment*, p. 9, correctly endorsed the conventional interpretation.

37. *Madison Papers*, 8:301–2.

38. James Madison to James Monroe, June 21, 1785, in ibid., 8:306.

39. Dreisbach, *Real Threat and Mere Shadow*, pp. 143–45; Cord, *Separation of Church and State*, p. 20; Malbin, *Religion and Politics*, p. 25.

history of an establishment of religion in Virginia. The Church of England had enjoyed an exclusive establishment; broadening the benefits of an establishment to include all churches ended the exclusive character of that establishment. In effect, the general assessment would have established every religious society in the state that had a meetinghouse and a clergyman.

Nevertheless, the bill did discriminate against non-Christians by purporting to benefit Christians only. Although Madison criticized it on grounds of religious "discrimination," he attacked it chiefly because it created an establishment of religion, not because it created a discriminatory establishment. Using every possible argument against the bill, however, Madison even found discriminatory a provision of the bill that was meant to be liberal. The bill taxed everyone for the support of a clergyman of the individual's choice, but because Quakers and Mennonites had no formal clergy, the bill provided that they could pay their taxes into a fund to be spent as they directed "to promote their particular mode of worship." In his "Memorial and Remonstrance," Madison converted that provision into the basis for an argument that the bill granted improper preference to those denominations, for they were not the only ones to oppose a "compulsory support of their Religions."[40]

That the bill discriminated was not, however, the main reason Madison attacked the bill. What kind of establishment the bill created did not matter to him, nor how inclusive or exclusive it was. He attacked the bill because as a matter of principle he opposed *any* kind of an establishment of religion. Had he opposed the bill only because it established the Christian religion exclusively, his arguments would have been directed, quite simply, to the reasons for amending the bill so as to cover all religions, including Judaism, Islam, Deism, Hinduism, and Zoroastrianism. He made no such argument. He opposed the bill in whole, not in part. Indeed, at only one point in his "Memorial and Remonstrance" did he mention that bill's exclusive character: "Who does not see that the same authority which can establish Christianity, in

---

40. For Madison on the discriminatory character of the bill, see his letter to Jefferson, Jan. 9, 1785, and his "Memorial and Remonstrance," in *Madison Papers*, 8:229, 300, respectively.

exclusion of all other Religions, may establish with the same ease any particular sect of Christians, in exclusion of all other Sects?"[41]

This sentence occurs, significantly, in the course of an argument in which Madison sought to convince his readers that the way to avoid the consequences of an infringement of liberty is to reject, on its first appearance, "the principle" that supports the infringement. The whole passage shows that Madison did not oppose the establishment because it was exclusively a Christian one. He opposed, rather, any government tax for religion because he feared a threat to liberty deriving from an unwarranted exercise of power in a domain forbidden to government.

That there can be no doubt of this is evident from Madison's fourteen other reasons for opposing the bill. Each was applicable to a bill supporting all religions or religion in general. The first of his fifteen arguments against the general assessment bill declared that the duty a person owes the Creator and the manner of discharging it must be voluntary, not coerced, and that religion is "wholly exempt" from the cognizance of government. Rhetorical questions about whether Madison was really an absolutist—would he have opposed a civil act against human sacrifice or polygamy?—are absurdly out of context. No answer to the question posed by nonpreferentialists alters the fact that Madison opposed all establishments, not just an establishment that favored Christianity over other religions. "Because if Religion be exempt from the authority of the Society at large [religion being a natural right], still less can it be subject to that of the Legislative Body" was Madison's second argument. The third was to "take alarm at the first experiment of our liberties" by "denying the principle" and thereby avoid the consequences of usurped power as well as entangling precedents.

Yet a scholar, having distorted one Madisonian argument after another, concluded: "In sum, only Madison's arguments against exclusive religious aid—in which he assailed the religious discriminatory Assessment Bill and the evils it was likely to produce—are germane in appraising Madison's attitude about the appropriate relationship between

---

41. "Memorial and Remonstrance," in ibid., 8:300; Irving Brant, *James Madison, The Nationalist, 1780–1787* (Indianapolis, 1948), p. 345.

Church and State."[42] The author of that absurd remark denied us the wonder of seeing how he could distort the meaning of the Virginia Statute for Religious Freedom, which Jefferson had drafted and whose passage Madison guided through the state legislature. That document, like Madison's "Memorial," also described freedom of religion as a natural right exempt from civil governance, contended that forcing people to support even the religion of their own persuasion was tyrannical and made the support of religion private and voluntary. It too expressed Madison's views.

Although the Reverend John Courtney Murray, S.J., did not approve of Madison's opinions, he granted the correctness of the statement that the "Memorial" discloses Madison's opposition to "every form and degree of official relation between religion and civil authority. For him religion was a wholly private matter beyond the scope of civil power either to restrain or support."[43] Father Murray added that the theme of the "Memorial" is that religion "must be absolutely free from governmental restriction and likewise *absolutely 'free' from governmental aid. . . .* For Madison, as for John Locke, his master, religion could not by law be made a concern of the commonwealth as such, deserving in any degree of public recognition or aid, for the essentially theological reason that religion is of its nature a personal, private, interior matter of the individual conscience, having no relevance to the public concerns of the state."[44]

In the same year as the "Memorial," 1785, Madison also expressed himself strongly against an abortive plan of the Continental Congress to set aside public land in each township in the western territories for the support of religion—any religion. To Monroe he wrote: "How a regulation, so unjust in itself, so foreign to the Authority of Cong[res]s . . . and smelling so strongly of an antiquated Bigotry, could have re-

42. Cord, *Separation of Church and State*, p. 23. For the "Memorial and Remonstrance," see *Madison Papers*, 8:298–314.

43. John Courtney Murray, "Law and Prepossessions," in *Law and Contemporary Problems* 14 (Winter 1949): 28, quoting J. Rutledge in the *Everson* case, 330 U.S. 1, 39–40 (1947).

44. Murray, "Law and Prepossessions," p. 29; emphasis added.

ceived the countenance of a Committee is truly a matter of astonishment."[45] Notwithstanding Madison's objections, Congress included in the Northwest Ordinance of 1787 a provision that schools should be encouraged because religion and morality, as well as knowledge, were necessary to good government.

In 1790, prior to the adoption of the Bill of Rights, Madison in Congress gave the following reason for omitting ministers from enumerated occupations in a census bill: "As to those who are employed in teaching and inculcating the duties of religion, there may be some indelicacy in singling them out, as the general government is proscribed from the interfering, in any manner whatever, in matters respecting religion; and it may be thought to do this, in ascertaining who, and who are not ministers of the gospel."[46] Surely one who opposed nonpreferential land grants for religious purposes and who objected to a federal census report of ministers cannot be regarded as an opponent of only that public aid to religion which failed to provide for non-Christians. Nor can he be regarded as a supporter of nonpreferential government aid to religion. Madison had such refined constitutional scruples on this matter that in his mature opinion he also regarded as unconstitutional such governmental, legal, or financial support to religion as presidential proclamations of Thanksgiving, tax exemptions for religious institutions, chaplains for Congress and the armed services, incorporation of churches by the federal government in the District of Columbia, and the grant of lands to a church of the land on which it was built.

In the First Congress Madison did not say that his proposed amendment should be construed as banning only preferential aid or an exclusive establishment. He was saying that, contrary to Anti-Federalist warnings, the government under the Constitution would not adopt an exclusive establishment, because it had no power whatsoever over the subject of religion. Anyone who maintains that Madison in 1789 "believed Congress was being denied the power to 'establish a national

45. James Madison to James Monroe, May 29, 1785, in *Madison Papers*, 8:286; see also Brant, *The Nationalist*, p. 353.

46. Quoted in Irving Brant, *James Madison, Father of the Constitution* (Indianapolis, 1950), p. 272.

religion' *not religion*"[47] seems to say that Madison believed that Congress could establish religions but not religion. This peculiarly fatuous view locks into the nonpreferential thesis the notion that, because the ban on establishments reached only preferential supports, the government could constitutionally support all religions without preference to any. Thus, when Walter Berns, an eminent constitutional scholar, examined the Senate's recommended draft of the establishment clause before the joint conference committee altered it, he said that its language would have "permitted federal aid to religion on a nondiscriminatory basis."[48] And when Madison made the remark about a ban on "a national religion," Berns took note of Madison's willingness to accommodate those who wanted "nondiscriminatory assistance to religion."[49] Similarly, Chief Justice Rehnquist has declared that "the Establishment Clause did not require government neutrality between religion and irreligion nor did it prohibit the Federal Government from providing nondiscriminatory aid to religion."[50] But *no one* in the debate on the proposal that became the First Amendment, least of all Madison, recommended any language that would empower the government to take any positive action favoring religion. Madison sought to accommodate only one group, those who wanted reassurance that the government would not legislate on religious matters. The one thing a ban on a national religion did not mean to him was the implicit power for the United States to foster religion or even accommodate its needs on a nonpreferential basis.

During the debate, Madison expressly disclaimed taking any position on the question whether an amendment on the matter was needed. When Roger Sherman declared that an amendment was "altogether unnecessary" because Congress had no power "to make religious establishments," Daniel Carroll replied that an amendment on the subject would "conciliate the minds of the people to the Government," and Madison agreed with Carroll. Although Madison would not say

47. Cord, *Separation of Church and State*, p. 11; Cord's emphasis.
48. Berns, *First Amendment*, p. 7.
49. Ibid., p. 9.
50. *Wallace v. Jaffree*, 472 U.S. 38, 106 (1985).

whether an amendment was necessary, he reminded the House that some state conventions had expressed the fear that Congress might establish a national religion by the exercise of a power under the necessary and proper clause. In his great speech of June 8, 1789, when he urged the House to consider amendments to protect "the great rights of mankind,"[51] he repeated seven times that amendments, whether needed or not, would allay public fears. People feared that Congress would establish a national religion, and he had introduced an amendment calculated to appease them.

Madison mentioned that some people feared the dominance of one sect or the possibility that two might combine to establish a religion to which others might have to conform.[52] Anti-Federalists had persistently expressed exaggerated fears about the way the new government would abuse its powers if the Constitution were ratified. In North Carolina, for example, Henry Abbot frenetically predicted, in his state's ratifying convention, that the treaty power would be used to make Roman Catholicism the established religion of the country,[53] and Major Lusk warned the Massachusetts ratifying convention that "Popery and the Inquisition may be established in America."[54] In his own ratifying convention, Madison had heard Patrick Henry prophesy that the United States would "extort confession by torture," perpetuate "the most tyrannical and oppressive deeds," and send taxgatherers into everybody's home to "ransack, and measure, every thing you eat, drink, and wear."[55] Madison and the Federalists could not swing sufficient votes to secure Virginia's ratification of the Constitution without first accepting recommendations for amendments submitted by Henry. His amendments included a proposed bill of rights, one provision of which declared that "no particular religious sect or society ought to be favored or established by law, in preference to others." After perfunctory

51. "Amendments to the Constitution," *Madison Papers*, 12:198; the speech is on pp. 197–209.

52. See above, chap. 5, debate of Aug. 15, 1789.

53. Elliot, ed., *Debates*, 4:192.

54. Ibid., 2:148.

55. Ibid., 3:436, 448–49.

endorsement by a committee on amendments, the state convention accepted all of Henry's proposals. That was the price of ratification by Virginia.[56]

Madison, therefore, did not express his personal opinion on how best to frame an amendment. His record on the point was clear: Congress had no power to meddle with or legislate on religion, so there was no need to limit nonexistent power. But he felt obligated to make an effort, concerning establishments of religion, to satisfy popular demand for something explicit on that subject as well as on religious freedom. His motives were more political than we like to recognize. Understandably, we exalt the Bill of Rights, which gives constitutional recognition to precious freedoms, and we assume that its framers were the wise statesmen who pondered just the right phraseology to make every provision possess a resonance and rightness for the ages. In fact they were more interested in discussing tonnage duties, and their debate was brief, listless, and unclear. Moreover, the Anti-Federalists, knowing that the adoption of a bill of rights would sink their movement for a second convention and make unlikely the amendments they really wanted, amendments that would cripple the powers of the national government, sought to scuttle Madison's proposals. Failing that, they tried delaying tactics, depreciated the importance of the very protections of individual liberty that they had formerly demanded as a guarantee against impending tyranny, and then tried to weaken the provisions.[57] Madison understood what the Anti-Federalists were up to and would not be put off. Privately, however, he said he was engaged in "the nauseous project of amendments." Among the reasons he gave for persisting in a policy that even some members of his own party opposed was his belief that the Anti-Federalists would make political capital out of a failure of Congress to propose amendments in the nature of a bill of rights. Moreover, he declared, the amendments "will kill the opposition everywhere, and by putting an end to disaffection to

56. Ibid., 3:593, 659.

57. Leonard W. Levy, "Bill of Rights," in *Encyclopedia of American Political History*, edited by Jack Greene, 3 vols. (New York, 1984), 1:104–25; or Levy, *Constitutional Opinions* (New York, 1986), pp. 105–34.

the Government itself, enable the administration to venture on measures not otherwise safe."[58]

From a constitutional standpoint, Madison believed that the entire enterprise was unnecessary; from a political standpoint, however, the stakes were high. He meant to give the people what they seemed to want, guarantees that nightmares pictured by demagogues would not become real. Politics had demanded that the ratificationist forces swallow Henry's recommended amendments in Virginia in return for crucial votes. Those amendments included some that Federalists vehemently opposed, such as the requirement of a two-thirds majority by Congress for the enactment of laws regulating commerce. Conversely, George Mason, who made much, publicly, of the absence of a bill of rights in the Constitution, had said at the Constitutional Convention that he would rather cut off his right hand than sign the Constitution without that two-thirds provision.[59] Henry's phrasing for the Virginia convention's recommendation against preferred sects ignored the language of Virginia's Statute of Religious Liberty, which went much further; Madison and the ratificationists did not take the no-preference language seriously as a reflection of Virginia's opinion, but it was harmless: who, after all, favored a preferential establishment? Madison, moreover, did not use the Virginia recommendation or the language of no preference when he made the proposal that became the establishment clause.

In any case, Virginia's nonpreferential language could not possibly have implied that Patrick Henry and his Anti-Federalist forces meant to empower Congress to assist or encourage religion. They sought to cripple the national government in every possible way, not to augment its constitutional authority on a subject reserved for state control. Least of all did they mean to authorize Congress to exercise its tax power,

58. James Madison to Richard Peters, Aug. 19, 1789, in *Madison Papers*, 12:346–47.

59. See Max Farrand, ed., *The Records of the Federal Convention*, 3 vols. (New York, 1911), 2:479, for the statement of Aug. 31, 1787, about his right hand, and 2:640, for the statement of Sept. 12 that congressional control over commerce by majority vote constituted "an insuperable objection."

which they feared and deplored, in order to enact anything like a nationwide general assessment or general establishment.

No credence can be attributed to the view of the scholar Charles Antieau, who concluded from a few state recommendations couched in nonpreferential language that the public demanded government aid to religion without preference.[60] "It is revealing," he added, "to note that in every state constitution in force between 1776 and 1789 where 'establishment' was mentioned, it was equated or used in conjunction with 'preference.'"[61] He meant, of course, that nonpreferential support was not considered to be an establishment; but the Massachusetts experience destroys that point.

Indeed the basic laws of New Hampshire, Vermont, Maryland, Georgia, South Carolina, and even Connecticut, all of which lawfully permitted multiple establishments, as did Massachusetts, mentioned no favored church. In the classic sense of an establishment of religion, one denomination received preference, not Christianity or Protestantism. There is no doubt whatever that establishments of religion existed in four New England states, actually as well as theoretically. They disprove the nonpreferentialist interpretation that the absence of preference in government aid to religion denotes the absence of an establishment.

Interestingly, when Antieau named the six states that supposedly mentioned "establishment" in connection with the idea of nonpreference, the five besides Massachusetts were Pennsylvania, New Jersey, North Carolina, Delaware, and New York.[62] That these were the five is interesting because none of them maintained an establishment after 1776, and yet all five, including the three that never had an establishment at any time in their histories, placed the support of religion on a purely private basis. In other words, they believed that a constitutional provision ensuring no subordination of one sect to another, or providing no preference of one over another, banned government aid to religion. Opponents of government aid to religion, especially of tax

60. Antieau, Downey, and Roberts, *Freedom from Federal Establishment*, p. 132.
61. Ibid.
62. Ibid., pp. 132–33.

support for religion, employed the language of no preference to achieve their objective of keeping religion and government in separate universes. According to Thomas Curry, the probable reason for such usage is that the classical concept of an establishment as a state church continued to dominate the American image of an establishment of religion. Apart from the fact that the image and the reality seemed so disparate, there is no explaining the fact that opponents of government aid, even nonpreferential aid, did not recommend or use language condemning nonpreferential aid. Condemning preferential aid and meaning a condemnation of even nonpreferential aid seems clumsy, perverse, and unlikely. Yet the fact is that the principle of voluntarism in the support of religion was most firmly entrenched for the longest time in Rhode Island, which recommended an amendment against government preference of one religion over another. Rhode Island meant to reaffirm its own principle of voluntarism and opposed any extension of national powers.[63]

The case of John Leland is similar to that of Rhode Island. A Baptist preacher who influenced James Madison, Leland advocated a radical separation of government and religion.[64] He rejected the commonly accepted belief that America was a Christian nation, and he contended that any sort of establishment of Christianity, including all state establishments, were "all of them, Anti-Christocracies." Legislative chaplaincies, to Leland, constituted establishments of religion. He favored equality in every sense for Deists, pagans, atheists, Jews, Turks, and Catholics. He advocated their right to hold public office and censured disqualifying test oaths as instruments of establishments. Above all, Leland insisted that "religion is a matter between God and individuals," not subject to the jurisdiction of government.[65]

The point is that Leland would have been the last person to approve

63. Thomas Curry, *The First Freedoms* (New York, 1986), pp. 192, 209–12.

64. L. H. Butterfield, *Elder John Leland, Jeffersonian Itinerant* (Worcester, Mass., 1953); William G. McLoughlin, *New England Dissent, 1630–1833: The Baptists and the Separation of Church and State*, 2 vols. (Cambridge, Mass., 1971), 2:928–35.

65. *The Writings of John Leland*, edited by L. F. Greene (reprint, New York, 1969), pp. 181, 184, 187, 191, 221, 281, 293.

of government aid to religion. Under no circumstances could he have implied that by his opposition to preferential aid he favored government assistance to religion on a nonpreferential basis. In 1794 he proposed, in the following language, an amendment to the Massachusetts constitution that he thought would have ended that state's nonpreferential establishment:

> To prevent the evils that have heretofore been occasioned in the world by religious establishments, and to keep up the proper distinction between religion and politics, no religious test shall ever be requested as a qualification of any officer, in any department of this government; neither shall the legislature, under this constitution, ever establish any religion by law, give any one sect a preference to another, or force any man in the commonwealth to part with his property for the support of religious worship, or the maintenance of ministers of the gospel.[66]

The facts show that the treasured principle of nonpreference, which nonpreferentialists converted wrongly into an allowance of government aid on an impartial basis, is, in effect, irrelevant. States with no history of establishments (Rhode Island, Pennsylvania, Delaware, and New Jersey) endorsed the no-preference principle yet kept religion privately supported, while Massachusetts, New Hampshire, and Vermont endorsed the same principle yet maintained tax-supported compulsory public worship. Or take Rhode Island and Connecticut, the two states that had no written constitutions. After 1784 the laws of neither provided preference, yet one always had an establishment and one never did.

Two hundred years ago, when the United States was substantially a nation of Protestants and the links between government and religion were close in many ways, people did not quibble as we do about whether the integrity of the principle of separation depended on the use of the definite or the indefinite article or whether the law provided for absolutist language or language that by logical deduction allowed for important exceptions. The significant case of Isaac Backus, the great Baptist leader of Massachusetts, illustrates that fact. It has been

66. Ibid., p. 229.

said of him that "no individual in America since Roger Williams stands out so preeminently as the champion of religious liberty."[67] Backus, a veteran of the struggle against the establishment provision of the Massachusetts constitution of 1780, was a member of the Massachusetts ratifying convention in 1788 and supported ratification of the Constitution secure in the knowledge that the United States had no power to legislate on the subject of religion. In his *History of New England, with Particular Reference to the Denomination of Christians Called Baptists* (3 vols., 1777–96) and in the later one-volume abridgment (1804), he misquoted the First Amendment entirely as stating the following: "Congress shall make no law, establishing articles of faith, or a mode of worship, or prohibiting the free exercise of religion."[68] The point is that he regarded such language, which the Senate had adopted at one point, as sufficient to condemn the establishments of religion in Massachusetts and Connecticut.[69] Nonpreferentialists would construe that language as the narrowest proposed during the entire legislative history of the First Amendment, logically allowing impartial government aid to religion of the sort that Backus opposed. Backus was misinformed but not naive; he was a veteran of the separationists' campaign to make the support of religion purely voluntary. As Thomas Curry noted, in his analysis of the original meaning of the establishment clause, "Eighteenth-century American history offers abundant examples of writers using the concept of preference, when, in fact, they were referring to a ban on all government assistance to religion."[70]

Curry also observed that the Senate debate in its historical context "represented no sharply divided opinions about the nature of the amendment on religion. Senators who believed that religion should be supported voluntarily could subscribe to the formula banning an establishment of 'One Religious Sect or Society in preference to others' as readily as their colleagues, especially from New England, who believed

---

67. *Dictionary of American Biography*, 1:470. William G. McLoughlin, *Isaac Backus and the American Pietistic Tradition* (Boston, 1967), and McLoughlin, *New England Dissent*, are the best works on Backus.

68. Quoted in McLoughlin, *New England Dissent*, 2:783.

69. Ibid., 2:783–84.

70. Curry, *First Freedoms*, p. 211.

that the states should make provisions for the support of religion." Senators from states whose constitutions had separated government and religion and left the support of religion to private conscience, Curry concluded, may well have preferred to use the no-preference language of those constitutions, just as New Englanders may have wanted the terminology most familiar to them, proscribing articles of faith or modes of worship.[71]

Curry observed that legislators in several states that opposed a preference for one religion did not propose assistance to all, and their constitutions "clearly banned any state support for religion whatsoever. On the other hand, proponents of a general assessment never viewed a ban on preferential establishments as enabling legislation for their cause." In no instance, he added, did such people claim that no preference could justify the establishment of several or all religions rather than one. "Opponents of tax support for religion," Curry showed, "never saw in the 'no subordination of any one sect' clause a threat to their own stance." Staunch separationists on matters of government-aided religion "not only avoided criticizing the provision, but clearly approved of it."[72] Massachusetts towns opposing the establishment article of the proposed state constitution of 1780 endorsed the nonpreferential principle on the supposition that it banned all establishments of religion.[73] Accordingly, as Curry concluded, although that principle denying preference "appears when lifted out of its historical context to favor or permit a broad involvement of government with religion, [it] meant quite the opposite in its time. Those most against any state support for religion used language prohibiting preferential establishment to express a negation of all state favors or financial assistance to churches."[74]

The debate in both houses of Congress revealed, according to Curry, "not a clash between parties arguing for a 'broad' or 'narrow' inter-

71. Curry, "First Freedoms" (Ph.D diss., Claremont Graduate School, 1983), p. 829. See also Curry, *First Freedoms*, p. 214.

72. Curry, "First Freedoms," pp. 649–50. See also Curry, *First Freedoms*, p. 213.

73. See above, chap. 2, note 8 and related text.

74. Curry, "First Freedoms," p. 651; see also pp. 783–84.

pretation or between those who wished to give the federal government more or less power in religious matters. It represented rather a discussion about how to state the common agreement that the government had no authority in religious matters."[75] Of course, the state governments had authority over religious matters, but not one had a constitution or law that embodied the narrow interpretation. Right as Curry is that no one in Congress wished to vest in the national government an authority over religion, the chief fact remains that the language employed by those favoring a narrow interpretation was defeated, allowing no basis for nonpreferentialism in the text of the Constitution.

Congress considered and rejected the phraseology that nonpreferentialists emphasize as indicative of narrow interpretation. The House rejected the Senate's version, showing that the House under no circumstances can be understood as having framed an amendment that merely banned preference. The Senate, having accepted a phrasing that lends itself to the narrow interpretation (when abstracted from its historical context), abandoned it in the face of uncompromising opposition from the House. When the amendment emerged from the joint conference committee and received approbation from both chambers, it meant something broader than no preference. And, however it was phrased, it made an exception to a power that did not exist. Construing the establishment clause as the nonpreferentialists do amends it by adding the word "exclusive," which is not there, so that it reads: Congress shall make no law respecting an exclusive establishment of religion. Awed stupefaction is an appropriate response to the nonpreferentialists' achievement in metamorphosing the clause into a source of positive power.

Black magic—not historical evidence, grammatical analysis, or logical deductions—black magic and only that can turn the First Amendment into a repository of government power. Plainly it limits power. The fact that Justices William Rehnquist, Antonin Scalia, and Anthony Kennedy as well as outstanding constitutional scholars like Charles Antieau, Walter Berns, or Daniel Dreisbach could even think that the First Amendment permits government aids to religion shows how desperately unable they were to control their policy preferences, which

75. Curry, *First Freedoms*, p. 215.

they read back into the past and into the words of the amendment.[76]
Antieau sought to avoid dogmatism when he declared that all historical
interpretations of the establishment clause seem reasonable and that all
are "conjectural."[77] Some interpretations, however, are more reasonable than others and less conjectural.

Indeed, it is a fact, not an interpretation, that the unamended Constitution vests no power over religion and that the First Amendment
vests no power whatever. It is a fact that the framers of the Constitution insisted that no limitations on the government's power over religion were necessary, because the government possessed only delegated
authority, plus the authority necessary to execute the delegated powers;
under no circumstances, argued the framers, could the government
legislate on the subject of religion. They believed that nonexistent powers could not be exercised or abused, thus making all provisions against
such a possibility superfluous. They believed that no need existed to
declare that things shall not be done which there is no power to do.[78]
They believed that the government, having no authority over religion,
was powerless, therefore, even if the First Amendment never existed,
to enact laws benefiting religion, with or without preference.

When introducing the amendments that became the Bill of Rights,
Madison explicitly said that the "great object" was to "limit and qualify
the powers of government" to ensure that powers granted could not be
exercised in forbidden fields such as religion.[79] He told Jefferson that a
Bill of Rights should be "so framed as not to imply powers not meant
to be included in the enumeration."[80] To argue, as the nonpreferentialists do, that the establishment clause should be construed to permit
nondiscriminatory aid to religion leads to the impossible conclusion
that the First Amendment *added* to the powers of Congress even
though it was framed to restrict Congress. It is not only an impossible
conclusion; it is ridiculous. Not one state would have ratified such an

76. Antieau, Downey, and Roberts, *Freedom from Federal Establishment*, pp.
160–63, 208; Berns, *First Amendment*, pp. 7, 9.
77. Antieau, Downey, and Roberts, *Freedom from Federal Establishment*, p. 142.
78. *The Federalist*, no. 84.
79. "Amendments to the Constitution," *Madison Papers*, 12:204, June 8, 1789.
80. James Madison to Thomas Jefferson, Oct. 17, 1788, in ibid., 11:297.

enhancement of national authority, especially if it increased the tax power. The nonpreferentialists' feat of transforming the words "Congress shall make no law" into an augmentation of power vindicates the prophecy of Federalist leaders who feared that, in Madison's words, "if an enumeration be made of our rights, will it not be implied, that everything omitted, is given to the general government?"[81]

Citing Justice Joseph Story's *Commentaries on the Constitution* is fashionable among the nonpreferentialists who think that his authority is on their side.[82] For example, Robert Cord invokes Story as part of his evidence that the First Amendment was not meant to "preclude Federal governmental aid to religion when it was provided on a nondiscriminatory basis."[83] Story did state that "Christianity ought to receive encouragement from the [national] State," but he did not mention which provision of the Constitution authorized that encouragement. In fact, Cord also quoted him as saying that "it was deemed advisable to exclude from the national government all power to act upon the subject. . . . Thus the whole power over the subject of religion is left exclusively to the State governments."[84] Cord also quoted Madison as saying that the national government had not the shadow of a power to meddle with religion, and Cord himself declared that "the First Amendment originally left the entire issue of governmental involvement with religion to the States."[85]

What then is the source of the government's authority to provide nonpreferential aid to religion? The nonpreferentialists, who tend to be conservatives, surely do not believe that the government can do whatever is not expressly prohibited to it; on the contrary, it should do only that which is enumerated or necessary to carry out delegated powers. It may benefit religion incidentally by the legitimate exercise of its powers, because a general enactment might apply to religious institutions.

81. Elliot, ed., *Debates*, 3:620.

82. Cord, *Separation of Church and State*, pp. 12–15; McClellan, "The Making and the Unmaking," p. 295; Berns, *First Amendment*, pp. 59–60, 71; Antieau, Downey, and Roberts, *Freedom from Federal Establishment*, p. 160.

83. Cord, *Separation of Church and State*, p. 15.

84. Ibid., quoting *Commentaries on the Constitution*, secs. 1874, 1879.

85. Ibid., p. 14.

The government might, for example, make grants to all nonprofit institutions if the grants are for secular services such as those provided by hospitals. Government may not use religious affiliation as a basis for the grants nor attempt to promote religion or aid a pervasively sectarian institution, but it may assist all hospitals, or orphanages, or colleges. In doing so, it is not exercising power over religion.

Nonpreferentialists show little real commitment to liberty, however, except rhetorically, so long as they insist on forcing religion and aid to religion on others, not just on those who do not want either but also on those who have conscientious objections. Those who believe in the sovereignty of private choice respecting religious matters rightfully resent coercion. The conservatism of the nonpreferentialists seems not to extend beyond matters involving the economy; they profess to favor minimalist government, keeping government off the backs of citizens, and deregulation wherever possible. In matters of religion, however, they are maximalist, eschewing laissez-faire and forcing the government on our backs.

Dean M. Kelley of the National Council of Churches has insightfully observed that the proponents of free enterprise in economics want to eradicate free enterprise in religion by having the government exercise an ever increasing role in "sponsoring, regulating, subsidizing, and assisting the people's religious activities." Kelley sees the establishment clause as "the perfect counterpart of the principle of 'free competition': the private parties in religion are to prosper or decline according to their own merits in the free marketplace . . . without governmental 'assistance,' restriction, regulation or interference."[86] The best way to help religion is "to *leave it alone.*" "For government even to try to help religion is to hinder it," according to Kelley, who for religious reasons opposes religious exercises in the public schools, municipal religious displays, and legislative chaplains. He properly points out that far from "being welcomed as laudable accommodations to the religious needs of the people, these practices should be rejected as state proprietor-

---

86. Dean M. Kelley, "Free Enterprise in Religion, or How the Constitution Protects Religion and Religious Freedom," in *How Does the Constitution Secure Religious Freedom?*, edited by Robert A. Goldwin and Art Kaufman (Washington, D.C., 1986), pp. 11–12.

ships in religion—*prima facie* violations of the principle of free enterprise in the realm of religion."[87]

Nonpreferentialists seem to have no historical memory. They write about the establishment clause as if it were an enemy of religion rather than religion's bulwark, and they convert the clause into an antithesis of religious liberty, when in fact it is an additional guarantor of the rights of conscience. As the Presbyterian minister of South Carolina declared in 1777, "All establishments . . . are an infringement of religious liberty."[88] The establishment clause, contrary to what the nonpreferentialists would have us believe, is a legacy not of Deists but of profoundly believing Christians who understood that religion should not be state-supported "for the essentially theological reason that religion is of its nature a personal, private interior matter of the individual conscience, having no relevance to the public concerns of the state."[89]

Nonpreferentialism, unfortunately, is but a pose for those who think that religion needs to be patronized and promoted by government. When they speak of nonpreferential aid, they speak euphemistically as if they are not partisan. In fact they really are preferentialists. Being on the side of the angels by preferring religion over irreligion, a nonpreferential boast, is not the issue. The issue, rather, is whether religion needs the state, whether pious people require Caesar's helping hand to serve God, and whether the rights of conscience thrive best when left alone. Nonpreferentialists prefer government sponsorship and subsidy of religion rather than allowing it to compete on its merits against irreligion and indifference. They prefer government nurture of religion because they mistakenly dread government neutrality as too risky, and so they condemn it as hostility. They prefer what they call, again euphemistically, accommodation. They reject the Madisonian view, which was actually no different from a conventional evangelical view, that religion will exist in greater purity without the aid of government. That was once a widespread religious belief. Nonpreferentialists prefer, however, to turn the clock back to the time when religion did not have to

---

87. Ibid., p. 19.

88. Newton B. Jones, ed., "Writings of the Reverend William Tennent, 1740–1777," *South Carolina Historical Magazine* 61 (1960): 197.

89. Murray, "Law and Prepossessions," p. 29.

rely on private, voluntary support. For them the golden age ended when Massachusetts, the last state to do so, disestablished its public support of religion and no longer required every citizen to support the religion of his or her choice.

In the opinion of former attorney general Edwin Meese, "one of the founding principles" was that "it was an unfair burden for people of one religion to have to bear, by their taxes, the cost of another religion to which they did not personally subscribe."[90] That misstates the founding principle. It was, rather, the one subscribed to by Jefferson, Madison, and Christian evangelists, namely, that to require people to support even the religion of their choice denied them their freedom of choice and their right to religious liberty; moreover such a requirement violated the wall of separation between government and religion by intruding government into a realm of sacred privacy.[91]

90. Meese, "Address before the Christian Legal Society," pp. 4–5.

91. Jefferson said so in his Virginia Statute of Religious Freedom, Madison in his "Memorial and Remonstrance" (both cited in chap. 2), and the fundamentalists in "Religious Petitions Presented to the General Assembly of Virginia, 1774–1802," Remonstrance of the Committees of the Several Baptist Associations in Virginia Assembled in Powhatan County, Virginia, Aug. 13, 1785, discussed in chap. 3 above.

7

The Supreme Court and the Clause: Judicial Tests and Aids to Parochial Schools

The First Amendment bans laws respecting an establishment of religion. Most of the framers of that amendment very probably meant that government should not promote, sponsor, or subsidize religion because it is best left to private voluntary support for the sake of religion itself as well as for government, and above all for the sake of the individual. Some of the framers undoubtedly believed that government should maintain a close relationship with religion, that is, with Protestantism, and that people should support taxes for the benefit of their own churches and ministers. The framers who came from Massachusetts and Connecticut certainly believed this, as did the representatives of New Hampshire, but New Hampshire was the only one of these New England states that ratified the First Amendment. Of the eleven states that ratified the First Amendment, New Hampshire and Vermont were probably the only ones in which a majority of the people believed that the government should support religion. In all the other ratifying states, a majority very probably opposed such support. But whether those who framed and ratified the First Amendment believed in government aid to religion or in its private voluntary support, the fact is that no framer believed that the United States had or should have power to legislate on the subject of religion, and no state supported that power either.

Those who framed and ratified the First Amendment meant that the establishment clause, like the rest of the Bill of Rights, should apply to the national government only. After all, the First Amendment explicitly levies a ban on Congress, in contrast to the later Fourteenth Amendment, which expressly limits the states. James Madison in 1789 proposed an amendment to the Constitution that prohibited the states from violating certain rights, including freedom of religion. Had that amendment been adopted, the federal courts could easily have construed it to prohibit the states from maintaining establishments of religion. Except, perhaps, for Congregational New England, most of the nation believed that an establishment of religion violated religious liberty.[1] The House approved of Madison's proposal, but the Senate voted it down. The fact that Congress considered an amendment limiting the states shows that the establishment clause, which limited Congress, could not have been meant to apply to the states. The fact that Congress considered and rejected a prohibition on the states showed, further, that so far as the U.S. Constitution was concerned, the states were free to re-create the Inquisition or to erect and maintain exclusive establishments of religion, at least until ratification of the Fourteenth Amendment in 1868.[2]

According to the Fourteenth Amendment, no state may deprive any

---

1. Thomas Curry, *The First Freedoms* (New York, 1986), pp. 204–5.

2. *Barron v. Baltimore*, 7 Peters (U.S.) 243 (1833), and *Permoli v. New Orleans*, 3 Howard (U.S.) 589 (1845).

person of liberty without due process of law. Is a state law respecting an establishment of religion a deprivation of liberty? Does the word "liberty" include within its meaning a right to be free from a law respecting an establishment of religion? There is a difference between the intent of the amendment's framers and the language that they used. The preponderance of evidence suggests that the framers of the Fourteenth Amendment intended its provisions neither to incorporate any part of the Bill of Rights nor to impose on the states the same limitations previously imposed on the United States only.[3] The Blaine Amendment of 1875 is proof that the establishment clause had not been incorporated in the Fourteenth Amendment. James G. Blaine proposed in 1875 an amendment to the Constitution providing that "No state shall make any law respecting an establishment of religion, or prohibiting the free exercise thereof. . . ." The proposal itself as well as comments made during the debates demonstrated without doubt that the framers of the Fourteenth had not meant to apply the establishment clause against the states. The amendment was defeated, although an overwhelming majority of Congress favored a public school system severed from religion. Congress required new states thereafter to agree that their public schools should be open to all children "free from sectarian control."[4]

Despite the defeat of the Blaine Amendment, the language of the Fourteenth Amendment—no state denials of liberty—allowed for the possibility that the Constitution prevented the states, as well as the United States, from violating the First Amendment. And in time the Supreme Court so held. A rule of constitutional interpretation known as the "incorporation doctrine" posits that the Fourteenth Amendment incorporates the rights protected by the First Amendment.

Does it matter that the framers of the Fourteenth Amendment did not intend that any part of it should incorporate provisions of the Bill

3. Leonard W. Levy, ed., *The Fourteenth Amendment and the Bill of Rights: The Incorporation Theory* (New York, 1970), pp. vii–xxv. But see Michael Kent Curtis, *No State Shall Abridge: The Fourteenth Amendment and the Bill of Rights* (Durham, N.C., 1986).

4. *Congressional Record*, 44th Cong., 1st sess., 4 (pt. 1) :5580; Anson Phelps Stokes, *Church and State in the United States*, 3 vols. (New York, 1950), 2:68–70.

of Rights generally or the establishment clause in particular? The amendment was adopted to protect the rights of black Americans, but its language does not refer to race. Accordingly, its principles have properly extended to protect other races, women, aliens, and other persons not meant originally to benefit from its provisions. The Constitution is not a static document whose meaning is fixed timelessly. So long as the Court relies on the text itself and the principles and purposes embodied in the text, the Constitution can legitimately grow in meaning, like Magna Carta.

Magna Carta, the foundation of English personal liberties, was originally a reactionary document whose purpose was to protect the feudal barons who framed it. But they could not control its evolution, and it eventually came to signify many things not in it and that were not intended. As Magna Carta approaches its 800th anniversary, it stands for government by contract of the people, for fundamental law, for the rule of law, for no taxation without representation, for due process of law, for habeas corpus, for equality before the law, for representative government, for trial by jury and a cluster of the rights of the criminally accused. No one cares, or should, that the original document signifies none of this.

The Constitution, which serves a nation whose history had made it increasingly democratic and heterogeneous, is equally dynamic. That the Fourteenth Amendment did not originally include the incorporation doctrine is an antiquarian point. In 1940, when the Supreme Court incorporated the free-exercise clause into the Fourteenth Amendment, the Court assumed that the establishment clause imposed upon the states the same restraints as upon the United States.[5] In the 1947 *Everson* case that *obiter dictum* became a holding of constitutional law. The Court unanimously agreed that the Fourteenth Amendment incorporated the establishment clause. Consequently the principle embodied in the First Amendment separated government and religion throughout the land, outlawing government support of religion, or, rather, outlawing laws respecting an establishment of religion.[6] But what con-

5. *Cantwell v. Connecticut*, 310 U.S. 296, 303–4 (1940).
6. *Everson v. Board of Education*, 330 U.S. 1, 31–32 (1947).

stitutes an establishment or prohibited support, according to the Supreme Court?

In the *Everson* case the court laid down principles for interpreting the establishment clause that it has never abandoned, despite its frequently perplexing application of those principles. One such principle is that an establishment of religion includes "aid to all religions" as well as aid to just one in preference to others; another principle is that no tax in any amount can be used "to support any religious activities or institutions." These principles express, in part, the broad interpretation of what the framers of the First Amendment intended by the establishment clause. Justice Hugo L. Black, speaking for the majority in *Everson*, stated the broad interpretation as follows:

> The "establishment of religion" clause of the First Amendment means at least this: Neither a state nor the Federal Government can set up a church. Neither can pass laws which aid one religion, aid all religions, or prefer one religion over another. Neither can force nor influence a person to go to or to remain away from church against his will or force him to profess a belief or disbelief in any religion. No person can be punished for entertaining or professing religious beliefs or disbeliefs, for church attendance or nonattendance. No tax in any amount, large or small, can be levied to support any religious activities or institutions, whatever they may be called, or whatever form they may adopt to teach or practice religion. Neither a state nor the Federal Government can, openly or secretly, participate in the affairs of any religious organizations or groups and vice versa. In the words of Jefferson, the clause against establishment of religion by laws was intended to erect a "wall of separation between Church and State."[7]

The Court has frequently quoted these words with approval, as recently as 1992.[8]

The dissenting justices in the *Everson* case, while disagreeing with the majority on the question of whether the "wall of separation" had in fact been breached by the practice at issue, concurred with the majority on

---

7. Ibid., p. 15.
8. *Lee v. Weisman*, 112 S.Ct. 2649, 2662 (1992).

the historical question of the intentions of the framers and the meaning of the establishment clause. The opinion of Justice Wiley B. Rutledge, which all the dissenting justices endorsed, declared: "The Amendment's purpose was not to strike merely at the official establishment of a single sect, creed or religion, outlawing only a formal relation such as had prevailed in England and some of the colonies. Necessarily it was to uproot all such relationships." Rutledge went on to say, "But the object was broader than separating church and state in this narrow sense. It was to create a complete and permanent separation of the spheres of religious activity and civil authority by comprehensively forbidding every form of public aid or support for religion."[9]

Thus the heart of this broad interpretation, endorsed by the entire *Everson* Court, is that the First Amendment does not permit government aid even if impartially and equitably administered to all religious groups.

The second or narrow interpretation of the clause, which a majority of the recent Court supported (Chief Justice Rehnquist and Justices Byron R. White, Anthony Kennedy, Antonin Scalia, and Clarence Thomas), is that of nonpreferentialism or accommodation to religion. The appointment of Justice Ruth Bader Ginsburg to succeed White will very likely make the narrow interpretation a minority view again. According to this interpretation, the First Amendment prevents the establishment by the government of a single state church that would have any sort of preference over other churches. Rehnquist accepts the proposition that the historical and proper definition of establishment of religion is "a formal, legal union of a single church or religion with government, giving the one church or religion an exclusive position of power and favor over all other churches or denominations."[10] Advocates of this view reject the contention that every form of public aid or support for religion is prohibited; they also reject Justice Black's opinion that government cannot aid all religions or levy a tax on behalf of religious activities or institutions.

9. *Everson v. Board of Education*, 330 U.S. 1, 31–32 (1947).

10. J. M. O'Neill, *Religion and Education under the Constitution* (New York, 1949), p. 56; *Wallace v. Jaffree*, 472 U.S. 38, 91–106 (1985), where Rehnquist takes the same viewpoint.

Rehnquist might rephrase the debatable part of Justice Black's statement to read as follows:

The establishment of religion clause of the First Amendment means this: Neither can pass laws which aid one religion or prefer one religion over another. No tax can be levied to support any religious activities or institutions unless apportioned in some equitable form and without discrimination in any form or degree. Government participation in the affairs of any religious organization or groups is prohibited unless with the consent and approval of such. The very phrase "wall of separation between Church and State" is ambiguous and misleading.

According to this view, the wall of separation merely keeps the government from abridging religious liberty by discriminatory practices against religion generally, or against any particular sects or denominations; the wall was not intended, however, to enjoin the government from fostering religion generally or all such religious groups or institutions as are willing to accept government aid, whether in the form of tax support, promotional activities, or otherwise. Nor was the wall meant to allow religious reasons to be the basis of denying the benefits of government services to schoolchildren or their parents.

That last point, which is accurate, makes us confront the fact that absolutes are as absent from the constitutional law of the establishment clause as from the law of search and seizure. Moreover, the jurisprudence of the establishment clause seems to be nearly as murky.

As early as 1930 the Supreme Court held that a state did not take property or deprive anyone of it by appropriating tax monies for the purchase of books for children in private sectarian schools. The Court announced the "child benefit" theory to support its decision. The free school books were meant for the benefit of the schoolchildren, not their schools.[11] Similarly, as if to prove that not even the broadest interpretation of the establishment clause prevents all aid, the *Everson* Court, no less, saw nothing unconstitutional in state-subsidized bus rides for children attending parochial schools. *Everson* showed how the Court can agree, unanimously, on principle yet disagree as closely as

11. *Cochran v. Louisiana*, 281 U.S. 370 (1930).

possible, 5–4, on the application of that principle in an actual case. Justice Black, for the majority, insisted that the wall of separation "must be kept high and impregnable" and that the Court "could not approve the slightest breach,"[12] yet he sustained the state practice in question, as well he should have. The township of Ewing, New Jersey, had authorized reimbursement of money spent by parents for the transportation of their children on public buses to attend school. To have prohibited repayment to the parents of parochial-school children would have denied a benefit extended for the safety and convenience of all children regardless of religion. They are as entitled to the bus service as they, their schools, and their church are entitled to such civic services as police and fire protection. In theory, then, free textbooks and free bus rides constitute only indirect or incidental aids to religion.

But even seemingly direct aids that endorse or reflect religious beliefs honeycomb official practices, despite the fact that the Supreme Court holds that the establishment clause prevents government sponsorship of religion. In 1963 Justice William J. Brennan observed, in the single opinion on the establishment clause most worthy of study, that its framers meant to prohibit involvements between government and religion that serve religion, employ government organs for religious purposes, or use religious means to serve government ends when secular means would suffice.[13] Yet witnesses in courts swear on the Bible and take an oath that concludes "So help me God." Presidential proclamations invoke God. The Supreme Court itself opens its sessions daily with the invocation "God save the United States and this honorable Court." Both houses of Congress and also our state legislatures daily precede their work with a prayer uttered by a legislative chaplain paid from our taxes. Our currency carries the motto "In God We Trust," and schoolchildren pledge allegiance to "one nation under God."

Except for sustaining the constitutionality of legislative chaplains,[14] the Supreme Court has had the good judgment to decline deciding cases that question whether such practices violate the establishment clause. If that question has to be decided, those practices should be

12. 330 U.S. 1, 16 (1947).
13. *Abington Township School District v. Schempp*, 374 U.S. 203, 294–95 (1963).
14. *Marsh v. Chambers*, 463 U.S. 783 (1983).

held unconstitutional as a matter of principle, although the rule *de minimis non curat lex* (the law does not bother with trifles) might justify a more practical judgment; the Court might hold that custom has so trivialized and secularized these practices that they do not violate the establishment clause. However, the Court has enough cunning to avoid rendering judgments in such cases. Principle, public opinion, and historical custom conspire to dictate a prudent abstention.

The Court has devised a variety of tests to determine the outcome of those questions arising under the establishment clause that the Court agrees to settle. The Court's tests in fact settle no more than did the original strict-separationist or impregnable-wall test of *Everson*. In that case, to quote Justice Robert S. Jackson, dissenting, the Court's actual decision violated its principle of "complete and uncompromising separation of Church and State." As a result, Black's opinion reminded Jackson of Byron's Julia, who, "whispering 'I will ne'er consent,'—consented."[15] Yet Justice John Paul Stevens of the present Court, who is highly respected for his intellectual qualities and well-wrought opinions, has become so disenchanted by intramural squabbles among the justices on the application of establishment-clause tests that he has plaintively yearned for the good old days of the *Everson* era. "I would resurrect the 'high and impregnable wall,'" he wrote in 1980, rather than try to justify various types of subsidies to parochial schools at the expense of having the Court look so fickle.[16] Stevens hardly needs to be reminded that the *Everson* Court was unanimous in opposing the slightest breach in the wall, yet divided 5–4 on the question of whether bus subsidies constituted a breach.

In 1977 the Court put aside its child-benefit theory when it ruled against the constitutionality of publicly paid bus rides for parochial-school children to take field trips during the school day. In that case the Court construed an Ohio statute, one of whose provisions authorized expenditures from tax funds to cover the costs of enriching the secular studies of the students of sectarian schools by visits to governmental, industrial, cultural, and scientific centers. The Court distinguished

15. 330 U.S. 1, 19.

16. *Committee for Public Education and Religious Liberty v. Regan*, 444 U.S. 646, 671 (1980).

Everson, which allowed payment for travel unrelated to any aspect of the curriculum, and voided the Ohio provision, first, because the schools, not the children, received the aid and, second, because the field trips were "an integral part of the educational experience," thus producing an "unacceptable risk of fostering religion." One might have thought, however, that a visit to a factory or a museum carried a smaller risk of fostering religion than busing a student to a religious school whose purpose is to integrate religion with all subjects and train students in the tenets and practices of a particular denomination. The Court, incidentally, divided 5–4 on the field-trip issue. In his opinion for the majority, Justice Harry A. Blackmun first observed that establishment-clause cases presented analytical difficulties; he drew the astonishing conclusion nonetheless that that Court's numerous precedents, having become firmly rooted, "now provide substantial guidance."[17]

Sometimes the justices make distinctions that would glaze the minds of medieval scholastics. Free textbooks to sectarian schoolchildren are surely constitutional if the textbooks are the same as those used by public schools. The books are for the benefit of the pupils and therefore only indirectly aid the parochial schools, even though no public officials monitor the use of the books to ensure that they do not assist the religious objectives of those schools.[18] According to the Court, however, instructional materials, no matter how "secular, neutral, non-ideological," and unrelated to religion, are unconstitutional.[19] In a 1971 case the Court voided a Pennsylvania statute providing direct aid to parochial schools by reimbursing the costs for teaching mathematics, foreign languages, physical sciences, and physical education. The act was unconstitutional because the subjects were "an integral part of the religious mission of the Catholic Church" and the subsidy required an "excessive entanglement" of church and state to be sure that the teaching as well as the books and instructional materials did not assist that

17. *Wolman v. Walter*, 433 U.S. 229 (1977); on field trips, see pp. 252–54; on precedential guidance, see p. 236.

18. *Board of Education v. Allen*, 292 U.S. 236 (1968); *Meek v. Pittenger*, 421 U.S. 349, 360–61 (1975).

19. *Meek v. Pittenger*, 421 U.S. 349, 354 (1975).

mission.[20] In that case, *Lemon v. Kurtzman*, the instructional materials could easily be seen as a direct aid to the parochial schools and not to its pupils.

In the later cases of 1975 and 1977, which did not involve reimbursement to the parochial schools for any part of their costs, the rulings became confusing. Free books are constitutional, although books are instructional materials; other instructional materials, such as periodicals, photographs, maps, charts, globes, recordings, cassettes, films, and slides, and instructional equipment such as movie projectors, test tubes, and record players, involve excessive entanglement and have the effect of advancing the religious mission of the schools. The Court reasons that the children get the books, but the schools get the instructional materials and equipment.[21] To monitor the use of other instructional materials necessarily requires excessive entanglement by government in religious affairs.

The test of excessive entanglement seems to carry the seeds of its own misconstruction. "Excessive," after all, is a relative term that cannot possibly have a fixed or objectively ascertainable meaning. Justice Sandra Day O'Connor has become so disillusioned by the use to which the Court has put the test that she favors scrapping it, on the supposition that the Court would thereby be enabled to reach more realistic decisions.[22] That is as realistic a view as Stevens's yearning for the impregnable-wall test. If the Court should repudiate the test of excessive entanglement, it would surely employ similar considerations when analyzing whether some aid to sectarian education had the impermissible effect of promoting religion. Moreover, tests have little to do with decisions; the use of a test lends the appearance of objectivity to a judicial opinion, but no evidence shows that a test influences a member of the Court to reach a decision that he or she would not have reached without that test. And justices using the same test often arrive at contradictory results.

Advancing a religious mission and the test of excessive entangle-

20. *Lemon v. Kurtzman*, 403 U.S. 602 (1971).

21. *Meek v. Pittenger*, 421 U.S. 349, 354–55, 363, 366 (1975); *Wolman v. Walter*, 433 U.S. 229, 248–51 (1977).

22. *Aguilar v. Felton*, 473 U.S. 402, 428–30 (1985).

ment are components of what the Court calls the three-part *Lemon* test, so named because it derived from a case of 1971 named *Lemon v. Kurtz-man.*[23] The Court uses that test for determining the constitutionality of government action challenged under the establishment clause. Although the individual parts of the test have their sources in cases decided before 1971, in that year an eight-member majority of the Court, speaking through Chief Justice Warren E. Burger, combined the parts in the comprehensive tool of analysis that the Court still employs as a means of enforcing the *Everson* interpretation. The *Lemon* test permits a finding of constitutionality if the government act fulfills three requirements: "First, the statute must have a secular legislative purpose; second, its principal or primary effect must be one that neither advances nor inhibits religion . . . ; finally, the statute must not foster 'an excessive government entanglement with religion.' "[24]

The Court usually accepts whatever secular purpose the government, whether local, state, or national, announces, but there are exceptions. In one case, for example, the Court ruled against the avowed secular purpose of posting the Ten Commandments on the classroom wall, because the actual purpose was to advance religion.[25] Similarly, a state act requiring a moment of silence for contemplation or prayer was said to have the actual purpose of serving religion.[26] But the Court does not often distinguish the avowed from the actual purpose. The requirement that the challenged government act must not have the primary effect of advancing religion has come to mean that government may not endorse or sponsor religion, or inhibit it by disapproving of it.

Excessive entanglement, which constitutes the third part, controlled the result in the 1971 *Lemon* case when the Court assembled the three parts to reach its ruling: state salary supplements paid to teachers of secular subjects in religious schools and state reimbursements to such schools for teaching services and for instructional aids unduly enmeshed state authorities in monitoring to prevent inculcation of religious beliefs. Moreover, the entanglement also involved a potential

23. *Lemon v. Kurtzman*, 403 U.S. 602 (1971).
24. Ibid., pp. 612–13.
25. *Stone v. Graham*, 449 U.S. 39 (1980).
26. *Wallace v. Jaffree*, 472 U.S. 38 (1985).

for political divisiveness over religion, contrary to a purpose of the establishment clause. The clause decreed that religion "must be a private matter for the individual, the family, and the institutions of private choice," Burger declared, without unnecessary government intervention. Burger acknowledged that the language of the clause seemed "opaque," but its framers "did not simply prohibit the establishment of a state church or a state religion," he explained. They commanded that there should be no law "respecting" an establishment of religion. That meant that a law might fall short of creating an establishment and yet be unconstitutional if it was a law "respecting" or concerning an establishment. It concerned an establishment if it inched toward one of the three "main evils" against which the establishment stood guard: sponsorship, financial support, and active involvement. At that point, significantly, Burger described the three-prong test.[27]

Use of the *Lemon* test does not really aid the Court in deciding establishment-clause cases. The justices frequently disagree on the test's application in particular cases. For example in two cases the Court split 5–4, the majority believing that an act of Congress squared with all three prongs of the *Lemon* test while the minority believed the opposite.[28] Disagreements of this sort are common, suggesting that the application of a particular test solves nothing; it is merely a point of analytical departure. What counts rather are the policy preferences of the individual judges.

No matter what test had been employed by members of the recent Court, Justices William J. Brennan, Thurgood Marshall, and John Paul Stevens usually found a violation of the establishment clause, while Justices William H. Rehnquist, Byron R. White, and Warren E. Burger usually did not. Justices Sandra Day O'Connor, Harry A. Blackmun, and above all, Lewis F. Powell usually held the balance of power that determined the result. If, as likely, Blackmun voted with Brennan, while O'Connor voted with White, Powell in effect decided the case. He very rarely was on the losing side in an establishment-clause case. The justices in the middle, surrounded by separationists on one side and accommodationists or nonpreferentialists on the other, profess to be-

27. *Lemon v. Kurtzman*, 403 U.S. 602, 612–13.
28. *Mueller v. Allen*, 463 U.S. 388 (1983); *Bowen v. Kendrick*, 487 U.S. 589 (1988).

lieve that the particular test that the Court should use has considerable importance. The use of a test conveys the impression of judicial objectivity or diminishes the impression of judicial subjectivity.

On the Rehnquist Court, Chief Justice William Rehnquist joined by Justices Byron White, Antonin Scalia, Clarence Thomas, and Anthony Kennedy vote most consistently in favor of religion. Usually opposed to them are Justices Harry Blackmun, John Paul Stevens, Sandra Day O'Connor, and David Souter, who have been pushed toward the separationist side by the extremist views of the Rehnquist-Scalia wing; that wing nudges even Kennedy toward the center. Kennedy joined that wing in wanting the Court to repudiate the *Lemon* test in favor of a test allowing nonpreferential aid to religion but prohibiting direct aid that establishes "a state religion or religious faith, or tends to do so."[29]

The Rehnquist-Scalia wing also favors a coercion test for determining violations of the establishment clause. But that test would gut the establishment clause by making it superfluous or repetitious, because the free-exercise clause protects against coercion that is based on religion. The Rehnquist-Scalia wing subordinates the establishment clause to the free-exercise clause in an effort to accommodate the interests of religion. They do not understand that the establishment clause has independent purposes distinct from that of the free-exercise clause. Separation of government and religion is a means of protecting each from the other as well as a means of ensuring that the support of religion be voluntary and private.

In a real sense all members of the Court, including even the separationists, have favored accommodation of religion, but they differ as to the meaning of accommodation. Justice Arthur Goldberg, in a school prayer case of 1963, for example, declared that although the attitude of the government toward religion should be neutral, that did not mean that government should be wholly secular or even passively hostile toward religion. Because so many Americans believe in God, government "must take cognizance of the existence of religion." Goldberg endorsed teaching about religion, yet even he concurred in the majority judgment that opening the school day with a prayer or Bible reading

---

29. *Allegheny County v. ACLU*, 109 S.Ct. 3086, 3136 (1989); *Board of Education v. Mergens*, 110 S.Ct. 2356, 2377 (1990).

directly involved government in sectarianism.[30] That was not accommodating religion; it was subordinating government to religion. Justice William O. Douglas, who had earlier declared that we are a religious people, voted the same way as Goldberg.[31] Thus, professed accommodationists can vote as separationists. The distinction between the two can fail to distinguish.

In a case in which the Court struck down as unconstitutional a state constitutional provision that disqualified clergymen from holding office, Justice William Brennan made this declaration: ". . . permissible government action under the Establishment Clause must reflect an appropriate accommodation of our heritage as a religious people. . . ." Government, he added, may take religion into account to advance secular purposes but not religious ones. But government may not use religion as the basis of imposing a penalty any more than granting a benefit.[32] Accommodation in this case constituted the emancipation of religion from a disqualification. Generally, the justices agree that accommodation means relieving religion of an improper burden that restricts its free exercise.

For example, the Court sustained a provision of the Civil Rights Act of 1964, which exempted religious organizations from the statute's prohibition against firing an employee on religious grounds. The Mormon church had fired a nonmember employee who held a secular job; claiming religious discrimination, he argued that the exemption granted by the statute amounted to an establishment of religion. Leaning over far, too far, to accommodate the church, the Court disagreed by ruling that the statute satisfied each prong of the *Lemon* test.[33] Thus, the exemption avoided a government burden on the church, by no means necessarily the same as avoiding a burden on religious freedom.

In 1990 the Court also rejected an establishment-clause claim by school officials who had refused to allow the formation of a Christian club on school premises, even without a faculty adviser. A congressio-

30. *Abingdon Township School District v. Schempp*, 374 U.S. 203 (1963).
31. *Zorach v. Clauson*, 343 U.S. 306, 313–14 (1952).
32. *McDaniel v. Paty*, 435 U.S. 618, 639 (1978).
33. *Corp. of Presiding Bishop v. Amos*, 483 U.S. 327 (1987).

nal statute, the Equal Access Act, required public schools to permit the existence of "noncurriculum-related" clubs on a nondiscriminatory basis. The Court supported the formation of the Christian club on the same basis as the stamp club or the chess club. Relieving a religious interest of a burden, the Court held that because the statute satisfied all parts of the *Lemon* test, it had not violated the establishment clause. Here the Court protected the religious interest against discrimination by the school authorities based on the religious content of speech.[34] Accommodation of religion must, therefore, uphold the free exercise of religion against some government-imposed disability founded on religious classification.

In a similar case of 1993 the Court held that if a public school permits its property to be used after hours for meetings by community organizations, such as the Girl Scouts, a dance group, and a baseball clinic, then the use of its facilities by a religious organization does not violate the establishment clause. Justice Byron White reasoned for the Court, properly enough, that the after-hours showing of a film by a church group would not have been school sponsored, would have been open to the general public, and scarcely created the risk that the community would think the school was endorsing religion. White found no violation of the *Lemon* test. The judgment was unanimous, although three justices separately dissociated themselves from the *Lemon* test.[35]

Justice White, long one of the Court's leading supporters of accommodation and aid to religion, could use the *Lemon* test to support his position when he wanted to, but he really disliked it. He objected particularly to the entanglement prong of the *Lemon* test. In effect, he said that it produced a catch-22 situation. "The Court," he wrote, "thus creates an insoluble paradox for the State and the parochial schools. The State cannot finance secular instruction if it permits religion to be taught in the same classroom; but if it exacts a promise that religion not be so taught—a promise the school and its teachers are quite willing and on this record able to give—and enforces it, it is then entangled in

34. *Board of Education v. Mergens*, 110 S.Ct. 2356 (1990).
35. *Lamb's Chapel v. Center Moriches Union Free School District*, 113 S.Ct. 2141 (1993).

the 'no entanglement' aspect of the Court's Establishment Clause jurisprudence."[36] The paradox does exist and can be unfair at times, but it
seems to be a necessary upshot of the First Amendment, which virtually dictates a constitutional jurisprudence of private choice and voluntarism in the support of religion. The majority of the Court confronted a need to keep the sacred and the secular in separate universes
for their own good. A Court sympathetic to the integrity of religion as
well as religious liberty devised the catch-22. The Burger Court could
not justly be accused of "hostility" to religion or of establishing "a
religion of secularism," as Justice Potter Stewart, dissenting alone, once
unfairly accused the Warren Court,[37] and as Burger in 1985 accused the
majority of his own Court.[38]

The three-part *Lemon* test has featured prominently in the Court's
deliberations involving three particularly knotty problems involving
public aid to private sectarian schools: reimbursing them for giving
standardized tests mandated by the state, allowing some reimbursement to the parents of children in such schools, and public provision of
various auxiliary services to children in those schools. The testing issue
first arose to perplex the Court in 1973. New York State had appropri-
ated $28,000,000 for the reimbursement to parochial schools of the
costs of administering and reporting the results of various records and
examinations required by state law. New York provided a fixed amount
per student to cover costs, but that amount seems to have been politically determined on the basis of what the state treasury could afford as
a subsidy to parochial schools. The state neither required audits of
financial records to determine actual costs nor a rebate of any sums in
excess of actual expenses. Chief Justice Burger for an 8–1 Court easily
detected a forbidden subsidy that advanced religious purposes.[39]

Four years later the Court upheld the constitutionality of Ohio's plan
for having the parochial schools administer to their pupils the standardized tests used in the public schools. Ohio simply supplied the

36. *Lemon v. Kurtzman*, 403 U.S. 602, 668 (1971).
37. *Abington Township School District v. Schempp*, 374 U.S. 203, 311, 313 (1963).
38. *Aguilar v. Felton*, 473 U.S. 373, 419–20 (1985).
39. *Levitt v. Committee for Public Education and Religious Liberty*, 413 U.S. 472
(1973).

secular-subjects tests, which the public-school personnel composed and scored; the state provided no money to reimburse the costs of giving or reporting the tests. Accordingly, the Court ruled that Ohio had avoided direct aid to religion as well as entangling supervision.[40] The Court could not, however, legitimate New York's initial attempt to patch up its scheme to reimburse the church schools for their costs in giving and scoring state-required tests. By a 6–3 vote the Court held that even if the state conducted an audit to determine actual costs, the schools could not receive the money without first proving that religion did not benefit from state financial aid. The state act, the Court held, necessarily had the primary effect of aiding religion, which was patently not so, and necessarily resulted in excessive state-church entanglement, thereby violating the establishment clause under the *Lemon* test.[41]

In 1980, however, a 5–4 Court ruled that New York had finally purged its reimbursement plan of any unconstitutional features.[42] The state had again revised its statute, reimbursing the church schools for costs in giving, grading, and reporting the state-mandated tests. This time, however, and for the first time, the act also required an audit to determine costs. Justice White, who had dissented alone in the first of the New York testing cases in 1973, spoke for the Court in 1980, without bothering to respond to the dissenting opinions or to explain why the state no longer had an obligation to disprove that any money supported religion or entangled church and state in its administration. White simply asserted what in fact seemed to be true, namely, that the tests had a secular purpose, did not advance religion, and did not involve the state with religion.

Justice Harry Blackmun, for the dissenters, did not have the better argument, but he explained why the 1980 decision differed from those in the previous New York testing cases: some members of the Court— Lewis F. Powell and Potter Stewart—had simply switched sides. The New York cases of 1977 and 1980 cannot be reconciled. Blackmun probably exaggerated when declaring that the majority opinion took "a

---

40. *Wolman v. Walter*, 433 U.S. 229 (1977).

41. *New York v. Cathedral Academy*, 434 U.S. 125 (1977).

42. *Committee for Public Education and Religious Liberty v. Regan*, 444 U.S. 646 (1980).

long step backwards in the inevitable controversy that emerges when a state legislature continues to insist on providing public aid to parochial schools."[43] But he had a good point in stating that to have parochial-school teachers grade subject-matter exams allowed them to exercise subjective judgment. As a result, excessive entanglement would result from state monitoring to ensure objectivity. In fact, though, the state did no monitoring. White emphasized that the test measured student achievement in secular subjects such as earth sciences, biology, and social studies; he ignored the fact that public- and parochial-school teachers might grade differently the answers to questions dealing with the origins of life, evolution, sexual behavior, and many other topics. Moreover, secular subjects in a very real sense do not exist in parochial schools because the entire curriculum is taught in a manner that will indoctrinate the beliefs of the denomination running the school.

The issue of excessive entanglement figured prominently in one of the most important establishment clause cases ever decided by the Court. By an 8–1 vote, it upheld the constitutionality of property-tax exemptions granted to religious organizations for properties used exclusively for religious worship.[44] Chief Justice Burger for the Court reasoned that the legislative purpose of a tax exemption neither advanced nor inhibited religion. That proposition amounted to what can kindly be called a constitutional fiction. As a purely economic matter, exempting churches from taxation constitutes an enormous financial aid to them, which could have no result other than advancing their religious functions. But Burger appropriately observed that the state had not granted the tax exemption to just houses of worship. They were merely one form of "non-profit, quasi-public corporations" that included hospitals, libraries, museums, symphonies, colleges, and scientific, professional, historical, and patriotic organizations, all of which the state considered as groups benefiting the community at large.

43. Ibid., p. 662.
44. *Waltz v. Tax Commission of City of New York*, 397 U.S. 664 (1970). See generally Dean M. Kelley, *Why Churches Should Not Pay Taxes* (New York, 1977); "Church/State Symposium: Whether Tax Exemptions for Religious Organizations Violate the First Amendment," *Cumberland Law Review* 22 (1991–92): 471–680.

Burger in effect had contradicted himself. Having declared that the tax exemption did not advance religion, he reasoned that the state had granted the exemption to advance the church's mission because it was worthwhile to the community. But the establishment clause imposes a restriction that does not inhibit hospitals, libraries, and other nonprofit institutions. The establishment clause operates peculiarly on religious agencies. Burger did not explain why churches should receive the aid given to other institutions that are not the subject of the establishment clause. Moreover, he recognized that the "good works" or social welfare services performed by churches, such as caring for orphans or the destitute, varied substantially. Some churches provided a good deal, others hardly at all. Burger used the point only to say the exemption could not be based on a determination of the services rendered, because that would involve the government in excessive entanglement. He claimed that to tax rather than exempt might involve still greater entanglement "by giving rise to tax valuation of church property, tax liens, tax foreclosures," and the conflicts that would ensue.[45] The entanglement is not self-evident. Burger should have explained and argued that exemption is the price paid by the community for services rendered to it.

When acknowledging that the exemptions operated as "an indirect economic benefit," Burger again claimed that the exemption gave rise to less involvement than taxing churches. He acknowledged too that a "direct" money subsidy would be impermissible sponsorship of religion, but he reasoned soundly that by a grant of taxation, "the government does not transfer part of its revenue to churches but simply abstains from demanding that the church support the state."[46] He detected no connection between tax exemption and an establishment of religion, but he botched his point by analogizing that fire and police protection were also "incidental" benefits consonant with the establishment clause. "Benevolent neutrality" rather than the advancement of religion or excessive entanglement was the Court's attitude toward tax exemptions for churches. By "neutrality" Burger meant neither ad-

---

45. *Waltz v. Tax Commission of City of New York*, 397 U.S. 664, 674 (1970).
46. Ibid., p. 675.

vancing nor inhibiting religion. He did not concern himself with the question of whether government exemption favored religious organizations over irreligious ones.

Justice Brennan, concurring, believed that never had the Court considered the constitutionality of a practice "for which the historical support is so overwhelming." Tax exemptions for churches went back to the colonial period and did not constitute an issue at the time of the framing of the establishment clause. Madison had been a member of the Virginia legislature that voted for exemptions, and Jefferson had been president when Congress exempted the capital's churches. No court had ever held such exemptions unconstitutional on establishment-clause grounds, and such exemptions were in force in all fifty states.[47]

To the historical evidence, Brennan added that churches performed secular services for the well-being of the community, but like Burger did not face the problem of whether the exemption could be justified for those churches that provided no services or few. Rather, Brennan justified tax exemptions on the grounds that churches "uniquely contribute to the pluralism of American society by their religious activities." But that would logically justify direct grants to churches notwithstanding the establishment clause, which uniquely singles out religion. Brennan's contribution to the case enhanced the constitutional fiction that the "principal effect [of tax exemptions] is to carry out secular purposes—the encouragement of public service activities and of a pluralistic society."[48]

Contrary to the Court, the best argument in favor of the constitutionality of tax exemptions for churches is that their property is so closely involved with religious practices that to impose a tax would violate the free exercise of religion. Tax exemption is a means of avoiding a burden on religious liberty, which is the reason that government accommodation in this instance made sense. Moreover, the Court decided as it did for an unspoken political reason: a contrary decision would have had bad results. Not only would the public services of

47. Ibid., pp. 681–85.
48. Ibid., p. 692.

churches be severely curtailed; the issue would have become a divisive political bombshell.

Justice William Douglas, dissenting, detected a discrimination in the statute. Nonbelievers who owned realty were taxed whereas churches were not, and the establishment clause banned aid to all religions as against nonbelievers. The point, of course, was misleading. Believers were taxed too; only certain nonprofit institutions enjoyed the exemption. Douglas discerned no practical difference between a subsidy for churches and exempting them from taxation. For Douglas the establishment clause required that public services rendered by private sectarian organizations remain private and not benefit from public subsidy.[49]

Another controversial and more important establishment-clause issue that has agitated the nation and divided the Court concerns state plans to underwrite part of the cost incurred by citizens who exercise their constitutional right to send their children to private sectarian schools, which charge tuition. Direct aid to the schools themselves is clearly unconstitutional because of their religious character. Therefore, the state cannot pay any part of teachers' salaries; building, maintenance, and repair costs; or even the cost of instructional equipment such as a chemistry lab that presumably might have only a secular purpose.[50] Consequently the price of free choice for parents of parochial-school students is, figuratively speaking, double taxation; they pay taxes for the public schools, as we all must and should, but they also pay for their parochial schools. And those schools, their sectarian mission aside, serve community and nation by performing essential secular educational functions, by enormously reducing the tax burden for the operation of the public schools, and by providing a salutary competition. Diversity and pluralism, which those schools enhance, are quintessentially American. Good education in an environment marked by better discipline; less violence, crime, and drug use; and better attendance records also speaks well for religious schools. It is

49. Ibid., pp. 700–16.

50. *Lemon v. Kurtzman*, 403 U.S. 602 (1971); *Meek v. Pittenger*, 421 U.S. 349 (1975); *Wolman v. Walter*, 433 U.S. 229 (1977).

easy, therefore, to understand a public effort to reduce the cost to parents who help pay the bills for those schools if it is possible to reduce that cost without breaching the wall of separation between government and religion.

However, the community has no obligation to underwrite any part of parochial schools, and the parents of parochial-school children voluntarily choose not to send them to public schools. The claim of "double taxation" is a misnomer. The cost of parochial schools is a self-imposed one. Citizens who do not use various public services, such as parks, schools, museums, and hospitals, must contribute to their upkeep through taxation. If the parents of parochial-school children chose to use the public schools, the cost to the community would be staggeringly enhanced. Fairness, then, seems to justify efforts for the public to ease the burden on those who support parochial schools. But this beguiling inducement or concern has distinct limits. The same logic would validate public underwriting of parochial schools, though as a matter of constitutional law the establishment clause and the justifiable policy considerations that underlie it bar such aid. Only aid that is directly for the benefit of the child and not the sectarian school can receive constitutional approbation. Even as to that, critics argue that the child-benefit theory is a subterfuge for indirectly aiding religious institutions. The hard fact remains, however, that certain aids do benefit children, such as those denominated as "auxiliary," which will be discussed below.

In 1973 the Court held unconstitutional two state plans for reimbursing part of the cost to parents of parochial-school tuition bills. New York's plan called for direct, unrestricted grants of up to $100 per child but not more than 50 percent of tuition to low-income parents and state income tax benefits for other parents of parochial-school pupils. Pennsylvania's reimbursement statute provided $75 for each child in an elementary religious school and $150 for each in a secondary school. Both states argued that the grants to the parents rather than to the schools made their plans pass constitutional muster. By 6–3 decisions, applying the *Lemon* test, the Court found that the reimbursements, no matter in what form, were offered as an incentive to parents to send their children to sectarian schools and therefore violated the establishment clause by advancing the religious mission of those schools just as if the aid had been given directly.[51]

Ten years later, in 1983, the Court uncapped the restriction on such reimbursements if they took the form of tax benefits that were available to the parents of all schoolchildren. The case that radically altered the constitutional law of the matter involved a Minnesota statute that allowed state taxpayers to deduct expenses for tuition, books, and transportation of their children to school, no matter what school—public, private nonsectarian, or private church-related. Justice Rehnquist ruled for a 5–4 Court that the Minnesota plan satisfied all three parts of the purpose, effect, and no-entanglement test.[52] That all taxpaying parents benefited from the statute made the difference between this case and the precedents, even though parents of public-school students could not take advantage of the major tax deduction—$500 per student through the sixth grade and $700 per student in grades seven through twelve. Public-school parents could, however, deduct for the cost of transportation and for the costs of uniforms and special equipment from calculators to gym shoes. That fact constituted the basis for the summary finding that the Minnesota plan did not have the primary effect of advancing the religious mission of sectarian schools.

The Court conceded that parents of sectarian schoolchildren benefited the most, by far, and that "financial assistance provided to parents ultimately has an economic effect comparable to that of aid given directly to the schools attended by their children."[53] Yet Rehnquist asserted that the state did not aid religion generally or any particular denomination. He added, in passing, that the statute did not excessively entangle the state in religious affairs, even though government officials had to disallow any tax deductions for instructional materials and books that were used to teach religious tenets, doctrines, or worship.

Justice Thurgood Marshall, speaking for the four dissenters, rejected the distinction between the precedents and the case before the Court,

51. *Committee for Public Education and Religious Liberty v. Regan*, 413 U.S. 756 (1973); *Sloan v. Lemon*, 413 U.S. 825 (1973).

52. *Mueller v. Allen*, 463 U.S. 388 (1983).

53. Ibid., p. 399.

and he was right. The precedents established that a state may not aid parochial schools by direct grants or by financial aids to the parents of parochial-school students, whether the aids were in the form of tax credits or reimbursements. Indirect as well as direct assistance to those schools came within the establishment clause, Marshall contended, and by such aid the state required all taxpayers to help underwrite religious schools and their religions. If the plans of New York and Pennsylvania unconstitutionally provided incentives to parents to send their children to parochial schools, so did the Minnesota plan.

Marshall repudiated the majority's point that the availability of the tax deduction to all parents differentiated this case from others. Parents of public-school children could deduct for pencils and notebooks, but they were "simply *unable*" to claim the large deduction for tuition. Because the benefit was not in fact available to all parents and because the assistance that parochial schools admittedly derived from the scheme could not be channeled into exclusively secular purposes, the minority urged that the state act violated the Constitution. They surely had a powerful case when making the argument that the Minnesota plan allowed reimbursement for books and instructional materials in a way that entangled the government in religious matters.

The Burger Court had agreed that instructional materials other than books could be used to advance the religious mission of church schools because of the integration, where possible, of the secular and sectarian in such schools.[54] The Court had also sustained the constitutionality of state-provided textbooks to parochial-school children when the same books were chosen by the state for use in the public schools.[55] And the Rehnquist-led majority did not alter the law in that regard but ruled, rather, that the tax deduction plan did not involve excessive entanglement. Marshall argued that it did. The statute did not restrict the parochial schools to books approved only for public-school use. When state authorities decided what was religious in nature and what was not, the

54. *Meek v. Pittenger,* 421 U.S. 349 (1975); *Wolman v. Walter,* 433 U.S. 229 (1977).

55. *Board of Education v. Allen,* 292 U.S. 236 (1968); *Meek v. Pittenger,* 421 U.S. 349, 360–61 (1975).

state became deeply enmeshed in religious matters. The Court should have voided at least that part of the Minnesota statute. The majority upheld it entirely because, the precedents notwithstanding, they obviously concurred in the public policy underlying the state act and cared little about convincing or consistent judicial opinions.

In 1986, the Court delivered a far more reasonable interpretation of the establishment clause when it upheld the constitutionality of a state vocational assistance program that allowed a blind person to study for the ministry at a Christian college. The state court had held the opposite, finding that the subsidy covering tuition "clearly has the primary effect of advancing religion." Justice Thurgood Marshall for the Court reasoned soundly that the aid provided by the state went to the religious institution "only as a result of the genuinely independent and private choices of aid recipients." The state had not created any financial incentives for students to take sectarian programs of study. The aid went to all qualified students, few of whom chose religious education. In any case the decision was theirs, not the state's.[56] The Court was right not to discover an establishment of religion in this case.

In 1993 a 5–4 Court found no violation of the establishment clause in its requirement that a school district must provide a sign-language interpreter to a deaf student who chose to attend a Catholic school. The dissenters, led by Justice Harry Blackmun, strenuously objected that the public employee's duty would be to relay religious messages, because the purpose of the school was to inculcate the faith and morals of the Roman Catholic church. But Chief Justice Rehnquist, for the majority, observed that the First Amendment did not disable religious institutions from participating in publicly sponsored welfare programs. In this case an act of Congress provided educational aid to individuals with disabilities and had paid for the sign-language interpreter when the student attended a public school. The government program provided its benefits to the handicapped without regard to religion. The money for the interpreter went to the interpreter for the benefit of the student, not the religious school, which at best was merely an incidental beneficiary. The majority had the best of the argument. To have de-

56. *Witters v. Washington Department of Services for the Blind*, U.S. 481 (1986).

cided otherwise would have penalized the student because of his religion. The dissenters' views would have been more convincing if the interpreter had been a teacher rather than a neutral conduit.[57]

Providing an interpreter for a deaf student is an auxiliary service paid by the public. The battle for auxiliary services sundered the Court and resulted in some of its most indefensible decisions. The first of these, *Meek v. Pittenger*, which was settled in 1975 by a 6–3 vote on the auxiliary services issue, struck down a comprehensive program of Pennsylvania whose purpose was to provide a variety of technical aids to parochial-school children with special needs.[58] Auxiliary services included remedial instruction for the disadvantaged or those for whom English is a second language; accelerated instruction for the intellectually gifted; guidance counseling and testing; and instruction for those with speech or hearing impairments. In addition, Pennsylvania provided free diagnostic services to identify students needing auxiliary aids and to determine their best treatment. Such services were available, of course, to public-school students. The state sent its professional staff from the public schools to the parochial schools, with all supportive materials and equipment, to test and treat students when requested by the parochial-school authorities.

Justice Potter Stewart for the majority delivered an unrealistic opinion that deprived needy students of auxiliary services and damaged the cause of separation by making it look absurdly dogmatic. Stewart reasoned that the auxiliary services program required "a constitutionally impermissible degree of entanglement between church and state." He insipidly remarked that "a teacher remains a teacher, and the danger that religious doctrine will become intertwined with secular instruction persists." If, as he observed, the state must be "certain" that its employees did not inculcate religion, many public schools would have to close. The fact that public employees provided the auxiliary services made no difference to the Court majority because that did "not substantially eliminate the need for continuing surveillance."[59] Thus, the auxiliary services program failed the *Lemon* test.

57. *Zobrest v. Cataline Foothills School District*, 113 S.Ct. 2462 (1993).
58. *Meek v. Pittenger*, 421 U.S. 349 (1975).
59. Ibid., pp. 370–71.

To Stewart, oversensitive to the need to keep religion uncontaminated by the state but even more oversensitive to the danger that a religious environment presented to public employees, the chances were too great that those employees would serve religion simply because they entered schools whose function was to advance religious belief. On the other hand, in a remark relegated to a footnote, the majority made an exception for diagnostic testing whose purpose was to determine which pupils needed speech and hearing services. Those services could not constitutionally be provided by public employees with state-owned equipment and materials on parochial-school premises. But singling out the students needing such services, which the Court made unavailable to them in their own schools, was constitutional.

A teacher is indeed a teacher, especially public employees professionally trained in special skills. A guidance counselor from the public schools might be seduced "on occasion" into inculcating religious beliefs, however unlikely that is in the real world, but conjecture about what might happen "on occasion" seems to be a contrived basis for holding unconstitutional all auxiliary services. Professionals, whether audiologists, speech therapists, remedial reading specialists who work with dyslectic children, psychologists who treat emotionally disturbed children, and even specialists in accelerated teaching of exceptional students simply do their jobs without proselytizing. No evidence whatever existed to show anything to the contrary. The expert staff that provides auxiliary services is as indifferent to religion as the public-school nurse. The child-benefit theory required a contrary decision.

Stewart's opinion shot the Court in the foot. Chief Justice Burger charged that the decision penalized the children, not the schools, and penalized them, he said, "because of their parents' choice" of religion.[60] Stewart's opinion also allowed Rehnquist to castigate the majority for siding with those "who believe that our society as a whole should be a purely secular one."[61]

Two years later the scales dropped from Stewart's eyes when he joined an 8−1 majority that upheld Ohio's diagnostic services.[62] Ohio

60. Ibid., p. 386.
61. Ibid., p. 395.
62. *Wolman v. Walter*, 433 U.S. 229, 241–48 (1977).

authorized diagnostic testing to be conducted by publicly employed professionals on the premises of parochial schools to determine which students needed special assistance. Diagnostic services survived the Court's scrutiny under the *Lemon* test because they seemed to be comparable to public health services and because they had nothing to do with the educational mission of the church schools. The benefit to those schools appeared incidental to whatever benefits accrued to the children. Ohio, mindful of the Court's 1975 decision in *Meek*, provided all treatment off the premises of those schools. The statute specified that "therapeutic, guidance, and remedial services" should be available to the parochial-school children only in public schools, public centers, or mobile units located off nonpublic-school premises. Notwithstanding that a teacher is a teacher, that fact persuaded all but Justices Brennan and Marshall that this case differed significantly from *Meek*, where the state provided the services "in the pervasively sectarian atmosphere of the church related school."[63] Therefore, Ohio, unlike Pennsylvania, had not advanced the cause of religion or entangled the government in a religious mission. Justice Marshall, dissenting, fretted about whether certain therapeutic and remedial services were meant to aid the sectarian schools to improve the performance of their students (as if that were unconstitutional), and Justice Brennan expressed anxiety about whether the auxiliary services caused too much danger of political divisiveness.

In 1985 Brennan spoke for the Court in two companion cases that involved the assignment of public-school teachers to parochial schools for special auxiliary services. In one of these cases the city of Grand Rapids sought to assist the parochial schools by adopting two so-called enrichment and remedial programs.[64] The Community Education Program did not use public-school employees at all. At public expense it employed the regular parochial-school teachers to offer a miscellany of after-school courses on chess, nature appreciation, home economics, arts and crafts, journalism, and gym. The Court, by a vote of 7–2, could not believe that the sectarianism of the teaching staff would suddenly disappear at 3:30 P.M. when they taught the same students in the same

63. Ibid., p. 247.
64. *Grand Rapids School District v. Ball*, 473 U.S. 373 (1985).

building as earlier in the day. White and Rehnquist, dissenting, said nothing of merit.

The second program provided by Grand Rapids, the Shared Time Program, employed the regular public-school teachers, who volunteered for extra duty to get extra pay, to teach reading, art, music, and gym on parochial-school premises. No evidence indicated that these enrichment and remedial courses required a staff with special skills or that the pupils had special needs. Brennan, speaking for a 5–4 majority on the Shared Time Program, found that it too had the primary effect of advancing religion by virtually subsidizing the religious mission of sectarian schools. Brennan did not write one of his better opinions. He repeated the simplism about a teacher being a teacher; insisted that public-school teachers "may well subtly (or overtly) conform their instruction to the environment in which they teach";[65] and worried about a symbolic union of church and state. As Justice Sandra O'Connor replied in dissent, nothing in the record validated the majority's fears.

The companion case of *Aguilar v. Felton* was tremendously important and the opinion by Brennan disastrous. The facts are undisputed. In 1965 Congress passed the Elementary and Secondary Education Act; Title I of the act authorized the secretary of education to distribute financial assistance to local schools to meet the special needs of "educationally deprived" children from low-income families by providing educational programs that supplement, not supplant, existing ones. Beginning in 1966 New York City used federal funds to provide auxiliary services to students on parochial-school premises. Regular public-school employees (teachers, guidance counselors, psychologists, psychiatrists, and social workers) taught remedial reading, remedial math, English as a second language, and provided guidance services. These professionals met in rooms cleared of all religious symbols in order to diminish the sectarian atmosphere; they worked under supervision similar to that which prevailed in the public schools; and the city monitored the instruction. They were not accountable to parochial-school officials, did the testing, chose the students for special education or treatment, and used only materials and equipment supplied by secular and professional authorities. They acted under explicit instructions not

65. Ibid., p. 388.

to participate in any way in the religious activities of the parochial schools that they visited, to eschew religion in their work, and to avoid teaching in collaboration with the parochial-school staff. Personnel of the city's department of education made at least one unannounced visit monthly and reported to supervisors who made "occasional" supervisory visits to monitor the operation of the program.[66]

From those facts and without any evidence to justify his speculations, Justice Brennan concluded for the Court that the supervisory system for the administration of the city's Title I program "inevitably results in the excessive entanglement of church and state," making it unconstitutional.[67] Justice O'Connor, dissenting, estimated that the Court's decision injured 20,000 disadvantaged schoolchildren in the city plus "uncounted" others elsewhere in the country. The U.S. Department of Education counted a total of 183,000.[68] O'Connor believed that for those children the decision was "tragic." "The Court," she declared, "deprives them of a program that offers a meaningful chance at success in life, and it does so on the untenable theory that public-school teachers (most of whom are of different faiths than their students) are likely to start teaching religion because they have walked across the threshold of a parochial school."[69] The records of the lower court showed that almost three-fourths of the instructors in the program did not share the religious affiliation of any school they taught in. The chief justice, in his dissenting opinion, sought to savage the majority opinion by remarking that it bordered on "paranoia" to see the pope lurking behind the program, and he absurdly stated that the Court "exhibits nothing less than hostility toward religion and the children who attend church-sponsored schools."[70]

The Court's spokesman, a Roman Catholic, insisted that entanglement must be avoided for two reasons. Those reasons explain why the majority justices, all church members who profoundly respect religion, traveled a far and doctrinaire path to find infirmities in the city's Title I

---

66. *Aguilar v. Felton*, 473 U.S. 402, 404–7, 428 (1985).
67. Ibid., p. 409.
68. Ibid., p. 432; *Los Angeles Times*, Aug. 16, 1985, pt. 1, p. 13.
69. *Aguilar v. Felton*, 473 U.S. 402, 431 (1985).
70. Ibid., pp. 419–20.

program. The first reason expressed a concern for the freedom of religion of all citizens not of the denomination with which the city had gotten enmeshed in the administration of the program. The point showed the Court's good intentions but seemed misdirected or far-fetched, and the same must be said of the second reason, offered by Brennan. It concerned the freedom of religion of those benefiting from the program. Governmental "intrusion into sacred matters" seemed alarming to the majority. To ensure the absence of a religious message, an "ongoing inspection" was required, making "a permanent and pervasive State presence in the sectarian schools receiving aid." Such heavy monitoring, Brennan said, infringed the values protected by the establishment clause.

But no evidence existed, and Brennan produce none, to show that "Agents of the State [Brennan made this sound like Orwell's Big Brother] must visit and inspect the religious school regularly, alert for the subtle or overt presence of religious matter in Title I classes. . . . In addition, the religious school must obey these same agents." Brennan declared that the religious school, which has a primary purpose of the advancement and preservation of a particular religion, must endure the ongoing presence of state personnel whose primary purpose is to monitor teachers and students in an attempt to guard against the infiltration of religious thought."[71] And, Brennan added, church and state got entangled in still another way: schedules had to be fixed, classrooms assigned, and reports made—as if that created a threat. Indeed, the Court depicted the city's Title I program as if it were a form of thought control that presented an actual threat to religious liberty.

Thus, if government fails to provide for some sort of surveillance to ward off the inclusion of religion, it behaves unconstitutionally because it aids the religious mission of the church school; but if government does provide for monitoring—once a month or occasional unannounced visits—it gets "excessively" entangled with religion. Either way, according to the Court, it behaves unconstitutionally; its aid violates the establishment clause. And Justice Lewis Powell, who provided the fifth vote in a concurring opinion of his own, asserted that a forbidden entanglement became "compounded by the additional risk of po-

71. Ibid., p. 413.

litical divisiveness stemming from the aid to religion at issue here."[72] That, of course, assumed that the auxiliary services, such as teaching reading to children suffering from dyslexia, advanced the religious mission of their school. Never had the *Lemon* test produced such inequitable results as in *Aguilar.*

Justice O'Connor, unlike her brethren Burger, White, and Rehnquist, does not luridly express herself in establishment-clause cases, nor did she do so here, a fact that enhances the persuasiveness of her argument. She quoted the U.S. district court that had heard voluminous evidence at the trial: "The presumption—that the 'religious mission' will be advanced by providing educational services on parochial school premises—is not supported by the facts of this case." O'Connor concluded, "Indeed, in 19 years there has never been a single incident in which a Title I instructor 'subtly or overtly' attempted to indoctrinate the students in particular religious tenets at public expense."[73] Although no one could know that for certain, the point was clear enough for her to speak of the "unblemished record" of the city's professional educators who did their jobs as experts under appropriate supervision without promoting a religion most of them did not share with their parochial-school students. O'Connor also expressed difficulty in understanding why auxiliary services on the school premises were more entangling or advanced religion more than the same services provided in a mobile classroom parked next door to the school. The Court, she declared, had "greatly exaggerated" the risks of entanglement and indoctrination.[74]

We may be sure that the question of auxiliary services has not been settled by the 1985 decisions. The Court did not hold Title I unconstitutional; it held unconstitutional New York City's implementation of that enactment. Conservatives who rage against the Court for such decisions do not question the constitutionality of Title I, although the authority of Congress to pass legislation that controls education throughout the nation does not seem evident from the Constitution. The situation has an additional complication: the act of Congress pro-

72. Ibid., p. 416
73. Ibid., p. 424.
74. Ibid., p. 421.

vides that federal funds shall be cut off to any school district that does not provide to disadvantaged children in private schools the services equal to those provided in the public schools. That provision of the statute, as well as the unconvincing character of the Court's opinion, ensures that ways will be found to circumvent *Aguilar v. Felton.* But the current Court, its conservative side strengthened by Reagan and Bush appointments, may find that aids previously regarded as unconstitutional do not violate the establishment clause. If proper restraints exist on the funds for parochial schools so that tax monies are not spent for religious purposes and the aid rendered is comparable to the value of the secular education provided by the schools, fairness seems to be on the accommodationist side. Similarly, if proper restraints exist on funds for auxiliary services for disadvantaged students, fairness again seems to be on the accommodationist side. A 5–4 decision of the Rehnquist Court in 1993 sustained the constitutionality of a federal grant to handicapped students to attend parochial schools. President Bill Clinton's nomination of Ruth Bader Ginsburg to replace Byron White will likely result in 5–4 or 6–3 decisions that ensure continuity as well as fairness.

The

Supreme Court

and the Clause:

Public Schools and

Public Creches

Attempts to conduct religious ceremonies and teach religious beliefs in the public schools have rivaled government aid to parochial schools as a source of constitutional litigation. Well-meaning zealots abound—they are never lacking in number—who want the public schools to teach religion. Loyal to the biblical axiom "He that is not for us is against us," they insist that a secular public school without religion is godless; government neutrality in religious matters is, for them, hostility to religion. As true believers who feel driven to proselytize and indoctrinate, they cannot comprehend that religious liberty flourishes best when the state does not embrace religion. They lack understanding that religion is not a matter of ritual or outward conformity. It is rather a matter of spirit and conviction that cannot be orchestrated. Religion is "too personal, too sacred, too holy" to permit its "unhallowed" nurturing by the state.[1] The state has a leaden touch. It can conscript, regiment, and compel obedience. It cannot and should not teach faith, govern conscience, require ritual, or sponsor religion.

As a secular institution the public school has no religious purpose or function. It is not antagonistic to religion or to its role in history or in society. Because those who framed the First Amendment understood the overriding importance of religion, they meant to create a state without a religion, although they did not believe that reference to God established religion; they wanted to be sure that religion flourished because it would not be an engine of the state. Indeed they sought to create a system in which neither religion nor government was sovereign, or slave, to the other. That is a prime reason why the state has an obligation not to teach religion and why religion has achieved an exalted place in our nation; it is the product of voluntary, private choice, not public sponsorship or coercion. The public school is a mirror of society. "Designed," as Justice Felix Frankfurter once wrote, "to serve as perhaps the most powerful agency for promoting cohesion among a heterogeneous democratic people, the public school must keep scrupulously free from entanglement in the strife of sects." He added that the preservation of society from divisive sectarian conflict and of government from irreconcilable pressures demands "strict confinement of the State to instruction other than religious, leaving to the individual's church and home indoctrination in the faith of his choice."[2]

Frankfurter made his statement in a concurring opinion in 1948 when the Court decided its first case on religion in the public schools. The question was whether Champaign, Illinois, violated the establishment clause by permitting clergymen of different faiths to give religious instruction in the public schools at no cost to the public. Denominational classes were made up of pupils whose parents approved. Other students were excused from participation but not from school. The

---

1. *Engel v. Vitale*, 370 U.S. 421, 432 (1962), opinion by Justice Black.
2. *McCollum v. Board of Education*, 333 U.S. 203, 216–17 (1948).

Court, voting 8 to 1, held the so-called released-time program uncon-stitutional because the state's compulsory education laws operated to enforce religious instruction. "Here," declared Justice Hugo Black for the Court, "not only are the state's tax-supported public school build-ings used for the dissemination of religious doctrines, the State also affords sectarian groups an invaluable aid in that it helps to provide pupils for the religious classes through the use of the state's compul-sory public school machinery."[3] Black repudiated the notion that gov-ernment was hostile to religion merely because the public schools did not teach religion.

Black was right. Government neutrality is not hostility to religion, nor is it an implication that religion is insignificant or should not pros-per. On the contrary, it prospers best without government aid to spon-sor, promote, or recognize it. The government must be independent and uncommitted to any religious practices or beliefs. The government is founded not on religious beliefs or revelation but on civil law but-tressed perhaps by natural law. As to religion, government must be silent because the subject lies beyond the jurisdiction of government. Thus it supports no religious faith, practices, or institutions. Neutrality is a form of nourishment for both government and religion.

In 1952, four years after its first released-time case, the Court de-cided another case on the issue in its leading opinion on the need for government to accommodate the needs of religion. The Court sus-tained New York City's program by finding a crucial distinction be-tween it and the 1948 precedent: New York actually released the par-ticipating students from the public schools so that they could attend religious centers of their choice for instruction and devotional ser-vices.[4] Justice William O. Douglas, speaking for the Court's six-member majority, saw no coercion in the city's program and no viola-tion of the establishment clause. Its prohibition, he wrote, "is absolute" (whatever that meant), but it "does not say that in every and all respects there shall be a separation of Church and State." If the separation were absolute, Douglas reasoned, government and religion would be hostile to each other. Municipalities could not offer police or fire protection—

3. Ibid., p. 212.
4. *Zorach v. Clausen*, 343 U.S. 306 (1952).

a farfetched proposition—and the Court could not begin its session with the supplication "God save the United States and this Honorable Court." In this case, Douglas asserted, the public schools did no more than "accommodate their schedules to a program of outside religious instruction." In words that nonpreferentialists or accommodationists would thereafter quote with some frequency, Douglas declared:

> We are a religious people whose institutions presuppose a Supreme Being. . . . When the state encourages religious instruction or cooperates with religious authorities by adjusting the schedule of public events to sectarian needs, it follows the best of our traditions. For it then respects the religious nature of our people and accommodates the public service to their spiritual needs. To hold that it may not would be to find in the Constitution a requirement that the government show a callous indifference to religious groups. That would be preferring those who believe in no religion over those who do believe. . . . But we find no constitutional requirement which makes it necessary for government to be hostile to religion and to throw its weight against efforts to widen the effective scope of religious influence.[5]

The government must be neutral, Douglas observed, and may not coerce anyone, and all that it did here, he added with astounding insensitivity, was close its doors for those who wished to attend their religious sanctuary.

Justices Black, Frankfurter, and Jackson dissented. Frankfurter said the facts showed that the school system did not close its doors and did not suspend operation. It remained very much open during the city's released-time program. Its doors were closed only to the nonparticipating students to keep them in school. Those whom the schools released also remained subject to the compulsory education laws, a fact that was the point of the program: schools did not close, allowing students to do as they wished; schools remained open to channel students into the churches and temples, as if the various denominations could not attract them to sectarian classes without relying on the state's coercive laws governing truancy.

5. Ibid., pp. 313–14.

Jackson, dissenting, observed that although the nonparticipating students remained in school, teaching was suspended so that they would not forge ahead of "churchgoing absentees." But the school "serves as a temporary jail for a pupil who will not go to Church." Speaking as one who sent his children to "privately supported Church schools," Jackson challenged Douglas's suggestion that opposition to released time "can only be antireligious, atheistic, or agnostic" (Jackson's language). The Court's "evangelistic" majority had confused an objection to compulsion with an objection to religion. One might hold religious beliefs deeply enough to think that the state had no business supervising them. And, Jackson added in a memorable line, "The day that this country ceases to be free for irreligion it will cease to be free for religion—except for that sect that can win political power."[6] Notwithstanding the powerful dissenting opinions, the Court's constitutional doctrine in this case remains law.

Ten years later, when the Court considered the constitutionality of a nondenominational prayer for New York's public schools, Douglas wrote an opinion in which he compared that prayer with the daily supplication uttered by the Court's own crier and the practice of each house of Congress in opening with a prayer. On deciding that "the principle is the same" in each case, which was simply not so (children are more impressionable than adults), Douglas inconsistently concluded that New York's law was unconstitutional.[7] He also opined that the Court had wrongly decided the *Everson* school-bus case; he had sided with the majority in 1947. In the second released-time case, Jackson concluded his dissent by remarking that the opinion by Douglas for the majority was better suited for study by students of psychology than students of constitutional law.[8] But Douglas spoke for himself in the New York school-prayer case, though he also joined in the judgment of the Court as announced by Black. Of the seven participating members of the Court, only Potter Stewart dissented.

The case involved what was known as the Regents' Prayer, composed by the state's educational authorities: "Almighty God, we ac-

6. Ibid., p. 325.
7. *Engel v. Vitale*, 370 U.S. 421, 437–44 (1962).
8. *Zorach v. Clausen*, 343 U.S. 306, 325 (1952).

knowledge our dependence upon Thee, and we beg Thy blessings upon us, our parents, our teachers and our Country." By using the public school system, Black declared that New York "has adopted a practice wholly inconsistent with the Establishment Clause."[9] The prayer was religious in nature and "composed by government officials as part of a governmental program to further religious beliefs."[10] Government, Black added, could not, under the establishment clause, influence the prayers uttered by any citizens. Newspaper headlines screamed that the Court had outlawed God from the public schools, and a U.S. senator reacted by saying, "The Supreme Court has made God unconstitutional." Both houses of Congress considered amendments to the Constitution designed to supersede the decision, but no proposal received the necessary two-thirds majority.[11] The Court's view remained the law of the land.

A year later, in 1963, an 8 to 1 Court declared unconstitutional state laws of Pennsylvania and Maryland requiring Bible reading in the public schools. Schools throughout the nation had students recite from the Bible, often in tandem with the pledge of allegiance to the flag.[12] In Pennsylvania the reading of verses from the Bible, followed by a recitation of the Lord's Prayer, was broadcast to every schoolroom via an intercommunications system. Each student chosen to do the daily reading could select the passages he or she wished from any version of the Bible, but the state provided schools only with the King James version. Pennsylvania's endorsement of Protestantism was more offensive by far than the requirement of Bible readings, but the Court addressed only those readings, which were offered without comment. Any student might be excused from the exercises at the written request of a parent. Because the intercom carried the reading throughout a school, no one excused could escape. More important by far, even the

9. *Engel v. Vitale*, 370 U.S. 421, 424 (1962).

10. Ibid., p. 425.

11. Leo Pfeffer, *Church, State, and Freedom*, rev. ed. (Boston, 1967), pp. 466–69. In 1983 the same senator, Sam Ervin of North Carolina, vigorously opposed school prayers and defended the Court from charges that it was hostile to religion. Leo Pfeffer, *Religion, State, and the Burger Court* (Buffalo, N.Y., 1984), p. 83.

12. *Abington Township School District v. Schempp*, 374 U.S. 203 (1963).

availability of a genuine alternative could not eliminate the school's influence in transmitting religious beliefs. As Justice Frankfurter once said, "The law of imitation operates, and nonconformity is not an outstanding characteristic of children. The result is an obvious pressure upon children to attend."[13] Worse by far, nonparticipating students call attention to themselves for reasons that ought to be none of the business of the school or of fellow students, who are liable to persecute the one or few who are different. The school becomes a place where individuals in a minority become stigmatized because of their beliefs.

Justice Tom C. Clark, speaking for the Court, did not, however, focus on elements of coercion present in the cases before the Court. The establishment clause, he maintained, is violated by any government sponsorship of religion in the public schools; it did not matter whether a showing of coercion exists. Clark agreed with Stewart, dissenting, that the state might not establish a religion of secularism in the sense of opposing religion or showing hostility to it, thus preferring irreligion to religion. But the neutrality demanded of the state by the Constitution extended to believers and nonbelievers alike, without the state being the adversary of one against the other. The majority cannot use the machinery of the state to further or practice its beliefs. Any governmental measure whose primary purpose and effect advances religion infringes on the establishment clause.

The public reaction to this decision was similar to the reaction to the first school-prayer decision, but again Congress failed to muster a two-thirds majority for a constitutional amendment. Outright defiance of the Court by school systems, especially in the Deep South, became rather common.[14] So have a variety of alternative means, which some schools have employed to circumvent the Court's decisions. Indiana, for example, permitted Gideon bibles to be distributed to fifth-graders,

13. *McCollum v. Board of Education*, 333 U.S. 203, 227 (1948). Brennan quoted Frankfurter in his concurring opinion in *Abington v. Schempp*, 374 U.S. 203, 291 (1963).

14. On compliance, see Pfeffer, *Church, State, and Freedom*, pp. 466–78; Richard Johnson, *The Dynamics of Compliance* (Evanston, Ill., 1967); Stephen L. Wasby, *The Impact of the United States Supreme Court* (Homewood, Ill., 1970), pp. 126–35.

but the Court let stand a lower-court ruling that the practice violated the establishment clause.

Similarly, in several cases that came before the Supreme Court after its early school-prayer decisions, the Court refused to review lower-court decisions holding unconstitutional various circumventive means devised to restore prayer to the public schools. Some of those lower-court decisions seem as farfetched as the stratagems resorted to by devisers of the proposals struck down. Even the "cookie prayer," purged of its original reference to God cannot constitutionally be said by kindergarten children receiving cookies and milk. That prayer goes: "We thank you for the flowers sweet, we thank you for the food we eat, we thank you for the birds that sing, we thank you [God] for every-thing." The cookie-prayer case was one that the Supreme Court might have safely reviewed and in which it could have sanctioned the prayer. The republic, religious liberty, and the establishment clause could have withstood the shock. Even voluntary prayers initiated by students and said well before the school day begins, or after it, without involvement of school authorities or teachers seem safe, but the Court, which found Sunday closing laws secular in purpose even though having a religious origin, refused to review the decision against the constitutionality of such voluntary prayers.[15]

The drive to insinuate religion in the public schools, especially pray-ers and Bible reading, is usually led by those who are ignorant of history and the fact that the establishment clause is the product of devout Christians who sought to protect religion, as well as religious liberty, by immunizing it from the state's guiding hand. Many mainline churches, belonging to the National Council of Churches, have understood and opposed the drive to have the schools teach or promote religion. Those who criticize the Court's decisions seem to forget the passage in Mat-thew 6:5–6: "And when thou prayest, thou shalt not be as the hypo-crites are: for they love to pray standing in the synagogues and in the corners of the streets, that they may be seen of men. Verily I say unto you, They have their reward. But thou, when thou prayest, enter into thy closet, and when thou hast shut they door, pray to thy Father which

15. Pfeffer, *Religion, State, and the Burger Court,* pp. 86–90.

is in secret; and thy Father which seeth in secret shall reward thee openly."

Some people support the Court out of a concern for the public schools: they do not want a civil and secular institution to introduce denominational hostilities and religious exercises among a heterogeneous population. To do so provokes intolerance and divisiveness. Others support the Court out of a concern for religion; they know that anyone with confidence in his or her faith does not need Caesar to collect what is due to God. They know also that the state helps itself, not religion, and that the state probably can only hurt religion by trying to help it. Still others support the Court out of respect for the feelings of the few who may be ostracized for being different. Excusal remedies solve nothing; they too frequently injure students of no faith or of faiths different from that of the majority. If excuses have to be offered, the exercise is wrong. Providing excusal remedies, as Justice Sandra Day O'Connor said in 1985, sends the wrong message to those who must ask to be excused. It tells them that "they are outsiders, not full members of the political community. . . ."[16] They are merely tolerated, because of their religion or lack of it. The school is not theirs, nor the government, so long as they have to take refuge elsewhere. They are not first-class citizens because they do not belong to the mainline community.

In 1968 the Court held unconstitutional a wholly different attempt by religious fundamentalists to use the public schools for religious purposes. They sought to influence the school curriculum by proscribing the teaching of Darwin's theory of evolution.[17] An old statute of Arkansas modified the famous "monkey law" of Tennessee that had figured in the Scopes trial.[18] Tennessee had made criminal the teaching of any theory that denied the Bible's story of divine creation of the human species and taught, instead, that human beings are descendants of apes. Arkansas merely made it criminal for anyone to teach the theory that the human species descended from a lower order of animals or to use

16. *Wallace v. Jaffree*, 472 U.S. 38, 69 (1985).

17. *Epperson v. Arkansas*, 393 U.S. 97 (1968).

18. Ray Ginger, *Six Days or Forever? Tennessee v. John Thomas Scopes* (Chicago, 1958).

any book that taught that theory. Without a dissenting vote, the Supreme Court declared that a state's legal authority to prescribe the public-school curriculum does not carry with it the right to prohibit the teaching of a scientific theory that supposedly denies biblical teaching. Arkansas offered no secular purpose for the statute. It was enacted to further fundamentalist sectarian conviction and therefore breached the constitutional obligation of the state, under the establishment clause, to maintain neutrality in matters of religion. Without doubt, religious motivations underlay the statute.

That 1968 decision spurred fundamentalist determination to find a way around the Court. "Equal time" was thought to be the way. Fundamentalists claim that evolution is teaching of the religion of "secular humanism." If secular religion can be taught, they argue, creationism or "creation science" should also be taught. But there is no such religion as secular humanism. It is not a religion because it lacks a theology, a concept of the sacred whether of books, or places, or beings, and it has no temples, no connection with faith, sacrifice, prophecy, miracles, mysticism, otherworldliness, or revelation. Its only connection with religion is a concern for ethics and morality. Its name derives from its this-worldliness and its preoccupation with people, contrary to the other-worldliness and preoccupation with God on the part of creationists.

According to creationism, the book of Genesis accurately describes the origins of human beings and deserves accordingly to be part of the curriculum. That equal-time claim seems misdirected, however. If evolution or secular humanism is a religion, steps should be taken to expunge it from the curriculum of the public schools for the same reason that the Court held the Arkansas statute void. Far more important is the fact that creationism, not evolution, is religious in nature. Creationism is based on a belief in the literal truth of the Bible as the word of God. Creationists accept the Bible as an article of faith, not on the basis of verifiable evidence. Scientific truth looks to proofs that can be tested and verified. Scientific truths are not right or wrong on the basis of faith; they are constantly subject to revision, questioning, and skeptical disbelief. They are not accepted on the basis of revelation of any kind or on any authority other than empirical proofs. Creationism is not only religious; it is unscientific, even antiscientific. To teach it is to teach religious faith as if it were scientifically as valid as a scientific theory founded on physical evidence.

Several suits involving efforts to teach creationism in the public schools and to use textbooks supporting it have resulted in lower-court decisions that follow the Supreme Court's doctrine that any act having the primary purpose or effect of advancing religious belief conflicts with the establishment clause. Arkansas enacted an equal-time creationist statute that a lower federal court condemned as unconstitutional in 1982 after a trial that provided nationwide adverse publicity for creationism.[19] The statute in that case assumed that "creation science" is as scientific as Darwinism. The 1982 opinion by U.S. district judge William Overton proved that "creation science" is not scientific and masked religious beliefs.[20] In 1985 another federal court struck down a Louisiana equal-time act of a different sort, and the case, *Edwards v. Aguillard*, went all the way to the Supreme Court.[21]

Edwards v. Aguillard, decided in 1987, was the Court's answer to the very narrow question of whether creation science must be taught if evolutionary theory is taught. The title of Louisiana's Balanced Treatment for Creation-Science and Evolution-Science in Public School Instruction Act revealed the purported objective of evenhandedness. The act did not require the teaching of creation science; rather, it required that, if evolutionary theory was taught, creation science also be taught. Moreover, the act did not mention the Book of Genesis's depiction of creation or in any way refer to religion or religious beliefs. It spoke, rather, about "protecting academic freedom" by the teaching of "the scientific evidences" for both theories "and inferences from those scientific evidences."

Creation science, sometimes called scientific creationism, distinguishes itself from religious creationism. The Arkansas equal-time statute, which Judge Overton voided in 1982, had declared, "Creation-science is an alternative scientific model of origins and can be repre-

19. *New York Times*, Jan. 6, 1982, pt. 1, p. 1; *Time*, Jan. 18, 1982, p. 63; *McLean v. Arkansas Board of Education*, 529 F.Supp. 1255 (E.D. Ark. 1982).

20. *McLean v. Arkansas Board of Education*, 529 F.Supp. 1255 (E.D. Ark. 1982).

21. *Aguillard v. Edwards*, 765 F.2d (5th Cir. 1985); *Edwards v. Aguillard*, 482 U.S. 578 (1987).

sented from a strictly scientific standpoint without any religious doctrine just as evolution-science can. . . ."[22] Creation scientists claim that the galaxy, the solar system, and all plant, animal, and human life were created suddenly, from nothing, and have changed little over time. They claim, too, that people and apes have different ancestry and that catastrophism, including the occurrence of a worldwide flood, explains earth's geology. They exploit the facts that the theory of evolution does not explain creation and advances the unproveable notion that every form of life derived from a single organism. Darwinian theory also presumes that life gradually evolved over millions of years; and according to creation science, which is flat wrong on the point, evolution does not explain the sudden appearance of rather complex fossils without previous fossil records.[23] In any case, creation science, unlike creationism based on Genesis alone, professes not to be religious in character. It claims, rather, to be scientific. But the federal courts believed otherwise. Louisiana's creation-science act never got a chance to operate. A federal district court enjoined its enforcement, a federal court of appeals affirmed, and so did the Supreme Court by a 7–2 vote in *Edwards v. Aguillard.*

Justice Brennan for the Court referred not to creation science but to creationism, as if they were no different. The public schools, he observed, must be free of religious views especially because students are impressionable and their attendance is compulsory. Scientific critiques of prevailing scientific theories can be taught, but the Louisiana act,

22. Sec. 7(j) of the Arkansas statute of 1981, reprinted in *Creationism, Science, and the Law: The Arkansas Case*, edited by Marcel C. LaFollette (Cambridge, Mass., 1983), p. 18.

23. Chris McGowan, *In the Beginning: A Scientist Shows Why the Creationists Are Wrong* (Buffalo, 1984), chaps. 6–9. See also L. Beverly Halstead, "Evolution— The Fossils Say Yes!," in *Science and Creationism*, edited by Ashley Montagu (New York, 1984), pp. 240–81; Roger J. Cuffey, "Palentologic Evidence," in ibid., pp. 255–81; Brian F. Blenister and B. J. Witzke, "Interpreting Earth History," in *Did the Devil Make Darwin Do It? Modern Perspectives on the Creationism-Evolution Controversy*, edited by David D. Wilson (Ames, Iowa, 1983), pp. 55–84; and Douglas J. Fuituyma, *Science on Trial: The Case for Evolution* (New York, 1982), pp. 68–92. For the view of creation science, see Duane T. Gish, *Evolution? The Fossils Say No!*, 3d ed. (San Diego, 1979).

said Brennan, did not ensure that they would be taught, only that if one was taught, so must be the other. But the act allowed the possibility that neither would be taught and so did nothing to teach all the evidence. Brennan also believed that because creationism advocated or indoctrinated religion, it conflicted with the establishment clause. He regarded creation science as if it were an oxymoronic term for a religious belief; he did not address himself to the fact that it claimed to be scientific and to rest on scientific evidence. He saw only the relation between creationism and the Book of Genesis. In that regard his opinion for the Court was unfair and misleading.

He noted that the stated purpose of the act was to protect academic freedom but thought that a sham. The goal of having a more comprehensive science curriculum, he said, was "not furthered either by outlawing the teaching of evolution or by requiring the teaching of creation science." But the act did not outlaw the teaching of evolution. Brennan nevertheless found that the legislature that adopted it had a religious purpose and discriminated against evolutionary theory. His proof was that the act required curriculum guides to be developed for creation science but not for evolution, and it required that only "creation scientists" could serve on panels supplying resource services, which were not provided for evolution. The act prohibited discrimination against creation science or creation scientists but not against evolutionary science or scientists. The act did not encourage the teaching of "all" scientific theories; instead, it "discredited" evolutionary theory by counterbalancing its teaching with the teaching of creationism. Thus, creation science, Brennan declared, embodied a religious belief. Its "primary purpose," contrary to the first prong of the *Lemon* test, was to change the science curriculum of public schools "to reflect endorsement of a religious view that is antagonistic to the theory of evolution."[24]

Brennan's opinion spoke for the Court; even Justice Byron White, the Court's senior accommodationist, said that the Balanced Treatment Act was unconstitutional because its primary purpose was to further a religious belief. Justice Lewis Powell, joined by Sandra Day O'Connor, concurring separately, said that the Balanced Treatment

24. *Edwards v. Aguillard*, 482 U.S. 578, 586, 593 (1987).

Act mandated the teaching of scientific evidence to present a theory of divine creation. That religious purpose, he believed, predominated. All creation scientists, he observed, belonged to either or both of two organizations. One, which was an affiliate of the Christian Heritage College of San Diego, declared its goal to be belief in a "personal, omnipotent Creator," while the other required members to subscribe to a statement that the Bible "is the written word of God," that "all of its assertions are historically and scientifically true," and that the account in Genesis is "a factual presentation of simple historical truth." Powell found also that the language and legislative history of the act "unquestionably demonstrate that its purpose is to advance a particular religious belief."[25] The strength of Powell's opinion derived from his reliance on the opinion of Judge Overton in the Arkansas case.[26]

Justice Antonin Scalia, joined by Chief Justice William Rehnquist, wrote a corrosive dissent that had some merit but was grossly overstated and prejudicial in the extreme. "The body of scientific evidence supporting creation science," he declared, "is as strong as that supporting evolution. In fact, it may be *stronger*." He called evolutionary theory merely a "guess." "It is a very bad guess at that."[27] Scalia produced only his *ipse dixit* as evidence. He had a legitimate point in saying that creation science could be presented without any religious content. But he kept revealing his own deep biases. Failure to teach creation science, he thought, not only deprived students of "one of the two scientific explanations" for the origin of life; it also unconstitutionally promoted the religion of secular humanism. The Court "has held that secular humanism is a religion," he said, and by teaching evolution as if it were a fact, the public schools "are *now* advancing religion in violation of the Establishment Clause."[28] The Court, as a matter of fact, had never "held" that secular humanism is a religion; it had merely said so in a footnote noticing the fact that several "religions," including "Secular Humanism," did not accept a belief in God. That superfluous remark was made in a case in which the Court held unconstitutional, as a violation

25. Ibid., pp. 597–608.
26. *McLean v. Arkansas Board of Education*, 529 F.Supp. 1255 (E.D. Ark. 1982).
27. Ibid., p. 623.
28. Ibid., p. 624.

of religious liberty, a requirement that state officeholders must swear to a belief in God.[29] Secular humanism was not an issue in the case and was not argued before the Court. Scalia's biases burst forth when he lost his capacity to distinguish a gratuitous aside from a judicial holding.

Scalia scourged the Court for not recognizing the secular purpose of the Balanced Treatment Act to promote the academic freedom of students, not of teachers. Although he completely rejected the "purpose" prong of the *Lemon* test, he insisted that the act passed that test and was secular, not sectarian in purpose. As for its supposed discrimination in favor of creation science, he argued that only its teachers needed protection and that in the absence of works on the subject suitable for the classroom, the legislature reasonably believed that a curriculum guide on creation science, but not on evolution, was needed and that creation scientists should provide it. In fact, Scalia was wrong. The Creation Research Society in Ann Arbor published high school texts, and the Institute for Creation Research published a book for teachers called *Scientific Creationism*, which instructed teachers "how to avoid references to religion and the Bible in presenting creationist arguments in the classroom and how to challenge the geological and biological sciences with respect to the antiquity of the earth and organic evolution."[30]

The opinions by Brennan and Scalia did nothing to increase respect for the Court's establishment-clause jurisprudence or its objectivity. Scalia was probably right in characterizing Brennan's opinion as reflecting an "instinctive reaction" that the statute manifested a "Christian fundamentalist reaction."[31] Scalia's opinion manifested antievolutionary beliefs run amok.

The Court reached the right judgment for the wrong reasons. Brennan wholly mischaracterized the Balanced Treatment Act. His opinion

29. *Torcaso v. Watkins*, 367 U.S. 488, 495 n. 11.

30. Norman D. Newell, *Creation and Evolution: Myth or Reality* (New York, 1982), p. 13, citing *Scientific Creationism*, edited by Henry M. Morris (San Diego, 1974), published by Creation Life Publishers, as the teacher's manual, and John N. Moore and Harold S. Slusher, eds., *Biology: A Search for Order in Complexity* (Grand Rapids, Mich., 1970), as a creationist text.

31. *Edwards v. Aguillard*, 482 U.S. 578, 634 (1987).

will hardly be the last word on the matter. It taught advocates of creation science how to enact a statute that might pass constitutional muster. The legislative history of another act should not refer to religion. The act itself should be more explicit about its secular purpose by stipulating its concern for the academic freedom of students to learn all scientific views on creation, and it should also state that its objective is to ensure that all scientific theories should be taught, rather than make the teaching of one theory dependent upon another. Moreover, the act should not include any provisions that seem to discriminate in favor of creation science or against evolution. A statute so drawn should pass the "purpose" prong.

If such a statute actually operated in a way that promoted a religious belief, it would be void. Seventy-five percent of school superintendents in Louisiana had believed creation science to be a religious doctrine,[32] but unless a statute becomes effective, no chance will exist of producing evidence that teaching creation science has the actual effect of teaching religious beliefs or, for that matter, scientific ones. In this case, as in the Arkansas case, sustaining an injunction that foreclosed the operation of the act made the Court's views seem speculative. On the other hand, in the Arkansas case, Judge Overton had masterfully relied on the testimony of experts to explain the reasons that creation science was in fact not a science. Overton directly confronted and refuted all creation-science contentions about its scientific character. Brennan referred to Overton's opinion only to make the minor and obvious point that antagonism exists between the theory of evolution and some religious denominations. He should have exploited the wealth of evidence in Overton's opinion that refuted creationism as a science.[33]

The Court also confronted religion in the public schools when de-

32. Ibid., p. 596 n. 18.

33. Overton's opinion in *McLean v. Arkansas Board of Education* has been reprinted in LaFollette, ed., *Creationism, Science, and the Law*, pp. 45–73; and in Montagu, ed., *Science and Creationism*, pp. 365–97. Other excellent books on the subject are Ronald L. Numbers, *The Creationists: The Evolution of Scientific Creationism* (Cambridge, Mass., 1992); Philip Kitcher, *Abusing Science: The Case against Creationism* (Cambridge, Mass., 1982); McGowan, *In the Beginning*; Wilson, *Did the Devil Make Darwin Do It?*; Futuyma, *Science on Trial*; and Newell, *Creation and Evolution*.

ciding the Ten Commandments case of 1980. In that case the Court judged the constitutionality of a Kentucky statute that required the conspicuous posting in every public schoolroom of a large blowup of the Ten Commandments.[34] The statute also provided that the blowup carry the notation at the bottom that purportedly showed a secular purpose for the display. The notation said that the common law of the United States and the legal codes of Western civilization show the secular applicability of the Ten Commandments, which in point of fact is true. The Court delivered a brief, unsigned opinion that spoke for a 5 to 4 majority. Of the four dissenters, two took no position on the merits, one implied that on full consideration he might sustain the Kentucky act, and only one, Rehnquist, wrote an opinion supporting its constitutionality.

The majority opinion called the notation "self-serving" and stated that "the pre-eminent purpose" of posting the Ten Commandments in the schools was religious. "The Ten Commandments are undeniably a sacred text in the Jewish and Christian faiths, and no legislative recital of a supposed secular purpose can blind us to that fact."[35] The religious purpose of the statute undid it, because the state impermissibly sought to further a religious cause. That conclusion, however true, in no way impairs the accuracy of Rehnquist's observation that "equally undeniable" is the fact that the Ten Commandments "have had a significant impact on the development of secular legal codes of the Western World." Rehnquist quoted from Jackson's concurring opinion in the first released-time case, in 1948, on the difficulty of respecting an educational system that would leave students ignorant of the importance of religion in our history.[36] But that did not answer the Court's declaration that the case would differ if the commandments had been integrated into the curriculum, because the Bible "may constitutionally be used in an appropriate study of history, civilization, ethics, comparative religion, or the like"—which has been the Court's consistent position.[37]

34. *Stone v. Graham*, 449 U.S. 39 (1980).
35. Ibid., p. 41.
36. Ibid., pp. 45–46.
37. Ibid., p. 42. See *Abington Township School District v. Schempp*, 374 U.S. 203, 225 (1963).

The real problem is that the Court's zealous application of the establishment clause seems to make little sense. In 1961 the Court sustained the constitutionality of Sunday closing laws, even though they have an admittedly religious origin.[38] If the Court could find a secular purpose in statutes once religiously motivated, it ought to be able to find a legitimate secular purpose in the public display by the state of the Ten Commandments. To put the establishment clause athwart that display by public schools raises the question whether the Court would find constitutional a similar display of the Declaration of Independence or the Virginia Statute of Religious Freedom, both of which refer to God. Would a government or school display of the nation's motto, "In God We Trust," or of "The Star-Spangled Banner" be constitutional? Congress made that song our national anthem in 1931, although one verse includes the words "And this be our motto, 'In God Is Our Trust.'" Would a photograph of a dollar bill or a Lincoln penny, with a similar motto, be constitutional if posted on public property? Is the pledge of allegiance constitutional as a result of the inclusion by Congress in 1954 of the words "one Nation under God"? Can a public school post a copy of the pledge? Presumably the answer to these questions is "yes" because the currency, the coinage, the pledge, and the anthem are not sacred texts, although from the standpoint of civil religion, the Declaration of Independence and the Virginia Statute of Religious Freedom are sacred texts. The Ten Commandments do bear a relationship to civilized secular conduct. Holding their school display to be unconstitutional does not inspire confidence in the separation of government and religion or in the good judgment of the Court.

The Court that found Christmas to be a national holiday for secular reasons or Sundays to be secular days ought to be clever enough to make reasonable distinctions, to be reasonably consistent, and to protect the public confidence in it. It should be able and willing, as Justice Arthur Goldberg once wrote, "to distinguish between the real threat and mere shadow."[39] Finding the public-school display of the Ten Commandments unconstitutional does not strike down a real threat, while finding the publicly sponsored display of a nativity scene consti-

---

38. Sunday Closing Cases, 366 U.S. 420 (1961).
39. *Abington Township School District v. Schempp*, 374 U.S. 203, 308 (1963).

tutional because it is secular when accompanied by Santa Claus is neither reasonable nor consistent, nor does it void a government endorsement of religion that can harm nonadherents.[40]

In 1985 the Court again confronted the school-prayer issue.[41] Alabama, seeking a constitutional way to reintroduce prayers, had first ordered a one-minute period of silence in the public schools, then a period of silence "for meditation or voluntary prayer," and finally a state-composed prayer. In 1984 the Court in one sentence—"The judgment with respect to other issues presented by the appeals is affirmed"—upheld a lower federal court ruling against the government prayer, which boldly defied the Court's 1962 decision against New York's Regents' Prayer.[42] The 1985 case dealt with the more complicated issue of the period of silence for meditation or voluntary prayer. Justice Stevens for a 6 to 3 Court held the act unconstitutional because it was "entirely motivated by a purpose to advance religion" and had "*no* secular purpose."[43] The evidence irrefutably proved that.

Stevens spoke for five members of the Court; Justice O'Connor, in a splendidly analytical opinion, concurred separately in the judgment. Rehnquist wrote fiction and passed it off as history, namely that the framers of the establishment clause merely intended to prohibit "the designation of any church as a 'national' one" and to prevent "a preference of one religious denomination or sect over others."[44] One of Rehnquist's footnotes seems representative of the quality of his history. On behalf of the proposition that establishments of religion were "prevalent" during the late eighteenth and early nineteenth centuries, he mentioned four examples, one of which is "Rhode Island Charter of 1633 (superseded 1842)." Rhode Island's first charter, dated 1663, guaranteed religious liberty; neither as a colony nor as a state did Rhode Island ever have an establishment of religion.[45]

---

40. See *Lynch v. Donnelly*, 465 U.S. 668 (1984), discussed below in text related to note 63.

41. *Wallace v. Jaffree*, 472 U.S. 38 (1985).

42. *Wallace v. Jaffree*, 466 U.S. 924 (1985); *Engel v. Vitale*, 370 U.S. 421 (1962).

43. *Wallace v. Jaffree*, 472 U.S. 38, 56 (1985).

44. Ibid., pp. 99, 113.

45. Ibid., p. 99.

Justice White flunked history when he complimented Rehnquist for his description of the background of the establishment clause. Burger splenetically scored the Court's hostility to religion and asserted that O'Connor had not gone far enough. She said she could not "discern a serious threat to religious liberty from a room of silent, thoughtful schoolchildren."[46] "I would add to that," Burger declared, "even if they chose to pray."[47] The chief justice willfully misunderstood or missed the point. No danger derived from praying pupils; it originated, rather, with the state's effort to further praying, which is no more the business of the state than whether a child has received the sacrament of baptism.

The fact is that no need existed for the state law. Alabama already had a law fixing an official minute of silence, during which time students could pray if they wished—or daydream if they wished. Indeed, a student might silently pray at any time during the school day. But the state wanted to orchestrate group prayer by capitalizing on the impressionability of youngsters. As O'Connor demonstrated, a state-sponsored moment of silence differed radically from state-sponsored religious exercises. A moment of silence need not be religious or compromise anyone's beliefs, or expose anyone to the prayers or thoughts of others, and it involves no state encouragement to pray. "The crucial question," she wrote, "is whether the State has conveyed or attempted to convey the message that children should use the moment of silence for prayer."[48] Candor, she insisted, demanded a single answer: the state "endorses the decision to pray during a moment of silence, and accordingly sponsors a religious exercise."[49] She rejected the claim that the statute accommodated religion. This statute removed no such burden. Because students who were inclined to pray silently already had the opportunity of doing so voluntarily, without the statute, its objective became clearer: to provide an official endorsement and promotion of religion, contrary to the establishment clause. Unfortunately President Ronald Reagan had not read the excellent opinion of his appointee, Justice O'Connor. In a radio speech to the nation, he made the state-

46. Ibid., p. 73.
47. Ibid., p. 90.
48. Ibid., p. 73.
49. Ibid., pp. 78–79.

ment, which was either ignorant or demagogic, that "the good Lord who has given our country so much should never have been expelled from our nation's classrooms." The good Lord was never expelled, nor, contrary to the president, had God been barred "from our public life."[50]

In retrospect, the case shows that the majority of the Court realized that big oaks grow from small acorns. If it yielded on the principle that government may not legislate on the subject of prayers, the Court would lose its foundation for striking down as unconstitutional still more serious infringements than state encouragement of prayer during a moment of silence in the public schools. That, perhaps, is why even the "cookie prayer" cannot pass the First Amendment's yardstick. Although shadows must be distinguished from real threats, in the presence of a real threat the time to take alarm, as Madison said in a remark quoted by Stevens, is "the first experiment on our liberties."[51]

In 1992 the Court decided that prayers at high school commencements violate the establishment clause.[52] The decision surprised Court watchers, who had expected a bench dominated by Reagan-Bush appointees to rule that nonsectarian prayers to God on a public ceremonial occasion had the sanction of tradition. Graduation exercises, unlike regular school days, were not governed by compulsory attendance laws and did not exploit a captive audience. Nevertheless the Court, voting 5–4, voided Providence's ceremonial prayers because of a pervasive government involvement with religious activity. Justice Anthony Kennedy, a Reagan appointee, spoke for Blackmun, Stevens, O'Connor, and Souter, all Republican appointees. David Souter had joined the Court in 1990. The other Bush appointee, Clarence Thomas, sided with the dissenters.

The Bush administration as *amicus curiae* had invited the Court to repudiate its three-prong *Lemon* test, which required that, in order for a government act to survive establishment-clause scrutiny, it must be secular in purpose; must not advance or inhibit religion, and must not

50. "Radio Address to the Nation," Aug. 24, 1985, in *Weekly Compilation of Presidential Documents* (Washington, D.C., 1985), p. 1001.

51. *Wallace v. Jaffree*, 472 U.S. 38, 53 n. 38.

52. *Lee v. Weisman*, 112 S.Ct. 2649 (1992).

foster excessive government entanglement with religion. The *Lemon* test did not require a showing of any government coercion. Indeed, the Court had frequently asserted that proof of coercion was unnecessary to establish an infringement of the establishment clause. But the solicitor general as well as the City of Providence argued that the Court should substitute for the *Lemon* test a requirement of coercion to prove unconstitutionality: unless government on pain of criminal penalty had compelled behavior conflicting with religious belief or prevented behavior consonant with that belief, the establishment clause had not been violated. The Court declined the opportunity to reconsider its *Lemon* test or to adopt the proposed coercion test, yet it decided the case primarily on the basis of the psychologically coercive nature of Providence's commencement prayers.

The city had long authorized school principals to invite clergymen to offer invocations and benedictions at graduation exercises. In this case a principal invited a rabbi to offer the prayers and instructed him to keep the prayers nonsectarian. The rabbi gave the invocation to a standing audience that had just recited the pledge to the flag, which refers to "one nation under God." Speaking for about a minute, the rabbi addressed the "God of the Free, Hope of the Brave." At the close of the ceremonies, the audience again arose to receive the rabbi's brief benediction. The Court acknowledged that the content of the prayers reflected a good-faith effort by the school to avoid sectarianism; the dissenters said that the rabbi's prayers were "so characteristically American they could have come from the pen of George Washington or Abraham Lincoln himself."[53]

Justice Kennedy, who delivered the Court's opinion, was on record as a critic of the *Lemon* test and a supporter of noncoercive government accommodations of religion. He did not think that the display of a creche or nativity scene was psychologically coercive to non-Christian observers, though it might make them feel like outsiders.[54] In the commencement-prayer case, however, he believed that state-sponsored religious activity breached the establishment clause and that co-

---

53. Ibid., p. 2684.

54. *Allegheny County v. ACLU*, 109 S.Ct. 3086 (1989), dissenting opinion, discussed below.

ercion of the students intensified the breach. As the swing man in the case, Kennedy apparently had his way with the other members of the majority who would have been on the losing side had they not capitulated to his views.

The school principal, Kennedy declared, "directed and controlled the content of the prayer" and assisted in its composition.[55] The principal, however, had done no more than offer the rabbi the standard instruction to be nonsectarian. Kennedy consistently overstated his argument. He was accurate, however, in describing the nonsectarian prayer as one that came within the ambit of the Judeo-Christian tradition, though he said nothing about the possible offense of such a prayer to the millions of Americans who do not share that tradition. His emphasis on the principal's involvement in the prayers, giving them the imprint of the state, in effect demonstrated an excessive government entanglement with religion, a violation of the third prong of the *Lemon* test. Indeed, government sponsorship of the prayers in a school ceremony violated the purpose and effects prongs too. So the lower federal courts had held. But Kennedy ignored the *Lemon* test.

Instead, he emphasized the "coercive pressure" of the school in exposing students to religious activity and to the risk of "indirect coercion" that might be as "real as any overt compulsion." Standing up for the prayers and even hearing them in silence, he thought, revealed "an expression of participation" in the rabbi's prayer. He drew tenuous conclusions from "research in psychology" to show that the government was using "social pressure to enforce orthodoxy." The fact that attendance at graduation ceremonies was voluntary did not lessen the compulsion, Kennedy believed, because graduation was so significant an occasion that students would not absent themselves. "The Constitution," he concluded, "forbids the State to exact religious conformity from a student as the price of attending her own high school graduation."[56]

The other four members of the Court who had joined Kennedy's opinion also spoke through concurring opinions by Blackmun and Souter. Blackmun conceded that proof of government coercion

55. *Lee v. Weisman*, 112 S.Ct. 2649, 2657 (1992).
56. Ibid., pp. 2649, 2660.

showed government endorsement or promotion of religion, a violation of the *Lemon* test. But proof of government coercion, he argued, was wholly unnecessary to show a conflict with the establishment clause. In thirty-two establishment-clause cases decided since the *Lemon* case of 1971, Blackmun observed, the Court had relied on the *Lemon* test in all but one and should have done so again here.[57]

Souter, in a splendid opinion, proved that in many of the precedents revealing religious endorsement, not only was coercion absent; the precedents also showed that nonpreferential religious endorsement was unconstitutional. Souter further stressed that accommodation to religion, to be constitutional, should remove a burden on the free exercise of religion, but religious students could not complain that the omission of prayers from their graduation ceremony burdened their freedom of religion.[58]

In a scathing opinion for the dissenters, an opinion not calculated to win friends and influence people in the majority, Scalia expatiated on the American history of public ceremonies featuring prayers and thanksgiving. Commencement prayers were as unconstitutional as those ceremonies and the pledge to the flag—not at all. Scalia ridiculed as "incoherent" and "ludicrous" Kennedy's emphasis on psychological coercion, and added that because many graduating seniors were old enough to vote, the Court ought not to treat them as impressionable first-graders. Nothing in the record, Scalia explained, suggested that the rabbi was the "mouthpiece" of school officials or that they had controlled graduation prayers. He slammed Kennedy's "boundless, and boundlessly manipulative test of psychological coercion," and he scored the *Lemon* test, whose infirmities had been demonstrated by the majority's having ignored it. Scalia had a stronger point when he concluded that far from the rabbi's prayers being divisive, as Kennedy

57. Ibid., pp. 2661–67. The exception was in *Marsh v. Chambers*, 463 U.S. 783 (1983), discussed below, in which the Court sustained legislative chaplaincies.

58. *Lee v. Weisman*, 112 S.Ct. 2649, 2667–78 (1992). Souter relied on the first edition of this book to prove his point about nonpreferential aid being unconstitutional; Scalia also relied on the book to acknowledge that nonpreferential aid was unconstitutional but only when it was coercive in character. Ibid., p. 2683.

suggested, "The Baptist or Catholic who heard and joined in the simple and inspiring prayers of Rabbi Gutterman on this official and patriotic occasion was inoculated from religious bigotry and prejudice in a manner that cannot be replicated."[59]

Like Kennedy, Scalia revealed no sensitivity to students who did not share the Judeo-Christian tradition. Indeed, some who shared it, like the girl who brought the suit, objected in principle to the state's sponsorship of religion. Some believe that government has no business promoting or endorsing religious beliefs. Such people as well as those who do not share the Judeo-Christian tradition should not be made to feel that they are un-American or outsiders. State-sponsored religion does more harm than good in a religiously pluralistic nation The establishment clause is supposed to protect the minority; the majority does not need it. Moreover, the Court's opinion, by needlessly undermining the *Lemon* test, further confused its establishment-clause jurisprudence.

Confusion is apparent in Scalia's opinion. Despite the majority decision, the dissenters believed that future graduation ceremonies throughout the nation might continue to offer prayers so long as school authorities announce that participation is voluntary and that no one is compelled to rise or be assumed to have participated in prayer even if he or she stood. But this view is mistaken. It does not meet Kennedy's objection that the state controlled the prayer by advising that it be nonsectarian. Even if such advice does not exist, the problems remain whether a Judeo-Christian prayer or any state-sponsored prayer conforms to the establishment clause. However, the majority opinion added no clarity to these problems or to establishment-clause jurisprudence. Cases involving prayers at commencements will continue to arise.

One case did arise in 1993, but the Court refused to decide it, allowing a Fifth Circuit Court of Appeals decision to stand, though it seems to conflict with decision of 1992 against commencement prayers. The Fifth Circuit case from Texas allowed for a distinction, however, because the prayer was offered by a student, not a clergyman, after the

59. Ibid., p. 2686.

senior class had voted in favor of having commencement prayer.[60] The role of the school, therefore, was comparatively minimal. Yet a majority vote by high school students seems to be a grossly inadequate justification for sacrificing establishment-clause values. The clause, like any provision of the Bill of Rights, functions to protect the minority from the majority. A prayer, even if student-led at student behest, can violate the beliefs of minority students and operates at a school-sponsored educational event. School prayers of any shape or sort should be held to constitute a violation of the establishment clause.

The failure of the Court to review the Fifth Circuit's decision will merely put off temporarily the need to settle the issue once and for all. Courts of appeals in other circuits will undoubtedly reach conflicting decisions, as will state courts, requiring the Supreme Court to address the issue in order to enforce a uniform interpretation of the establishment clause throughout the nation. The departure of Byron White from the Court after the term ending June 1993 more than likely means a weakening of the accommodationist wing of the Court. Justice Ruth Bader Ginsburg, President Bill Clinton's appointee, will probably reinforce the separationist wing.

In 1992 the Court refused to hear another case of considerable importance.[61] Hawaii by statute had designated Good Friday as a state holiday. Because that holiday commemorates the crucifixion of Jesus, it is clearly a religious holiday. State celebration of that holiday is clearly sectarian and directly conflicts with the establishment clause. However, because the state legislature professed that the holiday also had a secular aspect, giving people a day off from work, the lower federal courts sustained the statute. The Ninth Circuit Court of Appeals delivered a reprehensible opinion that had its ludicrous aspects. The court declared that the state merely had made a paid state holiday on Good Friday, giving "an extra day of rest for a weary public labor-force." The federal judges could not see an endorsement of religion. Rather, they stated that it was "of no constitutional moment that Hawaii selected a day of traditional Christian worship, rather than a neutral date, for its

---

60. *Jones v. Clear Creek Independent School District*, 977 F.2d 963 (5th Cir. 1992).
61. *Cammack v. Waihee*, 112 S.Ct. 3027 (1992).

spring holiday once it identified the need."[62] Of the nine justices on the Supreme Court, four—the number necessary to review a case—could not be found who thought that the establishment-clause issue deserved a final hearing. Denying *certiorari* in a case raising a trivial issue, such as whether the cry "God save this honorable Court" violates the establishment clause, is understandable and sensible; denying *certiorari* in a case raising a momentous establishment-clause issue is contemptible. By turning tail, the Court avoided a public showing that it was divided.

Publicly sponsored religious symbols as well as school prayers have publicly divided the Court and produced conflicting interpretations of the establishment clause. In 1984 the Court significantly lowered the wall of separation between church and state by sanctioning an official display of a sacred Christian symbol.[63] Pawtucket, Rhode Island, included a nativity scene in its annual Christmas exhibit in the center of the city's shopping district. The case raised the question of whether Pawtucket's creche violated the establishment clause.

Chief Justice Burger, for a 5 to 4 Court, ruled that despite the religious nature of the creche, Pawtucket had a secular purpose in displaying it, as evinced by the fact that it was part of a Christmas exhibit that proclaimed "Season's Greetings" and included Santa Claus, his reindeer, a Christmas tree, a wishing well, figures of carolers, a clown, an elephant, and a teddy bear. That the First Amendment, Burger argued, did not mandate complete separation is shown by our national motto, paid chaplains, presidential proclamation invoking God, the pledge of allegiance, and religious art in publicly supported museums.

Brennan, speaking for the dissenters and reading the majority narrowly, observed that the question was still open on the constitutionality of a public display on public property of just a creche or of the display of some other sacred symbol such as a crucifixion scene. Brennan repudiated the supposed secular character of the creche. "For Christians," he argued, "the essential message of the nativity is that God became incarnate in the person of Christ." Brennan lambasted the majority for their insensitivity toward the feelings of non-Christians.

A spokesman for the National Council of Churches complained that

62. *Cammack v. Waihee*, 944 F.2d 466 (1991).
63. *Lynch v. Donnelly*, 465 U.S. 668 (1984).

the Court had put Christ "on the same level as Santa Claus and Rudolph the Red-Nosed Reindeer." Clearly, the Court lacked understanding of what constitutes an establishment of religion, because Santa's presence in no way minimized, transformed, or secularized the Christian message of the creche. It put Christ's mass back into Christmas.

The Court understood that fact only when in 1989 it confronted a case that presented a creche on public property without any secular embellishments. During the Christmas season Allegheny County, Pennsylvania, conspicuously displayed a large creche on the grand stairway of the county courthouse, the seat of county government. Atop the creche an angel bore a banner proclaiming "Gloria in Excelsis Deo!" (Glory to God in the Highest) from the gospel of Luke. A sign indicated that the creche had been donated by the Holy Name Society, a Roman Catholic organization. The American Civil Liberties Union sued to enjoin the exhibition of the creche, and the Supreme Court, in an opinion by Justice Harry Blackmun for a bare majority, held that the establishment clause prevented the exhibit.[64]

Blackmun declared that the clause obligated the Court to determine whether a particular governmental practice had the purpose or effect of "endorsing" religion. Endorsement meant favoritism, preference, or promotion of religion, or any practice by which government sided with religious belief, or made adherence to a religion "relevant in any way to a person's standing in the political community." By that Blackmun meant that government endorsement of religion, as Justice O'Connor had declared in her concurring opinion in the Pawtucket creche case, "sends a message to nonadherents that they are outsiders, not full members of the political community, and an accompanying message to adherents that they are insiders, favored members of the political community."[65] The setting or context of the creche determined its effect. When surrounded by secular symbols, the creche lost its Christian endorsement, as in Pawtucket, but here the creche stood alone. It was unconstitutional because it communicated government sponsorship of religious beliefs. It sent the unmistakable Christian message that the county government endorsed praise to God for the birth of Jesus.

64. *Allegheny County v. ACLU*, 109 S.Ct. 3086 (1989).

65. Ibid., pp. 3101, 3102, quoting *Lynch v. Donnelly*, 465 U.S. 668, 688 (1984).

Government may celebrate Christmas as a "cultural phenomenon" but not as a Christian holy day.

After the Pawtucket case, Rehnquist had succeeded Burger as chief justice, and Antonin Scalia and Anthony Kennedy had joined the Court. With White, these four dissented in a strong and angry opinion by Kennedy. He insisted that the majority's view made the establishment clause reflect "an unjustified hostility toward religion." Government policies of "accommodation, acknowledgment, and support for religion" were part of the American heritage. In the absence of coercion, accommodation allowed latitude in recognizing the major role of religion in our society. The county merely celebrated a holiday with religious significance. Passersby who disagreed with the religious message were free to turn their backs. Moreover, the county did not proselytize. If government could commemorate the holiday only as celebrated by nonadherents, their views would fix government policy, and their reaction to the creche made its effect unconstitutional because it made them feel like outsiders. Then, legislative chaplains, Thanksgiving proclamations, the pledge of allegiance to the flag, and even the national motto could not escape invalidation as well. The Court, Kennedy concluded, should not lend its assistance to an "Orwellian rewriting of history."[66]

Blackmun, speaking for the majority, regarded some of the practices that Kennedy found in jeopardy to be no more than "ceremonial deism" meriting a *de minimis* attitude. Contrary to Blackman, deism is theistic and religious. However ceremonial, it raised questions that Blackmun chose not to confront in any principled manner; similarly, he dismissed Christmas caroling on public property as beyond constitutional challenge, though some of it is Christological in character and to nonadherents as objectionable as the creche. Activities of this sort, Blackmun declared on his own *ipse dixit*, "do not demonstrate the government's allegiance to, or endorsement of, the Christian faith." How the Court distinguished "Gloria in Excelsis Deo" (prohibited) from "Christ the Lord" in carols (allowed) is a mystery.[67]

66. *Allegheny County v. ACLU*, 109 S.Ct. 3146 (1989).
67. Ibid., pp. 3106, 3111.

To the extent that Kennedy had relied on history to legitimate Thanksgiving and other ceremonially deistic practices, Blackmun replied that history "cannot legitimate practices that demonstrate government's allegiance to a particular sect or creed," but he did not reconcile this statement with winking at ceremonial deism. Kennedy's view of the establishment clause, including his no-proselytizing test would "gut" the clause, said Blackmun.[68]

Kennedy's accusation that the Court was hostile to religion, Blackmun believed, was "offensive" and "absurd." Kennedy confused a respect for religious pluralism with hostility or indifference. If the government remains secular rather than affiliating itself with religious beliefs and institutions, Blackmun reasoned, it avoids discriminating among its citizens on the basis of religion. He responded also to Kennedy's view that prohibiting government from celebrating Christmas as a religious holiday "discriminated against Christians" in favor of non-Christians. The establishment clause, Blackmun stated, cannot allow government to celebrate Christmas as a religious holiday, because that would necessarily mean that "government really is declaring Jesus to be the Messiah, a specifically Christian belief." By contrast, government celebration of the secular aspects of Christmas did not favor nonadherents' beliefs over those of Christians.[69]

Finally, Blackmun responded to Kennedy's repeated interpretation of the creche as a mere government "accommodation" of religion involving no coercion. A legitimate accommodation, to the Court majority, was a government act that removed a burden on the free exercise of religion, usually by exempting a religious practice from coercive regulation. So understood, an accommodation of religion has no pertinence to the creche. Similarly, Justice O'Connor, concurring separately, observed that the Court had long taken the position that proof of coercion had relevance to a free-exercise claim but was "not a necessary element of any claim under the Establishment Clause."[70] The free-exercise clause would be a redundancy if there were a requirement that

68. Ibid., p. 3106.
69. Ibid., p. 3110.
70. Ibid., p. 3119, quoting *Engle v. Vitale*, 370 U.S. 421, 430 (1962).

coercion be shown as an element of an establishment-clause violation. In fact, however, a showing of coercion proved a violation of the free-exercise clause. Accordingly, Kennedy's requirement of proof of coercion in an establishment-clause case would make that clause redundant and utterly subordinate to the free-exercise clause.

On the same day and in the same set of opinions the Court disposed of an allied question involving the constitutionality of the display of a menorah on public property. A block away from the county court-house where the creche was on display, in downtown Pittsburgh, outside a city building, the city had erected a forty-five-foot Christmas tree and an eighteen-foot menorah, or giant candelabrum, that commemorated the Jewish holiday of Chanukah. The menorah was the property of Chabad, a small, Orthodox Jewish sect. The ACLU, joined by several Jewish organizations as *amici curiae*, objected to the menorah as a violation of the establishment clause. The Court held that the menorah was constitutional, though the creche was not.

The question on the menorah forced the justices to regroup. Of the five-member majority on the creche issue, only Blackmun and O'Connor thought the menorah was constitutional, but the four dissenters on the creche issue agreed with Blackmun and O'Connor on the menorah issue. Justices Brennan, Stevens, and Marshall, who voted against the creche, dissented on the menorah issue because they believed that the display of that religious symbol by government was also unconstitutional. Thus the Court split 6–3 on the menorah, but could not produce an official opinion for the Court.

Chanukah, which happens to fall around Christmastime, is a holiday celebrating an event when Jews rededicated their temple in Jerusalem after recapturing it from the Hellenic Syrians, following a political rebellion about a century and a half before the time of Christ. Antiochus IV, the Syrian despot, had decreed death for the observance of Jewish practices and had compelled loyalty to pagan abominations, which he substituted. To enforce his outlawing of Judaism, his army murdered thousands of Jews and dismantled their temple. When they finally triumphed in battle, regained independence, and rebuilt the temple, they had enough oil to burn for only one day, though the temple's menorah should have burned continuously for seven days. As Blackmun pointed out, according to the Talmud the oil miraculously burned for eight days.[71]

Thus Chanukah, which commemorates the survival of Judaism, lasts eight days and the Chanukah menorah has a candle for each day. Without doubt, in modern America the proximity of Chanukah to Christmas and the practice of giving gifts to children has secularized the holiday, making it seem a Jewish equivalent of Christmas. Nevertheless, Chabad, the Chasidic sect that owned the menorah displayed in Pittsburgh, celebrated Chanukah as a purely religious holiday and advocated public display of the menorah as part of its own proselytizing mission, as Blackmun noted. He dismissed that and the evidence that Chabad lit the menorah in a religious ceremony, which included the recital of traditional blessings, because the ACLU had not made it an issue and the lower courts had not considered it.

For Blackmun, the Christmas tree was a secular symbol and the predominant object in the display; at its foot was a sign, bearing the mayor's name, with a purely secular message concerning festive lights by which the city made its "Salute to Liberty" during the holiday season. Accordingly, the city did not celebrate Christmas or Chanukah as religious holidays but rather as cultural events with secular dimensions that honored religious diversity, not religion. The menorah might be a religious symbol but the city did not endorse Judaism.

Blackmun made much of the fact that the Court had to "interpret the menorah in the light of the tree, rather than *vice versa.*"[72] Presumably if the menorah had been forty-five feet tall and the tree eighteen feet, the secular character of the exhibit would have become sectarian, or if the menorah had stood alone, without the tree, it would have also been unconstitutional. Understandably Kennedy thought the Court's reasoning was ludicrous, for it could lead to trials in which witnesses testify that they were offended but might have been less offended if the religious symbol stood closer to a candy cane. Kennedy's opinion

71. Abraham Schalit, ed., *The World History of the Jewish People. The Hellenistic Age: Political History of Jewish Palestine from 332 B.C.E. to 67 B.C.E.* (New Brunswick, N.J., 1972), pp. 131–200.

72. *Allegheny County v. ACLU*, 109 S.Ct. 3086, 3114 (1989).

barely mentioned the menorah, but he clearly believed that government recognition of the Judeo-Christian tradition merely accommodated religion without implicating the establishment clause.

By contrast, Justices Brennan, Stevens, and Marshall, who agreed
that the display of the creche was unconstitutional, believed the same
about the menorah. They believed that the Christmas tree is a religious,
not a secular, symbol; Chanukah is a religious holiday symbolized by
the menorah; and government should not promote pluralism by sponsoring displays that have strong religious associations. Both Brennan
and Stevens, who wrote opinions, mocked Blackmun's views on the
tree and menorah. They thought that an eighteen-foot menorah, which
is enormous for a menorah, would more likely dominate the exhibit
than the tree and would give it religious significance. Brennan made the
best point concisely. He said that Blackmun at the outset of his opinion
"recognizes the menorah is a religious symbol. That should have been
the end of the case."[73]

Menorahs belong in private homes and synagogues. Public creches
belong on private property—on lawns and church fronts. People who
insist on displaying religious symbols on public property under government auspices are demanding government endorsement for their religious beliefs. They seem mean-spirited because they are free to exhibit
their religious symbols without government sponsorship and in hun-
dreds of places other than on public property. Moreover, these religious displays under government auspices are divisive. They send the
wrong message to nonbelievers, who should not be made to feel that
they do not belong equally to America. Moreover, many people of
strong religious beliefs, whether Christian or Jewish, may be as offended as nonbelievers. These displays associate sacred symbols with
the commercialization of religious holidays and expose those symbols
to misuse and insult. In 1992, for example, in Cincinnati, Chabad's
Chanukah display of its enormous menorah inspired the Ku Klux Klan
to win a city permit authorizing it to erect a cross. The cross provoked
vandalism by Klan opponents and public dissension at a time supposedly dedicated to good will among people.

Although the Court could see no law respecting an establishment of

73. Ibid., p. 3127.

religion in the Pawtucket creche or in the Pittsburgh menorah, its judgment of whether it understood what constitutes an establishment is questionable in the light of its previous decision in the tavern case. In that case the Court discerned a forbidden establishment in a police power measure aimed at keeping boisterous patrons of a tavern from disturbing a church. Dissenting in the tavern case, Justice Rehnquist observed that "silly cases" like this one, as well as great or hard cases, make bad law.[74] Chief Justice Burger aimed the Court's "heavy First Amendment artillery," in Rehnquist's phrase, at a statute that banned the sale of alcoholic beverages within 500 feet of a school or church should either of them object to the presence of a neighboring tavern. Rehnquist rightly believed that a sensible statute had not breached the wall of separation of church and state. Originally, Massachusetts had absolutely banned such taverns but found that the objective of the state police power, promoting neighborhood peace, could be fulfilled by the less drastic method of allowing schools and churches to take the initiative of registering objections. In this case a church objected to having liquor sold at a place located ten feet away.

Burger held that vesting the church with the state's veto power breached the prohibition against an establishment of religion, because the church's involvement in a decision not to issue a liquor license vitiated the secular purposes of the statute, advanced the cause of religion, and excessively entangled state and church. Burger even objected to the fact that the church had not guaranteed to employ its veto exclusively for "secular, neutral, and nonideological purposes." If Burger had used that standard in other cases, he would have supported the Court in striking down a variety of government aids to parochial schools (including New York's implementation of Title I programs and the shared-time program of Grand Rapids) and Alabama's requirement of a minute of silence for meditation or private prayer. And if he and the Court had employed that same standard, they would have found unconstitutional the Minnesota tax deduction for the costs of tuition and books for parochial schools, the publicly sponsored Pawtucket creche, and the publicly paid legislative chaplain in Nebraska.

As the creche and tavern cases suggest, the Court settles a miscellany

74. *Larkin v. Grendel's Den, Inc.*, 459 U.S. 1081 (1982).

of questions on the establishment clause. One of the more important questions concerned the constitutionality of Sunday closing laws. In four companion cases of 1961, the Court held that a secular purpose had long ago supplanted the religious origins and character of Sunday laws. What was once a compulsory day of rest on the Christian sabbath had become a day decreed by government as a day of rest to promote the public health, safety, and relaxation. Chief Justice Earl Warren espoused that view, and the secularity of Sunday seems tenable given the fact Communist Russia made Sunday a day of rest too. Although forced shutdown on the Christian sabbath does not necessarily advance religion, it certainly helps. In fact, Sunday remains for many Americans the churchgoing day and continues to have a religious character unlike other days of the week. Warren's four opinions for the Court appear difficult to reconcile with the effects test for determining whether a statute violates the establishment clause.[75] The Court should have ruled that forced Sunday laws have the effect of advancing religion.[76]

In two of the four Sunday-closing cases, forced closure penalized those for whom the sabbath comes on Saturday. The failure of the statutes before the Court to give observant Jews and Seventh-Day Adventists, among others, an alternative day of rest should have been held unconstitutional on grounds of preference of one set of religious beliefs over another. The state may have a legitimate stake in forcing all citizens to take a day off from work, but no argument can show that one's health or welfare is improved by resting on Sunday rather than Saturday.[77]

In the 1963 case of a Seventh-Day Adventist who lost employment benefits because she refused to work on a day that her religion regarded as God's day of rest, the Court upheld her claim that the state denied her religious liberty.[78] In 1985, however, the Court found unconstitutional, on establishment-clause grounds, a state act that authorized em-

75. *Abington Township School District v. Schempp*, 374 U.S. 203 (1963).

76. *McGowan v. Maryland*, 366 U.S. 420 (1961), and companion cases.

77. *Braunfeld v. Brown*, 366 U.S. 599 (1961); *Gallagher v. Crown Kosher Supermarket*, 366 U.S. 617 (1961).

78. *Sherbert v. Verner*, 374 U.S. 398 (1963).

ployees to designate a sabbath day and not work that day.[79] Chief Justice Warren Burger invoked the three-part *Lemon* test appropriate to establishment-clause jurisprudence.[80] He concluded that by giving employees an "absolute and unqualified" right not to work on his or her sabbath and by forcing businesses to adjust their work schedules to the religious practices of religious employees, the act respected an establishment of religion. In purpose and effect it advanced religion, preferring those who believe in resting on the sabbath to those who do not.

Ordinarily Burger voted on the other side and castigated the Court for preferring irreligion over religion. Here the Court struck down a preference for religion over irreligion, but only Rehnquist dissented, without opinion. No member of the Court defended the statute as an effort by the state not to discriminate against Christians and Jews by preventing the imposition of employment penalties on someone who acted in obedience to conscience by refusing to work on the sabbath. The notion that this state act was "a step toward creating an established church," to quote Burger from a different case decided the same month, "borders on, if it does not trespass into, the ridiculous."[81] The state act was, rather, an accommodation of religious freedom.

One of the most interesting establishment-clause issues of recent years produced an extraordinary opinion by Chief Justice Burger for the Court in the Nebraska legislative-chaplains case.[82] He completely abandoned establishment-clause jurisprudence in favor of historical custom in order to sustain the constitutionality of prayers by tax-supported legislative chaplains. Government may not officially authorize schoolchildren to pray, because they are impressionable and government is coercive. But government officials can officially pray at public expense. Legislators apparently need prayers more than do schoolchildren. Every legislative day begins with prayer said vocally by an official chaplain paid from the government treasury. It is unclear why legislators who feel the need for prayer cannot attend their own houses of worship before turning up for official duties. Why they must pray

79. *Thornton v. Caldor, Inc.*, 472 U.S. 703 (1985).
80. *Lemon v. Kurtzman*, 403 U.S. 602, 612–13 (1971).
81. *Wallace v. Jaffree*, 472 U.S. 38, 89 (1985).
82. *Marsh v. Chambers*, 463 U.S. 783 (1983).

collectively is equally unclear. Perhaps legislators want to look religious to their God-fearing constituents, at the expense of all taxpayers. Least of all is it clear that they receive divine guidance. But the legislators of Nebraska have, since statehood, opened with prayers. And for at least eighteen years, from 1965 to the decision of the case in 1983, the same Presbyterian minister served as the chaplain of the Nebraska legislature.

Burger, for a 6–3 majority, did not distinguish the purpose-effects-entanglement test, nor did he try to argue that prayers by tax-supported legislative chaplains had a secular purpose and effect and did not enmesh the state with religion. He just ignored the three-pronged *Lemon* test and found a validation of legislative chaplains in a tradition traceable in our national life to the First Continental Congress. Significantly, in 1790 the First Congress provided for legislative chaplains, proof, declared the chief justice, that the framers of the establishment clause did not understand it to prohibit the practice. And with the passage of time it had become "part of the fabric of our society." Did Nebraska's retention of the same Presbyterian minister for so long violate the establishment clause? Burger did not mention that the First Congress required that "two Chaplains of different denominations . . . shall interchange weekly." "Weighed against the historical background," said Burger in a nonsequitur, "these factors do not serve to invalidate Nebraska's practice."[83] Clearly the Court had a hot potato on its hands and, not wanting to stimulate a furious public reaction, as Brennan, dissenting, noted, took an unreasoned way to drop that potato.

Justice John Paul Stevens dissented briefly; ignoring the general issue of legislative chaplaincies, he focused on the Nebraska case. That a state should have as it sole official chaplain a member of the same denomination for so long, Stevens believed, showed a decided preference of one faith over others. Brennan, however, for himself and Thurgood Marshall, delivered a masterful treatiselike dissenting opinion that combined systematic coverage with incisive analysis. Having explained why legislative chaplaincies violated each of the three prongs of the conventional test, he reviewed the values that the establishment

83. Ibid., p. 793. Burger gave the date of the act as Sept. 25, 1789. It was Jan. 7, 1790. See *Annals of Congress*, 1:1077.

clause promoted—privacy in matters of religion, government neutrality, freedom of conscience, autonomy of religious life, the prevention of government trivialization of religion, and the withdrawal of religion from the political arena. He then found that a legislative act of worship infringes these values.

Burger had not confronted any of the issues raised by Brennan, but Brennan faced Burger's reliance on historical custom. Practices once constitutional can become constitutionally abhorrent, he argued, showing that the Constitution is not static in meaning. "Cruel and unusual punishment" once did not raise death-penalty questions; "the equal protection of the laws" once allowed compulsory racial segregation. The Court should be more faithful to the broad purposes of the framers than to their particular practices, Brennan asserted, if the establishment clause is to serve a vastly more religiously diverse society than they knew. "The Court's focus here on a narrow piece of history," he stated, "is, in a fundamental sense, a betrayal of the lessons of history."[84] "God save this honorable Court" and "One nation under God" had lost religious significance. Brennan refused to classify legislative prayer similarly as "*de minimis*" or a trifling violation. Prayer, unlike mottoes or a bailiff's invocation, is serious religious business beyond the competence of the government. Despite the public hullabaloo that might be engendered by a contrary decision, Brennan believed, it would have invigorated the spirit of religion. As usual, Brennan saw some government practice as a violation of the establishment clause because he believed he was protecting religion.

The Rehnquist Court, its conservative side reinforced by Anthony Kennedy, Antonin Scalia, and Clarence Thomas, accommodated religious needs far more easily by relaxing its establishment-clause standards when public tax dollars were at issue. A 1988 case sustaining the constitutionality of Congress's Adolescent Family Act illustrates the point.[85] The statute authorized federal funds for services, administered by nonprofit institutions, that related to the discouragement of premarital adolescent sexuality, pregnancy, and parenthood. The statute also encouraged adoption rather than abortion. A federal district court

84. *Marsh v. Chambers*, 463 U.S. 783, 812 (1983).
85. *Bowen v. Kendrick*, 487 U.S. 589 (1988).

found that the statute, on its face and as administered, advanced religion by subsidizing sectarian organizations and by allowing them to preach their message to adolescents; the statute, according to the district court, also unduly entangled the government with religion by requiring official monitoring to ensure that religiously affiliated grantees did not promote their religious missions. The Court, by a 5–4 vote, reversed and remanded the case for a determination whether it was unconstitutionally applied.

Chief Justice William Rehnquist, for the majority, ruled that the statute satisfied the *Lemon* test. Congress had a valid secular purpose in passing it. The act neither required grantees to be religiously affiliated nor suggested that religious institutions were specially qualified to provide the services subsidized by the government. Congress merely assumed that religious organizations as well as nonreligious ones could influence adolescent behavior. Congress impartially made the monies available to achieve secular objectives, regardless of whether the funds went to sectarian or secular institutions. This was not a case in which the federal subsidies flowed primarily to pervasively sectarian institutions; moreover, the services provided to adolescents, such as pregnancy testing or child care, were not religious in nature. Thus the statute did not advance or endorse religion. The establishment clause did not prevent religious organizations from participating in publicly sponsored welfare programs of a secular character.

The majority also held that the government monitoring required by the statute did not necessarily entangle it excessively with sectarianism. Conceding, however, that the act as applied could violate the establishment clause, the Court returned the case to the district court for a factual finding on that issue. The district court had already made factual findings that the administration of the act violated the establishment clause. Indeed, Rehnquist, for the Court majority, conceded that "the record contains evidence of specific incidents of impermissible behavior" by recipients of federal tax monies, and O'Connor, separately concurring, conceded that the act had been "administered in a way that led to violations of the Establishment Clause."[86] However, the Court believed that even if so, the proper remedy was not to void the

86. Ibid., pp. 620, 623.

statute but for the secretary of Health and Human Services to cancel grants that had been misused.[87]

The four dissenters, speaking through Justice Harry Blackmun, may have been influenced by the fact that the statute banned grants to institutions that advocated abortion. Blackmun, as devoid of doubts as was Rehnquist, deplored a decision that breached the *Lemon* test by providing federal monies to religious organizations, thereby enabling them to promote their religious missions in ways that were pervasively sectarian and, contradictorily, requiring intrusive oversight by the government to prevent that objective. The majority, Blackmun reasoned, distorted the Court's precedents and engaged in doctrinal missteps to reach their conclusion by treating the case as if it merely subsidized a neutral function such as dispensing food or shelter instead of pedagogical services that impermissibly fostered religious beliefs. The dissenters believed that the statute was unconstitutional because it authorized government funding for religious organizations to teach impressionable adolescents about matters of religious significance, often on the premises of a church or parochial school.

Catholic organizations receiving government aid prevented their employees from encouraging birth control methods in conflict with Catholic teachings. Almost 20 percent of the funds spent by the government up to the time of the case went to such religiously affiliated organizations.[88] This percentage is scarcely incidental; it is substantial. On the other hand, the primary effect of the act did not advance religion if only 20 percent of its funds went to religion.

The establishment clause allows government aid to religiously affiliated organizations that provide secular services. To hold otherwise would disadvantage or even penalize religiously affiliated organizations

---

87. For the district court's finding on the unconstitutionality of the statute as enforced, see *Kendrick v. Bowen*, 657 F.Supp. 1547, 1564–67 (1987). On remand, the district court failed to decide the case, while the parties negotiated for a settlement. In 1993, finally, they reached a settlement, in *Kendrick v. Sullivan*, Civil Action No. 83-3175 (CRR), Jan. 19, 1993, U.S. District Court, D.C. The settlement included instructions for Health and Human Services personnel explaining how they should administer the program to avoid problems with the establishment clause.

88. *Bowen v. Kendrick*, 487 U.S. 589, 629 (1988), note 3 of Blackmun's dissent.

because of their religious affiliation. That would burden religion or discriminate against it, showing government hostility rather than neutrality. But in this case the secular and the sectarian were intermeshed. The Court had abandoned its customary view that the establishment clause necessitates that government aid to religiously affiliated organizations be utilized only for secular activities. In previous cases in which the Court had sustained financial assistance to religiously affiliated institutions, the statutes, both federal and state, had stipulated that the aid be given only for secular activities of liberal arts colleges, and the Court, in each of the precedents, had found no evidence that the aid had been used otherwise.[89] In another allied case, state aid to a religious institution resulted wholly from the choice of the individual who had been the recipient of a grant.[90] Accordingly, upholding the 1981 act of Congress marked a significant departure in the Court's establishment-clause jurisprudence. Rarely had the Court adopted so cramped a view of the clause. This was a case most nearly like the classic ones, involving public tax dollars for religious institutions, that had given rise to the establishment clause, yet the Court could see no law respecting an establishment.

Within a year, however, the unpredictable Court justifiably found unconstitutional a state enactment that favored religious publications.[91] Justices White and O'Connor voted with the Brennan-Blackmun wing to make a 6–3 majority in this case, leaving Rehnquist, Scalia, and Kennedy to dissent. However, the eccentric White had not altered his nonpreferentialist or accommodationist views in establishment-clause cases; he and he alone in this case believed that the Texas act violated freedom of the press. In effect only a bare majority of the Court voted that the establishment clause had been violated.

The Supreme Court has been inexcusably inconsistent in its interpretation of the establishment clause. The constitutional law of the

---

89. *Tilton v. Richardson*, 403 U.S. 672 (1971), concerning federal aid to religiously affiliated colleges; *Hunt v. McNair*, 413 U.S. 734 (1973), and *Roemer v. Maryland*, 426 U.S. 736 (1976), concerning state aid to religiously affiliated colleges.

90. *Witters v. Washington Department of Services to the Blind*, 474 U.S. 481 (1983).

91. *Texas Monthly v. Bullock*, 109 S.Ct. 890 (1989).

Fourth and Fifth Amendments is also unpredictable and murky, but the establishment clause strikes closer to the personal affairs of ordinary citizens than does the right to be free from an unreasonable search of one's car or the right to be represented by counsel at a custodial interrogation. Every parent or citizen can be immediately concerned about whether the Constitution permits the public-school curriculum to include prayers or whether parochial-school children can benefit from tax dollars. The public, which has little patience with legal distinctions, is appalled by the contradictory results of the Court's various decisions on the establishment clause. New York's released-time program of religious education for public-school children does not violate the establishment clause, nor do compulsory Sunday closing laws, nativity scenes on public property, or free bus rides and secular books for parochial-school children. And taxpayers can write off the cost of tuition for private church schools if a state provides the deductions. But a brief nondenominational prayer, even if voluntary, violates the establishment clause, as do remedial reading lessons for dyslexic children in parochial schools if their teachers or lessons are paid by our taxes. The gift by the government of a globe of the world or a videocassette of inaugural addresses by presidents of the United States would be unconstitutional if a religious school were the recipient. Nor can the government underwrite the costs of a field trip for the pupils of that school to watch our courts in action: that would advance the religious mission of the school unconstitutionally, even though sending the child to that school at public expense so that the child can receive a religious education is constitutionally permissible as a benefit to the child rather than to the school. No one can make much sense out of the Court's establishment-clause opinions.

The Court has reaped the scorn of a confused and aroused public because it has been erratic and unprincipled in its decisions. It sometimes heeds history; other times it ignores history or distorts it. Sometimes the Court appeases public opinion, but other times it seeks a higher ground for its decision. Whatever approach it takes, whether in the application of one of its tests, such as examining whether the purpose of some measure advances religion or entangles state and church, the Court has managed to unite those who stand at polar opposites on the results that the Court reaches; a strict separationist and a zealous accommodationist are likely to agree that the Supreme Court would not recognize an establishment of religion if it took life and bit the justices. As a matter of fact, they themselves accuse each other of not knowing what an establishment of religion is. In 1989, for example, in the Pittsburgh creche case, Justice Kennedy made the following angry statement:

> The approach adopted by the majority contradicts important values embodied in the [Establishment] Clause. Obsessive, implacable resistance to all but the most carefully scripted and secularized forms of accommodation requires this Court to act as a censor, issuing national decrees as to what is orthodox and what is not. What is orthodox, in this context, means what is secular; the only Christmas the State can acknowledge is one in which references to religion have been held to a minimum. The Court thus lends its assistance to an Orwellian rewriting of history as many understand it. I can conceive of no judicial function more antithetical to the First Amendment.[92]

Justice Brennan responded that Kennedy's interpretation "would gut the core of the Establishment Clause, as this Court understands it." Kennedy's misreading, Brennan declared, "is predicated on a failure to recognize the bedrock Establishment Clause principle that, regardless of history, government may not demonstrate a preference for a particular faith. . . . Although Justice Kennedy repeatedly accuses the Court of harboring a 'latent hostility' or 'callous indifference' toward religion, nothing could be further from the truth." And, Brennan tartly added, Kennedy's "accusations could be said to be as offensive as they are absurd." Kennedy "misperceived a respect for religious pluralism, a respect commanded by the Constitution, as hostility or indifference to religion. No misperception could be more antithetical to the values embodied in the Establishment Clause."[93]

Despite the wrangling, on the two largest issues we can generalize and say that for the most part the Court has kept religion out of the public schools and has allowed only fringe benefits to parochial

92. *Allegheny County v. ACLU*, 109 S.Ct. 3086, 3146 (1989).
93. Ibid., pp. 3106, 3110.

schools or, rather, to their pupils. Even so, the exceptions and deviations are so significant, the members of the Court so divided, the reasoning in judicial opinions so unsatisfactory, and the number of separate concurrences and dissents so great that the Court scarcely gets adequate credit even when it is right or consistent or principled.

A problem wholly of the Court's own making results from the fact that whatever decision it reaches on an establishment-clause issue, it does not usually write convincing opinions, because its members do not habitually take into serious consideration the best arguments advanced by dissenters, by those separately concurring, or by losing parties. The justices are more adept at manipulating precedents and arguments in order to reach preconceived opinions than they are at fair, open-minded, carefully reasoned judgments. Too many opinions read as if they could have been written by legislators deciding on how to make the policy preferences of their constituents look as if they served the national interest. Too few judicial opinions conflict with the personal views of the justices as private citizens. A judge who does not with some regularity reach judgments that conflict with his or her private policy views is not confronting complicated constitutional questions with sufficient disinterestedness or intellectual rectitude. The justices would more effectively earn the public's respect by trying to convince critics on every side and by doing it with judicial analyses that face and evaluate the most powerful contentions of losers as well. Their analyses would gain most if they sought to reveal as best as possible the timeless purposes implicit in the history and language of the establishment clause.

9 Incorporation and the Wall

Establishment-clause cases rarely concern acts of the national government. The usual case involves an act of a state, and the usual decision restricts religion in the public schools or government aid to sectarian schools. The First Amendment, as incorporated within the Fourteenth Amendment, operates as a ban against state action, and nonpreferentialists hate that fact. They hate and deplore the incorporation doctrine. The incorporation doctrine is that the Fourteenth

Amendment's due process clause incorporates within its protection of "liberty" most of the provisions of the Bill of Rights, thereby imposing on the states the same limitations imposed by the Bill of Rights on the United States. In the absence of the incorporation doctrine, nothing in the U.S. Constitution would prevent a state from conducting an Inquisition, outlawing an unpopular religious sect, establishing a particular church, storming into private homes without a warrant, imprisoning people who speak their minds in unpopular ways, or taxing local newspapers too critical of the state government. The due process clause of the Fourteenth Amendment, which has been the basis of the incorporation doctrine, states that no state shall deprive any person of life, liberty, or property without due process of law.

Because the United States has no constitutional power to make laws that directly benefit religion and because under the incorporation doctrine the Fourteenth Amendment imposes upon the states the same limitations that the First Amendment places on the United States, the states have no constitutional power to aid religion directly either. It does not matter that the incorporation doctrine was not intended. Neither was a ban on compulsory segregation of the races in the public schools, the promotion of privacy values, or the protection of women or aliens against discrimination. But the language of the amendment allows for its extension beyond the original intent of its framers. So too its protection of liberty against state denial allows for the incorporation of the First Amendment's guarantees.

Original intent supports nonpreferentialist arguments against incorporation. Consequently, those who want the Constitution to permit state benefits to religion rely on original intent, and they break a lance against reading the First Amendment's establishment clause into the Fourteenth as a limitation on the states. If the Fourteenth Amendment did not incorporate the First Amendment, the states would be free from the restraints of the U.S. Constitution and would be able to enact any measure concerning religion, subject only to such limitations as might exist in the individual state constitutions. Some nonpreferentialists and accommodationists therefore advocate the overruling of the incorporation doctrine. In its absence, the establishment clause, said a nonpreferentialist judge, would "not prohibit the state from establishing a religion."[1] Such views are based on fantasy, self-delusion, and misconceptions.

To expect the Supreme Court to turn back the clock by scrapping the entire incorporation doctrine is so unrealistic as not to warrant consideration. Numerous reactionaries, including former attorney general Edwin Meese and Professors James McClellan, Robert Cord, Charles Rice, and Daniel Dreisbach, indulge their emotions when denouncing the Court for six decades of decisions based on a doctrine that has "shaky" foundations or for pursuing its "revolutionary course" in making the First Amendment applicable to the states. Poor historians that they are, the nonpreferentialists think that the incorporation doctrine originated in cases beginning with *Gitlow v. New York*[2] in 1925 and that the Court "arbitrarily" assumed that religious liberty and freedom from establishments of religion came within the meaning of the "liberty" of the Fourteenth Amendment's due process clause.[3] But such extravagance of language by the nonpreferentialists persuades no one who remembers that the revolutionists were led not by Chief Justice Earl Warren but by Justice Edward T. Sanford, joined by

1. *Jaffree v. James*, 554 F.Suppl. 1130, 1132 (S.D. Ala. 1983); *Wallace v. Jaffree*, 472 U.S. 38, 45 (1985).

2. *Gitlow v. New York*, 268 U.S. 652 (1952). In *Gitlow* the Court ruled that the word "liberty" in the Fourteenth Amendment incorporated the First Amendment's protection of freedom of speech, with the result that a state could not abridge freedom of speech any more than the United States could.

3. Edwin Meese III, "ABA Washington Speech," July 9, 1985 (U.S. Department of Justice, Washington, D.C., typescript), pp. 13–14; reported in *Los Angeles Times*, July 10, 1985, pt. 1, pp. 1, 6. Meese's speech is reprinted in *Interpreting the Constitution: The Debates over Original Intent*, edited by Jack N. Rakove (Boston, 1990), pp. 13–21. See also James McClellan, "The Making and Unmaking of the Establishment Clause," in *A Blueprint for Judicial Reform*, edited by Patrick B. McGuigan and Randall R. Rader (Washington, D.C., 1981), p. 296; Daniel L. Dreisbach, *Real Threat and Mere Shadow: Religious Liberty and the First Amendment* (Westchester, Ill., 1987), pp. 93, 94; Robert L. Cord, *Separation of Church and State: Historical Fact and Current Fiction* (New York, 1982), pp. 85–101, a discussion littered with misconstructions of Court cases; Charles Rice, "The Bill of Rights and the Doctrine of Incorporation," in *The Bill of Rights: Original Meaning and Current Understanding*, edited by Eugene W. Hickock Jr. (Charlottesville, Va., 1991), pp. 11–16.

fellow conservatives on the Supreme Court, including Justices James C. McReynolds, George Sutherland, Pierce Butler, Joseph McKenna, Willis Vandevanter, and William Howard Taft, among others; and the *Gitlow* Court was unanimous as to the incorporation doctrine. In 1940 the *Cantwell* Court, which incorporated the free exercise clause and, by obiter dictum, the establishment clause, spoke unanimously through Justice Owen Roberts, one-time nemesis of the New Deal.[4] And in 1947 the Court was unanimous too when holding that the incorporation doctrine applied to the establishment clause.[5]

As mentioned above, Meese, McClellan, Cord, Dreisbach, and others erroneously complain that incorporation began belatedly in 1925 with *Gitlow* and the free speech clause of the First Amendment.[6] In fact, as early as the late nineteenth century the Court used the incorporation doctrine to protect property rights; in 1894 the Court read the equal protection clause of the Fourteenth Amendment to include or incorporate the eminent domain or takings clause of the Fifth Amendment in order to strike down rate regulation,[7] and then in 1897 the Court crammed the eminent domain clause into the Fourteenth's due process clause to achieve the same end.[8] Protecting First Amendment freedoms from state abridgment seems no more radical or arbitrary than protecting property rights. Moreover, the incorporation doctrine has a history so fixed that overthrowing it is as likely as bagging snarks on the roof of the Court's building. Of all the amendments constituting the

4. *Cantwell v. Connecticut*, 310 U.S. 296 (1940).

5. *Everson v. Board of Education*, 330 U.S. 1 (1947).

6. Cord, *Separation of Church and State*, p. 99; Meese, "ABA Washington Speech," p. 12; McClellan, "The Making and Unmaking," p. 316; Dreisbach, *Real Threat and Mere Shadow*, p. 93.

7. *Reagan v. Farmers' Loan and Trust Co.*, 154 U.S. 362, 399 (1894).

8. In *Chicago, Burlington & Quincy RR. v. Chicago*, 166 U.S. 226 (1897), the Court read the Fifth Amendment's eminent domain clause into the due process clause of the Fourteenth Amendment. The Court officially dates the incorporation doctrine with this 1897 case. See *Hawaii Housing Authority v. Midkiff*, 104 S.Ct. 2321, 2331 n. 7 (1984). See also *Smyth v. Ames*, 169 U.S. 466 (1898). In *United Rys. v. West*, 280 U.S. 234 (1930), the Court struck down as *confiscatory* a government fixed-rate schedule that allowed a profit of 6.26 percent.

Bill of Rights, the First Amendment is the least likely to be thrown out of its nesting place within the word "liberty" of the Fourteenth. The Hughes Court unanimously awarded the First Amendment the laurels of uttermost fundamentality: no freedoms are more precious or more basic than those protected by the First Amendment.[9]

Even so, eminent constitutional scholars, including Edward S. Corwin and Robert G. McCloskey, have suggested that a principled distinction can be made between the establishment clause and the other clauses of the First Amendment, allowing the disincorporation of the establishment clause. Their point is that the clause does not protect an individual freedom; it does not provide a right to *do* something. Government may violate one's personal right to speak freely or worship as one pleases, but government cannot violate one's right not to be subject to an establishment of religion. Advocates of this view state it as if it were self-evidently true. As McCloskey said, "It requires a semantic leap to translate 'liberty' into 'disestablishment' when by definition the forbidden establishment need involve no restriction of the liberty of any individual."[10] By what definition? The semantic leap covers about a millimeter of space: freedom from an establishment, even a nonpreferential one, is an indispensable attribute of liberty. That was the principal theme of Madison's "Memorial and Remonstrance" and a theme of the Virginia Statute of Religious Freedom. An establishment, Madison argued, "violated the free exercise of religion" and would "subvert public liberty."[11]

The belief that freedom from an establishment of religion is indispensable was not just the product of rationalists who cared little about revealed religion. From the religious founders of Rhode Island, Roger Williams and John Clarke, to the leading American Baptists a century and a half later, such as Issac Backus and John Leland, evangelicals who

---

9. *Palko v. Connecticut*, 302 U.S. 319 (1937).

10. Robert G. McCloskey, "Principles, Powers, and Values: The Establishment Clause and the Supreme Court," in *1964 Religion and the Public Order*, edited by Donald A. Giannella (Chicago, 1965), p. 11. See also Edward S. Corwin, *A Constitution of Power in a Secular State* (Charlottesville, Va., 1951), pp. 113–16.

11. "Memorial and Remonstrance," in William T. Hutchinson et al., eds., *The Papers of James Madison*, ser. in progress (Chicago, 1962–), 8:300, 304.

profoundly cared about the purity of Christian faith had warned against the corrupting embrace of government, and they had advocated separation in order to *defend* religion. To them the integrity of religion and of religious liberty depended on the promptings of private conscience unsullied by the assistance of government. Madison's "Memorial and Remonstrance" bore the influence of his Orange County neighbor, the great Baptist preacher John Leland, as well as that of the deistic Jefferson, who cared more about the purity of public liberty.

The aggressive personal liberties of the First Amendment, we are also told, must be exercised to be enjoyed, and therefore they seem to be distinguishable from disestablishment as a form of liberty. Freedom *of* religion, from this viewpoint, is unlike freedom *from* disestablishment. But that is only a partial truth, because freedom of religion and the freedoms of speech, press, and assembly are also freedoms from government ("Congress shall make no law . . ."). They are freedoms from government impositions and measures that create a suffocating civic environment within which the possibility of exercising and enjoying personal freedoms has been diminished. Freedom from seditious libel laws, from taxes on knowledge, from prosecutions for blasphemy, from censorship, and from disabilities arising because of one's associations or religion are similar in nature to freedom from establishments in the sense that the First Amendment creates immunities that form a wall behind which freedom can flourish. What Zechariah Chafee, one of the leading civil libertarians of the twentieth century, called "the most important human right in the Constitution" is a "freedom from" or an immunity: the right to the writ of habeas corpus or freedom from arbitrary arrest.[12] That writ has a fragile existence in the Constitution, for Article I, section 9, protects not a right to the writ but the "Privilege of the Writ" and protects it against suspension only when the public safety does not require its suspension. Parsing that provision of the Constitution the way nonpreferentialists parse the establishment clause would reduce the "privilege" to a nullity.

Numerous rights deemed fundamental by the Supreme Court are immunities that cannot be exercised by individuals. No one can affir-

12. Zechariah Chafee, *How Human Rights Got into the Constitution* (Boston, 1952), p. 51.

matively exercise a negative right, such as the right to be free from compulsory self-incrimination or to be free from cruel and unusual punishments. These are, nevertheless, personal rights; only specific individuals can be denied freedom from compulsory self-incrimination or from cruel and unusual punishment.

There is another and equally important dimension to all rights, however personal, and that is the social or civic dimension. By imposing restraints upon government, rights make it possible for the body politic to be free for private and voluntary judgments by all members. Public as well as private liberty is the beneficiary. Taxes spent for religion violate the right to support religion voluntarily and privately. Religious exercises in the public schools are intimidating or humiliating to those who must voluntarily decline to participate. Such assistance to religion therefore damages public liberty. As Madison said, an establishment of religion "violates equality by subjecting some to peculiar burdens." The fruits of such an establishment, he argued, include "bigotry and persecution" and "will destroy that moderation and harmony which the forbearance of our laws to intermeddle with Religion has produced among its several sects."[13] Public liberty and personal civil liberty require an exemption from government-sponsored programs that spur bigotry.

Although Madison thought that taxes for the religion of one's choice (a general assessment bill aiding all Christian sects) differed only in degree, not in principle, from the Inquisition, Professor Robert McCloskey thought otherwise. He believed that no useful purpose is served to talk as if the evil of modern establishments, as the Supreme Court understands them, is comparable to that of persecutions or pogroms. The state-church involvements that the Court considers, he wrote, include "nudging of moppets in the direction of religion instruction classes, a modest amount of classroom praying and Bible reading." That, he added, "is not the stuff from which crusades and martyrs are made."[14] That judgment has little historical merit and probably no psychological merit. McCloskey himself admitted that it is wrong to contend "that such involvements are not noxious at all."[15] He mentioned

13. "Memorial and Remonstrance," in *Madison Papers*, 8:300, 301, 302.
14. McCloskey, "Principles, Powers, and Values," p. 25.
15. Ibid.

both the coercion of children and the harmful effect upon the political process. "It is arguable," he wrote with some equanimity, "that religion has a special propensity to stir emotions and breed animosities when it becomes a subject of political controversy" and, one should add, when it becomes a subject of educational controversy too.

McCloskey might not have spoken so lightly about nudging moppets had he remembered the history of religion in our public schools. In the nineteenth century, Catholic children were flogged for refusing to participate in Protestant services—just a "modest amount" of classroom prayer and reading from the King James version of the Bible. In Philadelphia in 1842 a Roman Catholic bishop asked that the Catholic children be allowed to use their own version of the Bible and be excused from other religious instruction in the public schools. The result was "two years of bitterness and mob violence, the burning of two Catholic churches and a seminary, and finally three days of rioting in which thirteen people were killed and fifty wounded in the City of Brotherly Love."[16]

Of course, in a different sense McCloskey was right: we are not talking about church-state involvements that threaten pogroms or inquisitions. Justice Lewis F. Powell correctly observed: "At this point in the 20th century we are quite far removed from the dangers that prompted the Framers to include the Establishment Clause in the Bill of Rights. . . . The risk . . . even of deep political division along religious lines . . . is remote."[17] Indeed, we have progressed so much that the fallout from a released-time program, which at least has the virtue of keeping religion out of the public schools, is merely some virulent anti-Semitism, evidenced by Jewish children being called "Christ killer" and "dirty Jew."[18] In sum, reading freedom from disestablishment into the

16. James O'Neill, *Religion and Education under the Constitution* (New York, 1949), pp. 26–27. See also Ray Allen Billington, *The Protestant Crusade* (New York, 1938), pp. 142–65, 220–37; Leo Pfeffer, *Church, State, and Freedom*, rev. ed. (Boston, 1967), pp. 416–44.

17. *Wolman v. Walter*, 433 U.S. 229, 263 (1977).

18. Affidavit of Leah Cunn in trial proceedings of *Zorach v. Clausen*, 343 U.S. 306 (1952), the second released-time case, quoted in Pfeffer, *Church, State, and Freedom*, p. 417. I know from personal experience something about the divisive and prejudicial effects that result from religious exercises in the public schools. In 1935–36, I went to school in DeKalb, Illinois, which had, in McCloskey's

meaning of the "liberty" protected against state infringement by the Fourteenth Amendment makes the same sense and stands on the same principle as reading the free exercise clause into "liberty."

Those who expect the Supreme Court to overrule the incorporation doctrine with respect to the establishment clause underestimate both the inherent conservatism of the Court and its political shrewdness. It does not matter whether liberal or conservative activists dominate the Supreme Court. The precipitous repudiation of entrenched doctrines would appear too obviously the result of subjective choices. That is why Justices David Souter, Arthur Kennedy, and Sandra Day O'Connor refused to overturn *Roe v. Wade*'s protection of the right of a woman to an abortion. Their discourse on the conditions justifying the overthrow of a fundamental principle, whether the right to an abortion or the incorporation doctrine, is a brilliant discourse on the rule of law and the role of the Court.[19] In effect it is an explanation why the incorporation doctrine will not be overturned.

Wherever possible, the Court has avoided a dramatic overruling of its precedents. In the art of judging, a proper regard for appearances counts. The Court must seem to appreciate the values of coherence, stability, and continuity with the past. Judges, especially conservative ones, prefer to avoid sudden shifts in constitutional law. Any person who reaches the highest court is sophisticated enough to appreciate the strategic and political values of achieving desired results by indirection. Overruling is a device of last resort, employed only when other alternatives are unavailable or unavailing. The Court will not overrule the incorporation doctrine; it will not turn back the clock. But it might reinterpret precedents, distinguishing away some, blunting others, and making new law without the appearance of overruling or disrespecting the past. The Court will nourish the impression that it is for standing

---

words, "a modest amount of praying and Bible reading" plus some christological celebration of Christmas; my refusal to participate stigmatized me and unleashed latent anti-Semitism. I learned to associate religion in the public schools with my gym teacher's motto for coaching softball, "No kikes on our team," and with getting beaten up regularly because I was "the Jew bastard" and "Christ killer" who refused to pray in school.

19. *Planned Parenthood v. Casey*, 112 S.Ct. 2791, 2814–16 (1992).

pat. It merely refuses to endorse further expansion of rights but faithfully hews to fundamental doctrines.

In a 1985 case the Supreme Court had to reconsider the incorporation doctrine because a federal district judge in Alabama expressly repudiated it in a bizarre opinion holding that the establishment clause did not bar states from establishing a religion. The Supreme Court, however, serenely continued to employ the doctrine after treating the lower-court opinion with something close to the contemptuous disdain it deserved. Not even the reactionary William Rehnquist, still a loose cannon on the Supreme Court, aimed at the incorporation doctrine. He utterly misconstrued the establishment clause in an interpretation not accepted by any other member of the Court and he grossly distorted history, but he embraced the incorporation doctrine, even if reluctantly, when he declared: "Given the 'incorporation' of the Establishment Clause as against the States via the Fourteenth Amendment in *Everson*, States are prohibited as well [as the United States] from establishing a religion or discriminating between sects."[20]

Another reason that the incorporation doctrine will continue undiminished in vitality is that no need exists to overthrow it in order to achieve the results that promote religious interests. One scholar got his history all wrong when he declared that the framers of the First Amendment did not mean to prevent the United States from giving nonpreferential aid to religion if the aid is incidental to the performance of a delegated power, but he stumbled on a truth about the

20. *Wallace v. Jaffree*, 472 U.S. 38, 113 (1985). The federal judge in *Jaffree v. Board of School Commissioners*, 553 F.Supp. 1104 (S.D. Ala., 1983), was W. Brevard Hand of the district court in Mobile, who relied on the unreliable works of James McClellan and Robert L. Cord, previously cited. Attorney General Edwin Meese also advocated the repudiation of the incorporation doctrine. See his "ABA Washington Speech," pp. 12–14. Meese believed that the establishment clause bans merely a "national church," and he did not even consider the words "no law respecting." As for Judge W. B. Hand, he was correct in declaring that the framers of the Fourteenth Amendment did not intend incorporation of the Bill of Rights. But he rejected evolutionary doctrine in favor of a Constitution whose meaning is forever fixed by the original intent of its framers.

politics of constitutional law. Power that is illegitimately exercised under one constitutional rubric may be valid under another.[21]

Although Congress has no constitutional authority to legislate on religion as such or make it the beneficiary of legislation or other government action, the blunt fact is that regardless of what the framers intended and regardless of the absence of a power to legislate on religion, the United States does possess constitutional powers to benefit or burden religion as an indirect or incidental result of the exercise of delegated powers. For example, the First Congress in the course of debating the amendments that became the Bill of Rights, recommended the presidential proclamation of a day of national thanksgiving and prayer, and it also reenacted the Northwest Ordinance. Passed originally in 1787 by the Congress of the Confederation, the Northwest Ordinance included a clause providing that schools and the means of education should be encouraged because religion, like morality and knowledge, is "necessary to good government and the happiness of mankind." And without doubt, religion (Protestantism) constituted an important part of the curriculum at that time. In 1789 Congress extended the statute by adapting it to the new Constitution but not to the First Amendment, which had not yet been recommended to the states by Congress. Even in the absence of that amendment, however, the extension of the ordinance was unconstitutional from Congressman Madison's standpoint because the Congress had no powers over religion. But his was a minority voice. "The vast majority of Americans," as Thomas Curry wrote, "assumed that theirs was a Christian, i.e. Prot-

---

21. Michael Malbin, *Religion and Politics: The Intentions of the Authors of the First Amendment* (Washington, D.C., 1978), pp. 14, 16–17. In *Gibbons v. Ogden*, 9 Wheaton 1 (1824), the Court denied that the states possessed a concurrent power over interstate commerce and held void a state act that conflicted with a federal coastal licensing act. However, in *Willson v. Blackbird Creek Marsh Co.*, 2 Peters 245 (1829), the Court held that a state exercising its police power might dam up a navigable stream, shutting out a vessel licensed under the same federal statute. Congress could not outlaw compulsory racial segregation in public accommodations under its Thirteenth or Fourteenth Amendment powers, but could effectuate the same purpose in the exercise of its interstate commerce power. Compare the *Civil Rights Cases*, 109 U.S. 3 (1883), with *Heart of Atlanta Motel v. U.S.*, 379 U.S. 241 (1964).

estant country, and they automatically expected that government would uphold the commonly agreed on Protestant ethos and morality. In many instances, they had not come to grips with the implications their belief in the powerlessness of government in religious matters held for a society in which the values, customs and forms of Protestant Christianity thoroughly permeated civil and political life."[22]

When the Congress that adopted the First Amendment promoted religion in the Northwest Ordinance by urging a national day of prayer, it surely acted unconstitutionally by later standards. The fact that the First Congress extended the Northwest Ordinance added nothing to its constitutionality. The constitutionality of several acts of the First Congress was in doubt and fiercely contested. Not everything done by the founding generation can be accepted as constitutional. Some early measures, such as the Sedition Act of 1798, were surely not. Specific practices of the founders do not guarantee the constitutionality of those practices if the text of the Constitution or a principle or purpose of it does not warrant them. The founders' preference for Protestant-ism or Christianity has not only passed out of date; it had no constitu-tional basis originally.

Nevertheless, some plausible pretext can often be found for the constitutionality of government action benefiting religion. For exam-ple, Congress could constitutionally have benefited religion indirectly in the extension of the Northwest Ordinance by virtue of an express power to make "needful rules" for the governance of the territories. In a real case Congress and the Supreme Court would have a difficult task to explain why territories could not be governed without official en-couragement of religion. Few real cases exist, however, and the Court, like the First Congress endorsing religion as necessary for good gov-ernment, rarely troubles to think seriously about the delegated powers that might be exercised legitimately in a manner benefiting religion. Indeed, no enumerated power justifies the declaration of a day of prayer. Moreover, the power to regulate the territories must be ex-ercised in subordination to constitutional limitations, including the es-tablishment clause. If the First Amendment was not yet part of the Constitution when the First Congress initially extended the Northwest

22. Thomas Curry, *The First Freedoms* (New York, 1986), p. 219.

Ordinance, it was part of the Constitution when Congress again extended the ordinance.[23]

What are those powers whose exercise might benefit religion even in the absence of a power over religion? Under the power to "make rules for the government and regulation" of the armed forces, Congress provided for military and naval chaplains and paid them from public taxes. Under the power to govern its own proceedings, both chambers of Congress have provided for legislative chaplains. Under the power to punish violators of federal laws by imprisonment, Congress has built prisons and provided chaplains for the inmates. Congress may close government buildings on the sabbath and on religious holidays because it controls federal property. Under the power to coin money, Congress has placed a theistic motto on U.S. coins and currency. That does not make the motto constitutional, given the fact that it is irrelevant to the power to coin money. Nor is "In God We Trust" necessary or proper to the fulfillment of any enumerated power. Enumerated powers must be exercised in subordination to express constitutional limitations. Much that we take for granted as constitutional can be challenged, even if good political sense and the *de minimis* principle argue that no issue should be made. The legal maxim *Lex non curat de minimis* means that the law does not bother with trifles.

Under the power to levy taxes, Congress has made exemptions for churches and clergymen. Under the power to raise armies and therefore the power to lay down the terms for conscription, Congress has exempted conscientious objectors and clergymen. By the exercise of the treaty power the government has made treaties with the Indians and has implemented those treaties by appropriations for religion, ostensibly for the purpose of civilizing, Christianizing, and pacifying the Indians. The examples can be extended.

Unfortunately, the Supreme Court does not bother to explain much when it sustains some "accommodation" to religion, other than to argue whether the act in question has the primary purpose or effect of aiding religion or involving government entanglement with religion. Moreover, the existence of a power that might be exercised to benefit religion indirectly does not alter the fact that the limitations imposed by

23. I Statutes 50 (1789), reenacted 1800, chap. 41, and 1802, chap. 40.

the establishment clause are paramount. Many accommodations of religion cannot be justified constitutionally; most show an absence or abuse of power.

The Northwest Ordinance directly benefited religion, and it was a declared purpose and effect of the statute to do so. By contrast, aid that might be legitimate must be the incidental or indirect result of general secular legislation. For example, government may include religiously affiliated organizations in a grant program if the grant furthers the wholly secular functions of those organizations. To exclude a Catholic relief organization from a grant program because of its religious affiliation would be hostile to religion rather than neutral to it. If the mission of a Yeshiva is to train rabbis and teach Judaism, a grant to that educational institution could not subsist under the establishment clause; but if the same organization runs a Jewish hospital whose mission is medical research and care of the sick, a grant to all hospitals conducting medical research would not violate the establishment clause if the Jewish hospital were a recipient. Even so, no power exists to regulate religion as religion.

The same authority that can indirectly benefit religion by the exercise of legitimate powers may also injure religion. A power to help is also a power to hinder or harm. Congress could draft conscientious objectors or tax church property, for example. That it does not do so is a matter of politics, not the result of constitutional power. Those who clamor for additional government support of religion should beware of the risks to religion from government entanglements. Those damaging risks are possible.[24] The damage includes trivializing, making bland, or secularizing religion. Government aids religion for the government's sake—that is, for secular reasons. The same reasons might require re-

---

24. See the forebodings of Dean M. Kelley, "Confronting the Danger of the Moment," in *State and Public Policy*, edited by Jay Mechling (Washington, D.C., 1978), pp. 13–14, 16–18. On the same point, see also William Bentley Ball, "Mediating Structures and Constitutional Liberty," in ibid., pp. 49–59. See also Ball's "Religious Liberty: New Issues and Past Decisions," in *A Blueprint for Judicial Reform*, edited by Patrick B. McGuigan and R. R. Rader (Washington, D.C.; 1981), pp. 327–49. Ball writes from the standpoint of an accommodationist or nonpreferentialist; Kelley is a Christian separationist whose intellectual ancestors designed the establishment clause.

strictions or regulations damaging to the sacred character of religion. Only the innocent trust Caesar. The purpose of the Constitution is to impose limitations on government because it cannot and should not be trusted.

From a constitutional standpoint, government can go too far in implementing a spirit of "benevolent neutrality," to use a phrase of Chief Justice Warren Burger,[25] by purportedly serving religious needs. Benign "accommodation" is one thing; its purpose should be to protect religious freedom. If that is not its purpose, it should be held unconstitutional. An implicit alliance with religion or state encouragement or sponsorship of religion is not legitimate accommodation.

Unfortunately, the Supreme Court has not distinguished the two in any consistent manner. Congress cannot constitutionally spend tax monies for the erection or maintenance of houses of worship, although it can tax almost as it pleases and spend almost as it pleases for "the common defense and general welfare." Nor can government financially assist a private sectarian school that is integrally a part of the religious mission of the denomination operating that school. The limits on the employment of authorized powers include the proscription against establishments of religion.

The establishment clause is over two centuries old. At the time the First Amendment was framed, government and religion were much closer than they are today, but nothing was clearer than the fact that financial aid to religion or religious establishments constituted an establishment of religion. On that point the founding generation had given systematic thought to the meaning of an establishment of religion; it had scarcely thought at all about government chaplains, fast days, or the many other aids to religion that were taken pretty much for granted. The establishment clause should be far broader in meaning now than it was when adopted. The nation was relatively homogeneous in religion then; it is astoundingly heterogeneous today and is growing ever more religiously pluralistic. Then, for all practical purposes, religion meant Christianity and Christianity meant Protestantism. But Roman Catholics now compose the largest denomination in the nation, and about 6,000,000 American citizens are Jews, and Mus-

25. *Walz v. Tax Commission*, 397 U.S. 664, 676–77 (1970).

lims are as numerous. In addition, there are several scores of sects and substantial numbers of adherents to religions that were unknown in 1789, including Mormons, Christian Scientists, Pentecostalists, Jehovah's Witnesses, Eastern Orthodox, members of the Unification Church, and Hare Krishnas. The number of Muslims, Buddhists, Confuscianists, Hindus, Sikhs, and Taoists is increasing.

We should not want the ban on establishments of religion to mean only what it meant in 1789 or only what its framers intended. Oliver Wendell Holmes said, "Historical continuity with the past is not a duty, it is only a necessity."[26] That delphic statement can be construed to mean that we cannot escape history because it has shaped us and guides our policies, but we are not obliged to remain static. Two hundred years of expanding the meaning of democracy should have some constitutional impact. We are not bound by the wisdom of the framers; we are bound only to consider whether the purposes they had in mind still merit political respect and constitutional obedience. History can be only a guide, not a controlling factor. If we followed the framers of the Constitution blindly, we would be duplicating the method of the *Dred Scott* decision by freezing the meaning of words at the time they became part of the Constitution. Holmes wisely declared that courts—and he might have added scholars—are apt to err by sticking too closely to the words of law when those words "import a policy that goes beyond them."[27] The significance of words, he taught, is vital, not formal, and is to be gathered not simply by taking dictionary definitions "but by considering their origin and the line of their growth."[28]

The broad purpose of the establishment clause should not be the only thing kept in mind. A little common sense helps too in the constitutional politics of its interpretation, and that common sense should come from public-interest lawyers and counsel representing defense organizations, such as the ACLU and the Rutherford Institute, as well as from courts. Those who profess to be broad separationists ought to understand that popular government will continue to aid religion and

26. Oliver Wendell Holmes, *Collected Legal Papers*, edited by Harold Laski (New York, 1920), p. 191.
27. *Olmstead v. U.S.*, 277 U.S. 438, 469 (1928).
28. *Gompers v. U.S.*, 233 U.S. 604, 610 (1914).

show respect for it and that not every accommodation with religion, deriving from incidental assistance, is necessarily unconstitutional. Indeed, separationists ought to understand that even if they profoundly believe that a practice is unconstitutional, wisdom sometimes dictates against pressing a suit. Trying to ensure that the wall of separation is really impregnable might be futile and dangerously counterproductive. Indeed, the cracks in the wall might be more numerous than at present without seriously harming it or the values that it protects. A moment of silence in the public school for meditation or prayer, posting the Ten Commandments on the school bulletin board, or even saying a bland interdenominational prayer would not really make much difference if they were not omens that the cause of religion would be still further promoted by government.

Accommodationists seem insatiable and use every exception as precedents for still more exceptions. The moral majority does not compromise. Consequently, passionate separationists who see every exception as a disaster tend to run around, like Chicken Little, screaming, "The wall is falling, the wall is falling." It really is not and will not, so long as it leaks just a little at the seams. If it did not leak a little, pressure on the wall might generate enough force to break it. The *de minimis* principle has some value, as Madison understood and as the Supreme Court occasionally has understood too; it has referred to "ceremonial deism" as a way of sweeping under the rug theistic practices like the invocation "God save this honorable Court" or "In God We Trust."[29]

The American Civil Liberties Union has not always understood. Suits brought by the ACLU to have courts hold unconstitutional every cooperative relationship between government and religion can damage the cause of separation by making it look overrigid and ridiculous. One of the principal arguments of separationists against certain practices that breach the wall of separation, particularly in the field of education, is that those practices are divisive and stimulate conflict among people of differing faiths. Some silly suits, such as those seeking to have declared unconstitutional the words "under God" in the pledge of allegiance or in the money motto "In God We Trust," have the same deleterious effects. The Court had the political good sense in 1993 to

29. *Allegheny County v. ACLU*, 109 S.Ct. 3086, 3102 n. 46 (1989).

refuse consideration of a case in which an atheist, with ACLU support, sought to prevent daily recitation of the pledge of allegiance because of its "one nation under God" language. If the Court faced the issue, it might have to rule such language unconstitutional, even if only a "ceremonial deism." Such a decision would publicly discredit the Court and the wall of separation. Public opinion, which is extremely conservative in matters involving public recognition of God, should not be tempted to retaliate on such an inconsequential issue.

Separationists who cannot appreciate the *de minimis* concept ought to appreciate a different motto, "Let sleeping dogmas lie." The logic of the ACLU position is that a reenactment of the Declaration of Independence or of the great Virginia Statute of Religious Freedom would be unconstitutional because both refer to God. In effect, such references to God, as in the pledge, though literally religious, have lost all religious significance and ought not be taken seriously. Indeed, atheists should be howling in glee at the corruption of religion by irrelevant ceremonial references to God on our money or in our pledge of allegiance that schoolchildren so often garble.

The *de minimis* principle, of course, has two sides. People who are eager to have nativity scenes displayed at Christmas in publicly owned places tend to say "*de minimis*." Their insensitivities are about on a par with that of the Supreme Court when it decided that Pawtucket's creche was as nonsectarian because of the accompanying figures of Santa Claus and Rudolph the Red-Nosed Reindeer. *De minimis* can doubtlessly be made to cover practices damaging to the salutary benefits of separation between government and religion. Protestants used to respond *de minimis* when Roman Catholics objected to the use of the King James Bible in the public schools. In 1854, for example, a Maine court upheld the expulsion of a Catholic child for refusing to read that Bible, even though the court acknowledged that the law regarded every religion as having equal rights. However, added the court, "reading the Bible is no more an interference with religious belief, than would reading the mythology of Greece and Rome be regarded as interfering with religious belief or an affirmance of the pagan creeds."[30] Whether a practice seems *de minimis* may depend on the perspective from which it

---

30. *Donahoe v. Richards*, 38 Maine 379, 399 (1854).

is seen. What is trifling to the majority may be threatening and offensive, even persecuting, to a minority.

Accommodationists and nonpreferentialists such as the Rutherford Institute also go too far and can be equally insensitive to the rights of others in the overaggressive pursuit of their own interests. Like separationists, they too press suits to have the fundamental law enshrine their beliefs. In a case left unresolved by the Supreme Court, the issue was whether religious-minded citizens can force the public display of a Christmas creche on public land contrary to the decision of the town government.[31] Those who wanted the creche on public land, notwithstanding the unlimited opportunity to display creches on church and private property, won a federal Court of Appeals decision against the town of Scarsdale, New York, on the grounds that the town had denied free speech in a public forum. That proposition is not meritless. If nude dancing, flag burning, and the Nazi marches are symbolic speech worthy of constitutional protection, so too is a nativity scene at Christmastime in a public park. But a creche on public property during a religious holiday and without Santa and his cohorts is a sacred symbol that has a religious, not a secular, purpose. Nude dancing, flag burning, and marches by Nazis, being without religious significance, cannot possibly violate the establishment clause. The status of a public park as a public forum cannot justify its unconstitutional use. But the Court of Appeals, relying on the Supreme Court's offensive creche precedent of 1983, found no infringement of establishment-clause values.[32] Zealots demand the right to spread their prayer rugs in the midst of traffic. Mean-spirited zealots also demand government-sponsored creches when the front lawns of their homes and religious institutions are available. They need to be reminded about the virtues of limits even on devotional exercises. There may also be virtue in adhering to town-government decisions or local option, which some conservative judges claim on occasion to respect.

Strategists in the opposing camps see every nonpreferential aid to

31. *Board of Trustees of Scarsdale v. McCreary*, 471 U.S. 83 (1985).

32. *McCreary v. Stone*, 739 F.2d 716 (C.A. 2 1984). On nude dancing, see *Schad v. Mt. Ephraim*, 452 U.S. 61 (1981); on flag burning, *Street v. New York*, 394 U.S. 576 (1969).

religion as a precedent that might warrant still further aid. The non-preferentialists too often are really preferentialists seeking a bigger cut of the pie. They care as little for minorities as a former majority cared about them, and they eagerly claim that every existing aid proves the invalidity of an overbroad principle of separation. But exceptions to the principle do not impair its enduring value. If history teaches anything, Madison touched truth when he declared that "religion and government will both exist in greater purity, the less they are mixed together."[33] Fortunately, the opposing forces in our system have courts to resort to rather than bats and bricks, but the losing side in any case tends to react like Bret Harte's M'liss. Upon being told that the sun had obeyed Joshua's command to stand still in the heavens, she slammed her astronomy book shut with the defiant assertion, "It's a damned lie. I don't believe it."[34] The Court rarely convinces those who think it wrong, perhaps because no establishment-clause question can be dissected so precisely that it has only one side and because religion is a subject that is overladen with emotion. Religion goes to the core of human existence.

Americans ought to keep in mind that forbearance is sometimes better than disputation or litigation. They should realize that a faulty political compromise may be better than judicial dictation, which does not satisfy the loser and can corrupt the spirit of the victor. We profess to respect majority rule and minority rights, but when the minority wins, the majority claims that the minority rules, and when the majority wins, the minority feels oppressed. Circumventing the courts, demonstrating the civility due to one another, and making a deal might not be a bad idea. "Accommodation" can work both ways. In his old age, Jefferson wisely observed: "A Government [or society] held together by the bands of reason only, requires much compromise of opinion; that things even salutary should not be crammed down the throats of dissenting brethren, especially when they may be put into a form to be willingly swallowed, and that a good deal of indulgence is necessary to

33. James Madison to Edward Livingston, July 10, 1822, in *The Writings of James Madison*, edited by Gaillard Hunt, 9 vols. (New York, 1900–1910), 9:100.
34. Bret Harte, "M'Liss" (1873), in *The Luck of Roaring Camp and Other Tales* (New York, 1892), p. 171.

strengthen habits of harmony and fraternity."[35] Such a homily has meant so little to us that we now are where we are. We are common victims of our Supreme Court, which thinks a publicly sponsored menorah or creche can be secular and therefore not an establishment of religion,[36] but thinks too that it saw a forbidden establishment in a state police power measure aimed at keeping boisterous patrons of a tavern from disturbing a church.[37]

The principles of forbearance, mutual compromise, and indulgence might be well served by court decisions that keep religious exercises completely out of public schools and conspicuous public places, but that opens the doors wide to public support of everything secular in the private sectarian schools and to secular measures that aid those schools. The Court possesses the craft and authority to reach any result it wants, and it ought to relieve the burden of so-called double taxation on those who pay to send their children to private school. Private sectarian schools fulfill the goals of education at much savings to the public. So too the Court should keep the public schools free from sectarianism to fulfill their mission as the common meeting ground of the citizens of a pluralistic democracy.

The words of the establishment clause are not empty vessels into which judges may pour nearly anything they wish. Some justices of the Supreme Court, however, in candid moments have confessed that they believe otherwise. In 1948 Justice Robert Jackson wrote of the difficulty of separating the secular from the religious: "It is idle to pretend that this task is one for which we can find in the Constitution one word to help us as judges to decide where the secular ends and the sectarian begins in education. Nor can we find guidance in any other legal source. It is a matter on which we can find no law but our own presuppositions."[38] Similarly, Justice Byron White later declared:

35. Thomas Jefferson to Edward Livingston, Apr. 4, 1824, in *The Writings of Thomas Jefferson*, edited by Andrew A. Lipscomb and Albert E. Bergh, 20 vols. (Washington, D.C., 1903–4), 16:25. Hereafter cited as *Jefferson's Writings*.

36. *Lynch v. Donnelly*, 465 U.S. 668 (1984).

37. *Larkin v. Grendel's Den, Inc*, 459 U.S. 116 (1983).

38. *McCollum v. Board of Education*, 333 U.S. 203, 237–38 (1948).

No one contends that he can discern from the sparse language of the Establishment Clause that a State is forbidden to aid religion in any manner or, if it does not mean that, what kind of or how much aid is permissible. And one cannot seriously believe that the history of the First Amendment furnishes unequivocal answers to many of the fundamental issues of church-state relations. In the end, the courts have fashioned answers to these questions as best they can, the language of the Constitution and its history having left them a wide range of choice among many alternatives. But decision has been unavoidable; and in choosing, the courts necessarily have carved out what they deemed to be the most desirable national policy governing various aspects of church-state relationships.[39]

Whether Jackson and White were right about the guidance available from the Constitution or from history, the reality is that the Court exercises a freedom almost legislative in character, bringing us close to the intolerable, a Humpty Dumpty court. Humpty Dumpty told Alice scornfully that when he used a word, it meant just what he chose it to mean, neither more nor less. "The question is," said Alice, "whether you can make words mean so many different things." "The question is," said Humpty Dumpty, "which is to be master, that's all."[40] In our system of government the Supreme Court tends to be master on domestic issues. But the judges of the highest tribunal are supposed to enforce constitutional limitations, not make national policy or determine what policy is desirable for the nation.

The establishment clause may not be self-defining, but it embodies a policy that time has proved to be best. Despite continuing complaints about the wall of separation between government and religion, that is the policy embodied by the establishment clause. The Constitution erected that wall. If the fact that it is the policy of the Constitution does not satisfy, history helps validate it. A page of history is supposed to be worth a volume of logic, so let us consider a page from Tocqueville.

39. *Committee for Public Education v. Nyquist*, 413 U.S. 756, 820 (1973), dissenting opinion.

40. Lewis Carroll, *Through the Looking-Glass*, in *The Annotated Alice*, edited by Martin Gardner (New York, 1963), p. 269.

Slightly more than half a century after independence he wrote that "the religious atmosphere of the country was the first thing that struck me on my arrival in the United States." He expressed "astonishment" because in Europe religion and freedom marched in "opposite directions." Questioning the "faithful of all communions," including clergymen, especially Roman Catholic priests, he found that "they all agreed with each other except about details; all thought that the main reason for the quiet sway of religion over their country was the *complete separation of church and state*. I have no hesitation in stating that throughout my stay in America I met nobody, lay or cleric, who did not agree about that."[41]

Because the domains of religion and government remain separated, religion in the United States, like religious liberty, thrives mightily, far more than it did 200 years ago when the vast majority of Americans were religiously unaffiliated. In a famous letter to the Baptist Association of Danbury, Connecticut, President Jefferson spoke of the "wall of separation." After declaring that religion belonged "solely between man and his God," Jefferson added: "I contemplate with sovereign reverence that act of the whole American people which declared that their legislature should 'make no law respecting an establishment of religion, or prohibiting the free exercise thereof,' thus building a wall of separation between church and state."[42] The usual interpretation of Jefferson's Danbury Baptist letter by those who seek to weaken its force is either to minimize it or to argue that he was here concerned only with the rights of conscience and that these would "never be endangered by treating all religions *equally* in regard to support" by the government.[43] Neither interpretation is valid.

The rights-of-conscience argument ignores the fact that Jefferson quoted the establishment clause in the very sentence in which he spoke

41. Alexis de Tocqueville, *Democracy in America*, edited by J. P. Mayers and Max Lerner, translated by George Lawrence (New York, 1969), pp. 271–72; emphasis added.

42. Thomas Jefferson to "A Committee of the Danbury Baptist Association," Jan. 1, 1802, in *Jefferson's Writings*, 16:281–82.

43. O'Neill, *Religion and Education*, p. 81.

of a wall of separation, indicating that he was concerned with more than protection of the free exercise of religion. In any case, Jefferson most assuredly did believe that government support of all religions violated the rights of conscience. His Statute of Religious Freedom expressly asserts that "even forcing him [any man] to support this or that teacher of his own religious persuasion, is depriving him of the comfortable liberty of giving his contributions. . . . [No] man shall be compelled to frequent or support any religious worship, place, or ministry whatsoever."[44]

The second technique of robbing the Danbury letter of its clear intent to oppose any government support of religion belittles it as a "little address of courtesy" containing a "figure of speech . . . a metaphor."[45] Or, as Edward S. Corwin suggested, the letter was scarcely "deliberate" or "carefully considered"; it was rather "not improbably motivated by an impish desire to heave a brick at the Congregationalist-Federalist hierarchy of Connecticut."[46] Jefferson, however, had powerful convictions on the subject of establishment and religious freedom, and he approached discussion of it with great solemnity. Indeed, on the occasion of writing this letter he was so concerned with the necessity of expressing himself with deliberation and precision that he went out of his way to get the approval of the attorney general of the United States. Sending him the letter before dispatching it to Danbury, Jefferson asked his advice as to its contents and explained:

> Adverse to receive addresses, yet unable to prevent them, I have generally endeavored to turn them to some account, by making them the occasion, by way of answer, so sowing useful truths and principles among the people, which might germinate and become rooted among their political tenets. The Baptist address, now enclosed, admits of a condemnation of the alliance between Church

44. Julian Boyd et al., eds., *Papers of Thomas Jefferson*, ser. in progress (Princeton, N.J., 1950–), 2:545.

45. O'Neill, *Religion and Education*, pp. 83, 81–82.

46. Edward S. Corwin, "The Supreme Court as National School Board," *Law and Contemporary Problems* 14 (Winter 1949): 14.

and State, under the authority of the Constitution. It furnished an occasion, too, which I have long wished to find, of saying why I do not proclaim fast and thanksgiving days, as my predecessors did.[47]

On the matter of proclaiming fast and thanksgiving days, President Jefferson departed from the precedents of Washington and Adams, and went even further than Madison, by utterly refusing on any occasion to recommend or designate a day for worship, citing as a reason, among others, the clause against establishments of religion.[48]

However, even Jefferson was not wholly consistent when it came to an establishment of religion. He used the treaty power to make an Indian treaty that provided federal monies to serve the religious needs of a tribe, and he approved of legislation, under the power to regulate Indian affairs, that underwrote missionary expenses to "propagate the Gospel among the Heathen."[49] But contrary to the present chief justice, a former attorney general, and numerous nonpreferentialist scholars, what the government could do under the Constitution in regard to Indians it cannot constitutionally do by treaty or statute in regard to American citizens. Nonpreferentialists grossly exaggerate the significance of federal aid to religion among Indians as if it somehow justified aid to religion among citizens.[50] Aid to Indians under either the treaty power or the power to regulate Indian affairs is not worth two cents as a precedent for anything else. The Fourteenth Amendment, which granted citizenship to anyone born or naturalized in the United States, did not apply to Indians, who had an anomalous status as members of domestic, dependent nations, neither citizens nor aliens. The case of

---

47. Thomas Jefferson to Levi Lincoln, Jan. 1, 1802, in *Jefferson's Writings*, 10:305.

48. See Anson Phelps Stokes, *Church and State in the United States*, 3 vols. (New York, 1950), 1:490–91, 335–36.

49. Cord, *Separation of Church and State*, pp. 261–64, 268–70, reprints the documents. See also pp. 57–80 for an exaggerated emphasis on federal aid to religion among Indians.

50. Edwin Meese III, "Address before the Christian Legal Society," San Diego, Calif., Sept. 29, 1985 (U.S. Department of Justice, Washington, D.C., transcript), pp. 9–10.

the Indians was exceptional. Congress did not extend American citizenship to all American Indians until 1924.

Another way of minimizing the Danbury letter is to contend that Jefferson meant the wall only against aids to religion by the national government, not by the states. In view of the fact that at the state level he favored not only private and voluntary support of religion but also Sunday laws and proclamations of fast and thanksgiving, the proposition has a historical basis. But history provides no iron rule. Two centuries of experience have altered the constitutional status of the original widespread state support of religion, just as history has wiped out formal state establishments. Moreover, the incorporation doctrine of the Fourteenth Amendment, nationalizing the First Amendment, has superseded the original federal principle that kept the establishment clause as a limitation on only the national government.

As for Jefferson, he cared deeply about the rights of conscience, but he cared too for the government's freedom from religion. However, Roger Williams, who cared even more deeply about religion, had spoken of the "wall of separation" more than a century and a half before Jefferson. In 1644 Williams wrote that the wall existed to preserve the integrity of religion by walling out corrupting influences:

First, the faithful labors of many witnesses of Jesus Christ, extant to the world, abundantly proving that the church of the Jews under the Old Testament in the type and the church of the Christians under the New Testament in the antitype were both separate from the world; and that when they have opened a gap in the hedge or *wall of separation* between the garden of the church and the wilderness of the world, God hath ever broke down the wall itself, removed the candlestick, and made His garden a wilderness, as at this day. And that therefore if He will ever please to restore His garden and paradise again, it must of necessity be walled in peculiarly unto Himself from the world; and that all that shall be saved out of the world are to be transplanted out of the wilderness of the world, and added until His church or garden.[51]

51. Roger Williams, "A Letter of Mr. John Cottons" (1643), in *The Complete Writings of Roger Williams*, 7 vols. (New York, 1963), 1:392. I have followed the

Thus, the wall of separation had the allegiance of a most profound Christian impulse as well as a secular one. To Christian evangelists of the framers' time, the wall of separation derived from the biblical injunction that Christ's kingdom is not of this world. The wall of separation ensures the government's freedom from religion and the individual's freedom of religion. The individual's freedom and religion's freedom from government cannot flourish without the government's freedom from religion.

Separation has other bountiful results. Government neutrality toward religion does not hurt it; it aids it. Conversely, genuine harm can come to religion from government authority over it. Fortunately, government and religion in America are mutually independent of each other, much as Jefferson and Madison hoped they would be. Government maintains a benign neutrality toward religion without promoting or serving religion's interests in any significant way except, perhaps, for the policy of tax exemption. To be sure, government's involvement with religion takes many forms. The joint chiefs of staff supposedly used to begin their meetings with prayer, as do our legislatures. The incantation "God save the United States and this honorable Court" and the motto "In God We Trust" and its relatives are of trifling significance in the sense that they have little genuine religious content. Caesar exploits, secularizes, and degrades or trivializes religion in such instances, but leaves organized religion alone. Free of government influence, organized religion in turn does not use government for religious ends.

Thus, history has made the wall of separation real. The wall is not just a metaphor. It has constitutional existence. Even Chief Justice Burger approvingly referred to Jefferson's "concept" of a wall as a "useful signpost" to emphasize separateness.[52] Despite its detractors and despite its leaks, cracks, and its archways, the wall ranks as one of the mightiest monuments of constitutional government in this nation. Robert Frost notwithstanding, something there is that loves a wall.

---

modernized version of Perry Miller, *Roger Williams: His Contribution to the American Tradition* (New York, 1962), p. 98; emphasis added.

52. *Larkin v. Grendel's Den, Inc.*, 459 U.S. 116, 123 (1982).

Epilogue

On June 26, 1994, the Supreme Court decided *Board of Education of the Kiryas Joel Village School District v. Grumet.* Kiryas Joel, a village in Orange County, New York, about forty miles north of New York City, has a population of about 12,000 inhabitants, all of whom are Orthodox Jews who belong to the Satmar Hasidic sect. They speak Yiddish, dress like their eighteenth-century forebears in unusual-looking garments, segregate the sexes when outside of the home, and avoid English-language publications, radio, and television. Their strict adherence to Mosaic law separates them from the overwhelming majority of American Jews, particularly of the Reform and Conservative branches of Judaism.

All of Kiryas Joel's Satmar children attend yeshivas or Hasidic parochial schools, except about forty who are mentally retarded or have special learning disabilities. Until 1985 these children attended special-education classes in an annex to one of the parochial schools and were taught by public school employees from the nearby Monroe-Woodbury Central School District, all specialists in teaching mentally handicapped children. In 1985 the Supreme Court held in *Aguilar v. Felton* that the employment of public school specialists to teach Catholic children with special educational needs violated the establishment clause if conducted in parochial schools.[1] Thereafter the learning-disabled children of Kiryas Joel attended special-education classes at a public school in the Monroe-Woodbury district, but the experience proved to be traumatic for them. They were jeered at and insulted because of their appearance, customs, and Yiddish language. They were expected to watch Christmas skits held at the school, one student even being cast as Rudolph the Red-Nosed Reindeer. The school fed them nonkosher junk food from McDonald's and exposed them to television. As a result, their parents removed them from the public school.

The village then won from the state legislature a special enactment creating a school district of its own, congruent with village lines,

---

1. *Aguilar v. Felton,* 473 U.S. 402 (1985).

whose purpose was to teach the mentally retarded children. The school district received government aid to employ public school staff members who were experts in teaching the learning-disadvantaged. Only handicapped children attended the public school of Kiryas Joel; all other children attended private yeshivas. Well over a hundred handicapped Hasidic children from outside the village also attended the Kiryas Joel public school.

The high court of the state of New York ruled that the creation of a public school district with the same boundaries as the Hasidic enclave was unconstitutional. Because the public school population and the village board of education were Hasidic, the statute created a symbolic union of church and state. Consequently, the primary effect of the statute was an endorsement or advancement of religious belief, according to the ruling.

The question presented by the case can be framed in a variety of ways. If the question is, may the government take account of religion and accommodate religious needs by creating a religiously gerrymandered school district, the statute creating the Kiryas Joel school district surely was unconstitutional. It was also unconstitutional if the question is, may the demands or needs of the religious community be met educationally? If the question is, did the Kiryas Joel school district exclusively benefit the children of a particular religion, then the state court surely decided rightly. But all these ways of framing the question dictate the result and are misleading. The question was whether the state may create a secular school district that coincided with the boundary lines of a village to teach the learning disabled of that village. Religion was irrelevant, but the case became a cause célèbre as one that posed a major church-state issue, pitting liberals against conservatives.

The American Jewish Committee, the Anti-Defamation League, and the Jewish Reform Movement, among others, sided with Americans United for Separation of Church and State; they believed that the school district was unconstitutional. Christians of the religious right, including the Rutherford Center, the Christian Legal Society, Roman Catholic authorities, the National Association of Evangelicals, and Pat Robertson's Center for Law and Justice, supported Kiryas Joel.

The Kiryas Joel school district was wholly secular. The law creating it was completely neutral, like any law creating a school district, and the district in fact did not teach, reflect, or endorse Satmar Hasidism or Judaism in any way. Indeed, the district integrated the handicapped Satmar children into a secular experience that they otherwise do not know, and in most classes, it mixed the sexes, which the Satmar do not otherwise allow. The school building was not located next to any religious institution and housed no religious symbols. None of the teachers were Satmar Hasids, and none lived in the village. All teachers were state licensed and hired without regard to religious affiliation, although many understood Yiddish, the language of the children. As in any bicultural program, in which English is supplemented by the language spoken at home by the children, most teachers were bilingual. Instruction for the most part was in English. The school offered no religious instruction of any sort. The school calendar was the same as that of other public schools. The superintendent of the school district, a twenty-year veteran of the New York City public school system who specialized in bilingual-bicultural education for the handicapped, testified that Kiryas Joel was a secular school. An official of the Monroe-Woodbury Central School District swore, "I regard the [Kiryas Joel] school as a secular institution, staffed by public employees performing the public function of educating children."[2]

The Supreme Court, which so often finds an establishment of religion where one does not exist and which often cannot see an establishment of religion where it does exist, by a vote of 6 to 3 held unconstitutional the state statute creating the public school district of Kiryas Joel. Justice David Souter, for the majority, saw the question as whether the statute created a school district along religious lines. He believed that the statute allocated political power on a religious basis, in violation of the establishment clause. The statute, he wrote, delegated "the State's discretionary authority over public schools to a group defined by its character as a religious community" in a context that gives no assurance that governmental power has or will be exercised neutrally. However, Souter showed nothing to prove that the statute in any way mentioned religion, and he offered no evidence to

2. *Board of Education of the Kiryas Joel Village School District v. Grumet,* brief of the Rutherford Institute, amicus curiae, p. 21.

demonstrate that the statute had not been exercised neutrally. He found an analogy with a case—*Larkin v. Grendel's Den*, the tavern case—in which the Court had decided that an establishment existed because of the delegation of government powers to religious bodies, thus impermissibly entangling government and religion.[3] But Souter offered not an iota of data to show a religious basis for the statute or an actual entanglement. He kept repeating that the state had granted political control to a religious group by creating the village school district, but his only evidence was the fact that the school district's population was exclusively Satmar Hasids. Under the statute, "the boundary lines of the school district divide residents according to religious affiliation" and therefore, he believed, reflected a "religious criterion for identifying the recipients of civil authority." Thus the statute created a "fusion of governmental and religious functions" benefiting only one sect.[4] Souter seemed to attribute to the school district the problem of the village: the legislature had created a religiously segregated village; that may have been a mistake but had nothing to do with its subsequent creation of a school district for the village.

Souter was sure that alternatives existed to provide bilingual and bicultural special education to Satmar children. Their needs could be met, he suggested, by the Monroe-Woodbury Central School District; he failed to add that the Satmars had tried that option and found the experience insulting and traumatizing. Alternatively, Souter declared, the Monroe-Woodbury district could provide "a separate program of bilingual and bicultural education at a neutral site near one of the village's parochial schools." Souter did not attempt to answer Justice Antonin Scalia's dissenting query: "If a State can furnish services to a group of sectarian students on a neutral site adjacent to a private religious school . . . how can there be any defect in educating those same students in a public school?" In conclusion, Souter restated that the statute failed the test of neutrality because it provided authority "to an electorate defined by common religious belief and practice, in a manner that fails to foreclose religious favoritism."

3. *Larkin v. Grendel's Den*, 459 U.S. 1081 (1982).
4. The copy of the opinions that I received is unpaginated, disallowing me from providing page citations for quotations.

A curious aspect of Souter's opinion was his failure to make explicit its reliance on the controversial *Lemon* test, a fact that allowed Justice Harry Blackmun, who joined Souter, to write a separate concurrence rejecting any suggestion that the Court had departed from the principles of that test. Another curious aspect of Souter's opinion is the fact that the majority slighted *Aguilar v. Felton*, the 1985 case that should have been the governing precedent. The reason is that Souter would have lost his majority had he relied on *Aguilar*, from which Justice Sandra Day O'Connor had dissented and which Justice Anthony Kennedy opposed. Although O'Connor believed that the Kiryas Joel statute singled out a particular sect for favorable treatment, she scored the *Lemon* test and inconsistently adhered to her dissent in *Aguilar*. Because government provided handicapped children with special education in public schools and nonsectarian private schools, she asserted, "it is only fair that it provide it on-site at sectarian schools as well." Kennedy, separately concurring, also believed that the state had drawn a political boundary "on the basis of religion." He wrote at length, however, on behalf of accommodating the needs of religion.

Justice Scalia, joined by Chief Justice William Rehnquist and Justice Clarence Thomas, wrote a scathing dissent that repeatedly described the majority opinion as "astounding." First, he explained that the Kiryas Joel public school was strictly secular, concluding: "There is no suggestion, moreover, that this public school has gone too far in making special adjustments to the religious needs of its students." Indeed, he described the school as being as "public as can be" and wholly lacking in the danger that it would educate students in religion.

Scalia attacked Souter's view that vesting power in the village school district was the same as vesting it in a religious group. The tavern case on which the majority relied, he argued, showed power vested in a church, which was not the case here. Scalia distinguished a church from its members. Depriving a group of its rights because of its religious beliefs, he declared, was as pernicious as denying an individual's rights for reasons of religion. Scalia also attacked Souter's assumption that the state's creation of the village school district was religiously motivated. To Scalia, the problems that the Satmar Jews had in the adjoining public school district were cultural, not religious or theological; matters of dress, language, and cultural alienation, not matters of faith, posed the problems confronted by Satmar children in the Monroe-Woodbury district. Also, the legislature was motivated by cultural, not religious, considerations, acting just as if the beneficiaries of the school district act had been Native Americans, for example.

Scalia saw no statute that gave religious preference, only a statute creating a school district that was congruent with the boundaries of the existing village. Allowing a village to have its own school district posed no establishment clause issue for him.

He did not believe that the state had created an exclusive establishment of religion favoring the Satmar Hasids. The rabbi who had founded the Satmars would be astounded to learn, Scalia sarcastically declared, that after escaping brutal persecution in Europe and coming to America, "the Satmar had become so powerful, so closely allied with Mammon, as to have become an 'establishment' of the Empire State." The framers of the Constitution would also be astounded to learn that their establishment clause had been employed to prohibit accommodating the cultural peculiarities of a tiny minority sect.

Neither the majority nor the dissenting opinion focused on, let alone even dealt with, the child-benefit theory. The case should have been decided in favor of Kiryas Joel on the ground that the school district, which was secular in every respect, had been created to serve the special needs of handicapped children. The Court recognized form over substance and abstract principle over reality. It also distorted the facts concerning the wholly secular statute creating the secular school district. As a result, the public has been deceived into believing what an Associated Press subheadline announced: "High Court Says Public Money Can't Be Used for Religious Education." The case was not at all about religious education.

Appendix

The principal sources for an inquiry into the original meanings of the establishment clause should be (1) the records of the First Congress, which framed and submitted for ratification the first ten amendments to the U.S. Constitution, and (2) the records of the state legislatures that engaged in the process of ratification. But the records of the state legislatures do not exist, and the sources for the study of Congress's part are incomplete and yield few definite answers.

No official records were kept of the debate in either the Senate or the House. Because the Senate during the First Congress met in secret session, no reporters were present to take even unofficial notes of the proceedings. A valuable record of the proceedings of the Senate for this time is *The Journal of William Maclay*,[1] U.S. senator from Pennsylvania, 1789–91. Unfortunately, however, Maclay was absent during most of the time the Senate debated the Bill of Rights, and he mentioned the subject merely in passing. No account of the debates exists, and the only Senate document we have is a meager record of action taken on motions and bills, *The Journal of the First Session of the Senate of the United States of America*.[2]

The situation for the House is considerably better but unsatisfactory. In addition to a House journal, comparable to that of the Senate, we have a version of the House debates because the House, unlike the Senate, permitted entry to reporters who took shorthand notes. But these unofficial reports, which were published in the contemporary press, have numerous deficiencies. The reporters took notes on the debates "and rephrased these notes for publication. The shorthand in use at that time was too slow to permit verbatim transcription of all speeches, with the result that a reporter, in preparing his copy for the press, frequently relied upon his memory as well as his notes and gave what seemed to him the substance, but not necessarily the actual phraseology, of speeches. Different reportings of the same speech exhibited at times only a general similarity and details often recorded by

1. Edgar S. Maclay, ed., *Journal of William Maclay* (New York, 1890).
2. Printed by Thomas Greenleaf (New York, 1789).

one reporter were frequently omitted by another."[3] Volume 1 of *The Debates and Proceedings in the Congress of the United States*, commonly known by its binder's title as the *Annals of Congress*, was published in 1834.[4] The information it includes about Senate proceedings is "only an abstract of the scanty record that was written in the Senate's journal."[5] The House debates, as recorded in the *Annals of Congress* for the session of the Congress that framed the Bill of Rights, derive from contemporary newspaper accounts, especially from the pages of a weekly periodical known as Lloyd's *Congressional Register*. Despite its name, it was not an official publication. The reports of these House debates "were so condensed" by the compilers of the *Annals of Congress* "that much information about the debates was omitted entirely or was presented only in garbled form."[6] Lloyd recorded "skeleton" versions of speeches, which he could make intelligible only by imaginative and knowledgeable editing. He used few connectives or articles, and he embellished considerably. Madison spoke of his "mutilation & perversion."[7] To another correspondent Madison observed of Lloyd that he "was indolent and sometimes filled up blanks in his notes from his memory or *imagination*," and added that Lloyd had become "a votary of the bottle and perhaps made too free use of it sometimes at the period of his printed debates."[8]

Thus, our record of the House debates does not necessarily reveal all

3. *A National Program for the Publication of Historical Documents*, a report to the President by the National Historical Publications Commission (Washington, D.C., 1954), p. 92.

4. *The Debates and Proceedings in the Congress of the United States, Compiled from Authentic Materials*, edited by Joseph Gales and W. W. Seaton, 42 vols. (Washington, D.C., 1834–56).

5. *A National Program*, p. 93.

6. Ibid.

7. James Madison to Thomas Jefferson, May 9, 1789, quoted in Marion Tinling, "Thomas Lloyd's Reports of the First Federal Congress," *William and Mary Quarterly*, 3d ser., 18 (Oct. 1961): 533. See also pp. 521, 530–38, for criticism of Lloyd's reporting by contemporaries and by Tinling, an expert on early shorthand who was an editor for the National Historical Publications Commission.

8. Ibid., p. 536.

that was said about the Bill of Rights, nor is the report necessarily accurate as far as it goes. Accordingly, quotations from the *Annals of Congress* purporting to represent a speaker's words must be regarded with some skepticism, a fact of particular importance in cases where slight changes in phraseology may shift the speaker's meaning, as in the debate on the establishment clause. Relying on one article rather than another in a motion that was not adopted, as nonpreferentialists are wont to, is absurdly naive.

Finally, there is no record of the minutes of the special House committee on amendments; it was this committee that, using Madison's original proposals, drafted the version of the Bill of Rights submitted to the House for approval. Nor is there any existing record of the minutes of the joint Senate-House conference committee that worked out a compromise draft between Senate and House versions of the proposed amendments.

Nor do other sources offer much enlightenment. The fact that Congress was drafting a bill of rights during the summer of 1789 prompted no analytical comment by the press that published the House debates. Moreover, as a historian who scoured the sources has pointed out, "The finished amendments were not the subject of any special newspaper comment, and there is little comment in the available correspondence."[9] As for the records of the state legislatures that ratified the Bill of Rights, the situation is hopeless. Because no records were kept of the debates, we do not know what the legislators of the various states understood to be the meanings of the various parts of the Bill of Rights. Nor has any scholar who has read the contemporary newspapers uncovered anything particularly revealing as to these meanings. Public interest in the proposed amendments was desultory, and public discussion of them largely confined to generalities.

9. David M. Matteson, "The Organization of the Government under the Constitution," in *History of the Formation of the Union under the Constitution*, directed by Sol Bloom (Washington, D.C., 1943), p. 316.

Selected Bibliography

Berns, Walter. *The First Amendment and the Future of American Democracy.* New York: Basic Books, 1976. Includes two pertinent chapters by a good nonpreferentialist scholar.

Antieau, Chester James, Arthur T. Downey, and Edward Roberts. *Freedom from Federal Establishment: Formation and Early History of the First Amendment's Religion Clauses.* Milwaukee: Bruce Publishing Co., 1964. A nonpreferentialist legal brief in thesis but much good research.

Buckley, Thomas E., S.J. *Church and State in Revolutionary Virginia, 1776–1787.* Charlottesville: University Press of Virginia, 1977. A model state study.

Cobb, Sanford H. *The Rise of Religious Liberty in America.* 1902. Reprint, New York: Cooper Square Publishers, 1968. Still useful though sometimes factually unreliable.

Cord, Robert L. *Separation of Church and State: Historical Fact and Current Fiction.* New York: Lambeth Press, 1982. Mostly historical fiction masquerading as scholarship.

Curry, Thomas J. *The First Freedoms: Church and State in America to the Passage of the First Amendment.* New York: Oxford University Press, 1986. The best book on the subject. But see my criticisms in this book, chap. 1, notes 24 and 42, and chap. 2, note 6.

Dreisbach, Daniel L. *Real Threat and Mere Shadow: Religious Liberty and the First Amendment.* Westchester, Ill.: Crossway Books, 1987. Splendid research marred by narrow nonpreferentialist axe-grinding.

Estep, William R. *Revolution within the Revolution: The First Amendment in Historical Context, 1612–1789.* Grand Rapids, Mich.: Eerdmans, 1990. A short separationist history stressing Baptist contributions.

Ivers, Gregg. *Lowering the Wall: Religion and the Supreme Court in the 1980s.* New York: Anti-Defamation League, 1991. A brief and pessimistic separationist book that has a Chicken Little tone.

Laycock, Donald. "'Nonpreferential' Aid to Religion: A False Claim About Original Intent," *William and Mary Law Review,* vol. 27 (1986), pp. 875–923. Influential article in legal circles but untrustworthy: loaded with inaccuracies and misrepresentations.

Malbin, Michael J. *Religion and Politics: The Intentions of the Authors of the First Amendment.* Washington, D.C.: American Enterprise Institute, 1978. A slight nonpreferentialist pamphlet.

McBrien, Richard P. *Caesar's Coin: Religion and Politics in America.* New York: Macmillan, 1987. A well-intentioned and intelligent accommodationist view.

McConnell, Michael. "Accommodation of Religion." In *The Supreme Court Review 1985.* Edited by Philip B. Kurland et al., pp. 1–60. Chicago: University of Chicago Press, 1988.

———. "Religious Freedom at the Crossroads." In *The Bill of Rights.* Edited by Geoffrey R. Stone et al., pp. 115–94. Chicago: University of Chicago Press, 1992. Two essays by the best and most challenging of the accommodationists. For an effective rebuttal, see Kathleen M. Sullivan, "Religion and Liberal Democracy," in the same volume, pp. 195–223.

McLoughlin, William G. *New England Dissent, 1630–1833: The Baptists and Separation of Church and State.* 2 vols. Cambridge, Mass.: Harvard University Press, 1971. Superb scholarship.

Morgan, Richard E. *The Supreme Court and Religion.* New York: Free Press, 1972. Perceptive analysis but needs updating.

O'Neill, James M. *Religion and Education under the Constitution.* New York: Harper & Bros., 1949. Pioneering nonpreferentialist book.

Pfeffer, Leo. *Church, State, and Freedom.* Rev. ed. Boston: Beacon Press, 1967. The best separationist study by the distinguished separationist lawyer.

———. *Religion, State, and the Burger Court.* Buffalo: Prometheus Books, 1985. Updates the preceding book's discussion of judicial decisions.

Pratt, John Webb. *Religion, Politics and Diversity: The Church-State Theme in New York History.* Ithaca, N.Y.: Cornell University Press, 1967. Worthwhile monograph.

Reichley, James. *Religion in American Public Life.* Washington, D.C.: Brookings Institution, 1985. Only partially on First Amendment problems, but a valuable account sympathetic to accommodationist views.

Souraf, Frank. *The Wall of Separation: Constitutional Politics of Church and State.* Princeton, N.J.: Princeton University Press, 1976. Effective scholarship by a political scientist.

Stokes, Anson Phelps. *Church and State in the United States.* 3 vols. New York: Harper & Bros., 1950. Classic, monumental, comprehensive study by a moderate preferentialist. Invaluable.

Swomley, John M. *Religious Liberty and the Secular State: The Constitutional Context.* Buffalo: Prometheus Books, 1987. A slight and shallow separationist account.

Tribe, Laurence. *American Constitutional Law.* 2d ed. Mineola, N.Y.: Foundation Press, Inc., 1988. Inexplicably ignorant on the historical background of the establishment clause but technically outstanding on Court opinions—for law students.

Whitehead, John W. *The Rights of Religious Persons in Public Education.* Wheaton, Ill.: Crossways Books, 1991. By the advocate who heads the Ruthford

Institute. Wholly one-sided presentation, important and able, but ignores contrary views.

Wood, James E., Jr. *Religion and the State: Essays in Honor of Leo Pfeffer*. Waco, Tex.: Baylor University Press, 1984. A large collection of essays by various separationist scholars.

Index